THE GOSPEL OF PEACE

Studies in Peace and Scripture
Institute of Mennonite Studies

THE GOSPEL OF PEACE

A Scriptural Message for Today's World

Ulrich Mauser

Westminster/John Knox Press
Louisville, Kentucky

Scripture quotations from the New Revised Standard Version of the Bible are copyright © 1989 by the Division of Christian Education of the National Council of the Churches of Christ in the U.S.A., and are used by permission.

Book design by Gene Harris

First Edition

Published by Westminster/John Knox Press
Louisville, Kentucky

This book is printed on acid-free paper that meets
the American National Standards Institute Z39.48 standard. ♾

PRINTED IN THE UNITED STATES OF AMERICA

9 8 7 6 5 4 3 2 1

Library of Congress Cataloging-in-Publication Data

Mauser, Ulrich, 1926–
    The Gospel of peace : a scriptural message for today's world /
Ulrich Mauser. — 1st ed.
        p.   cm. — (Studies in peace and scripture)
    Includes bibliographical references and indexes.
    ISBN 0-664-25349-0

    1. Peace—Biblical teaching.   2. Bible.   N.T.—Criticism,
interpretation, etc.   I. Title.   II. Series.
BS2545.P5M28 1992
261.8′73′09015—dc20   91-32251

Contents

Series Preface

Visions of peace abound in the Bible, whose pages are also filled with the language and the reality of war. In this respect, the Bible is thoroughly at home in the modern world, whether as a literary classic or as a unique sacred text. This is, perhaps, a part of the Bible's realism: bridging the distance between its world and our own is a history filled with visions of peace accompanying the reality of war. That alone would justify study of peace and war in the Bible. However, for those communities in which the Bible is sacred scripture, the matter is more urgent. For them it is crucial to understand what the Bible says about peace—and about war. These issues have often divided Christians from one another, and the way Christians have understood them has had terrible consequences for Jews and, indeed, for the world. A series of scholarly investigations cannot hope to resolve these issues, but it can hope, as this one does, to aid our understanding of them.

Over the past century a substantial body of literature has grown up around the topic of the Bible and war. Studies in great abundance have been devoted to historical questions about ancient Israel's conception and conduct of war, and about the position of the early church on participation in the Roman empire and its military. It is not surprising that many of these studies have been motivated by theological and ethical concerns, which may themselves be attributed to the Bible's own seemingly disjunctive preoccupation with peace and, at the same time, with war. If not within the Bible itself, then at least from Aqiba and Tertullian, the question has been raised whether—and if so, then on what basis—God's people may legitimately participate in war. With the Reformation, the churches divided on this question. The division was unequal, with the majority of Christendom agreeing that, however regrettable war may be, Christians have biblical warrant for participating in it. A minority countered that, however necessary war may appear, Christians have a biblical mandate to avoid it. Modern historical studies have served to bolster one side of this division or the other.

Meanwhile, it has become clear that a narrow focus on participation in war is not the only way—and likely not the best way—to approach the Bible on the topic of peace. War and peace are not simply two sides of the same coin; each is broader than its contrast with the other. In spite of broad agreement on this point, the number of studies devoted to the Bible and peace is still very small, especially in English. Consequently, answers to the most basic questions remain to be settled. Among these questions is that of what the Bible means in speaking of *shalom* or *eirene,* the Hebrew and Greek terms usually translated into English as "peace." By the same token, what the Bible has to say about peace is not limited to its use of these two terms. Questions remain about the relation of peace, in the Bible, to considerations of justice, integrity, and—in the broadest sense—salvation. And of course there still remains the question of the relation between peace and war. In fact, what the Bible says about peace is often framed in the language of war. The Bible very often uses martial imagery to portray God's own action, whether it be in creation, in judgment against or in defense of Israel, or in the cross and resurrection of Jesus Christ—actions aimed at achieving peace.

This close association of peace and war, to which we have already drawn attention, presents serious problems for the contemporary appropriation of the Bible. Are human freedom, justice, and liberation—and the liberation of creation—furthered or hindered by the martial, frequently royal, and pervasively masculine terms in which the Bible speaks of peace? These questions cannot be answered by the rigorous and critical exegesis of the biblical texts alone; they demand serious moral and theological reflection. But that reflection will be substantially aided by exegetical studies of the kind included in this series—even as these studies will be illumined by including just that kind of reflection within them.

Studies in Peace and Scripture is sponsored by the Institute of Mennonite Studies, the research agency of the Associated Mennonite Biblical Seminaries. The seminaries and the tradition they represent have a particular interest in peace but, even more so, a shared interest in the Bible. We hope that this ecumenical series will contribute to a deeper understanding of both.

Ben C. Ollenburger, Old Testament Editor
Willard M. Swartley, New Testament Editor

Preface

During initial studies which eventually led to the writing of this book, a post–World War II Bible dictionary was consulted whose first edition did not contain an entry on "peace" in the main body of the work; only in an appendix was an article on the subject found, and that appeared almost like an afterthought. The fact of this omission is revealing. Into the 1970s, in spite of two devastating global wars, the attention given to the subject of peace in New Testament theologies, in scholarly monographs, and in articles was virtually nonexistent. Since then, some of the neglect of the subject in New Testament studies has been remedied. Some monographs on the topic of peace in the New Testament have been published, and the greatly increased interest in peace-making in church and society during the last two decades has produced some contributions in which the biblical voices were given a fair hearing.

The present study on peace in the New Testament seeks to strengthen the existing contributions by giving greater recognition to some factors which, in my view, have often been given insufficient attention. First, the attempt is made to correlate Old and New Testament studies on the topic more intentionally. Only in this way is it possible to come to grips with the fact that in important traditions in the New Testament peace is so often expressed in military metaphors and through images of conquest and victory. Second, the problems and demands of our time are not divorced from a supposedly purely objective and descriptive approach to biblical interpretation: this book begins and ends with chapters facing contemporary issues. One of the hazards of this approach lies in the occasionally very rapid developments in the political constellations. It is obvious that chapter 1 was written before the current disintegration of the communist central power in the U.S.S.R. I make no apologies for this procedure; the problems addressed in chapter 1 are not eliminated by the metamorphosis of the communist giant, although the conditions affecting their solution are greatly changed. Third, in spite of the acknowledged differences between several distinct concepts of peace in the New Testament, the thesis is here advanced that the subject of peace is approached in the New Testament in a manner that allows the construction of a meaningful synthesis. I have therefore emphasized the large contours of basic aspects of peace, omitting some details (such as the Johannine teaching on peace), and putting aside all technical discussion of exegetical minutiae, the inclusion of which would have swelled the size of this book to twice its present pages.

Several colleagues have helped me greatly in the last stages of work on this book. Professor Willard M. Swartley read the entire draft, giving significant help for improvement in substance and style. Professor Ulrich Luz offered his criticisms of an earlier form of chapter 8 which prompted me to recast the whole chapter. Professor William Klassen gave me excellent suggestions, several of which have been adopted in revisions of the original draft. I deeply appreciate the help of these colleagues. My thanks to them do not, of course, imply that they are in any way responsible for the views advanced in this book.

I thank Cynthia L. Thompson and Carl Helmich of the Westminster/John Knox Press for their unfailing helpfulness and encouragement.

My thanks are also due to the Board of Directors and the Faculty of Pittsburgh Theological Seminary for releasing me from the duties of Dean during the Winter Term of 1988/89, at which time the first seven chapters were written.

My former Pittsburgh secretaries, Mrs. Debora R. Sampson and Mrs. Nancy L. Fraker, have assisted me in every stage of the work. They have not only extended to me every form of secretarial care and courtesy, but accompanied the whole production with keen and understanding participation. I can't thank them enough for their help.

The Rev. Patricia Nelson has read most of an earlier draft. I am indebted to her for her frank criticism.

This book is published in the series *Studies in Peace and Scripture* sponsored by the Institute of Mennonite Studies. As child and heir of the mainstream Protestant tradition I want to express the hope that these pages may in a small way contribute to overcoming the injustices and condemnations, indeed the shedding of blood, which our forebears in the Calvinistic and Lutheran families of the Reformation inflicted on the peace churches in the past.

Ulrich Mauser

Princeton, September 1991

1

A Time for Peace

Concern for peace, efforts to secure peace, and the dedication to study issues bearing on peace have become a matter of survival. Millennia of human history have known deadly feuds, tribal wars, and armed conflicts between nations that were restricted to small spots on the map and did not endanger the continuance of human history and civilization. But in the last half of the twentieth century, even the remotest conflict is made known the world over, and local wars far away from the territories of the superpowers are now enmeshed in a network of global policies and strategies that threaten to escalate at any moment into a conflagration of horrifying magnitude. The successful containment of the recent war in the Persian Gulf cannot provide the assurance that similar military conflicts in the future will also remain under the control of an exceedingly fragile and tenuous multinational alliance.

The advent of a technology that has produced the nuclear threat has also brought about an irreversible situation in which the alternative between peace and war is indissolubly linked to economic, social, and environmental realities. Work for peace can no longer address itself solely to problems of armaments and military strategy if it hopes to proceed with any chance of success. Because of the advances in science and in the resultant technology, and because of the human drive for mastery over nature and the marshaling of nature's forces for our benefit, we have come to the point where a conscious decision for definite limits has become a necessity for the continuation of human history. Nuclear arsenals can serve peace, at best, only if they are never used. By the same token, available means for the use of energy resources can benefit human civilization only if the existing capabilities for exploitation are energetically and intentionally curbed. There need to be clear boundaries to what, while technologically possible, is driven by the production of escalating demands. If peace is understood—through the guidance provided by its biblical definition, or at least in factual parallel with it—as the well-being of human society within the functioning support of nature, peace efforts today must not isolate the military aspect of the task from its several correlated issues. The goal of peace in our world demands a total human effort. The goal will be unattainable if it is not accompanied by a reformation of consciousness. There must be a recovery of the truth that human life, including its intellectual powers and its ability to master nature, is essentially life within boundaries. Although the past few years have presented us with amazing political developments that have greatly reduced the tension between the United States and the Soviet Union, vigilance for peace remains a necessity because military facts have been created which in the long run can only be met by a transformation of attitudes toward war and peace.

This book looks for guidance for our peace efforts in the Bible, and particularly in the New Testament. But the quest is not undertaken in isolation from the conditions of the last decade of the twentieth century. We are looking for instruction from the vantage point of our present situation; although we will make every effort to listen to the Bible on its own terms, we will not seek to arrive at an abstract "biblical ideal" divorced from our own condition. It is therefore necessary that this present condition be first sketched with a few broad strokes of the brush. And in conclusion we will return to our time, in the final chapter of this book.

1. The Nuclear Threat

Since the explosion of nuclear bombs over Hiroshima and Nagasaki in 1945, human warfare has been revolutionized. It may be doubted whether the effects of this revolution have so far been adequately assimilated into the consciousness of a world population that has for thousands of years developed a corporate consciousness that mortal conflict can be conducted with no harm to the existence of the human race within nature, and that indeed such conflict is inevitable. But today the facts show a new and unprecedented situation that demands rethinking from the ground up.

Nuclear and thermonuclear devices exist today which in destructive potential dwarf even the most fearsome weapons used in so-called conventional warfare. In addition, nuclear and thermonuclear technology has, over the past forty years, rushed headlong into the construction of ever more insane monsters of death. The latest forms of these weapons far overshadow their first awful revelation in Japan. In the 1980s, a single salvo from one submarine, either American or Russian, equipped with nuclear missiles, could unleash more destructive force than was ever used in all previous wars throughout human history (McNamara, *Blundering Into Disaster,* 14; see Select Bibliography at the end of this chapter for this and all following references to sources). The bomb dropped on Hiroshima, sarcastically called "Little Boy," which started the nuclear revolution, killed an estimated 75,000 people; yet the MX missile of the 1980s, capable of striking within 100 yards of its target, owing to its computerized guidance system, can wipe out an area sixty times as large as that destroyed in Hiroshima (R. L. Sivard, *Expenditures,* 17). The firepower of a single nuclear submarine of the Poseidon class is sufficient to cripple the industrial capacity of the entire Soviet Union. Fitted with 24 Trident II missiles, each containing 17 individually targeted atomic warheads, the boat can trigger one blow against 408 different targets in Russia, each warhead packing a power five times as great as the "Little Boy" (Wallis, *Peace,* 37).

The estimates of military and civilian losses even in a limited nuclear confrontation between the superpowers, using only tactical nuclear arms in a policy of "flexible response," are horrendous and escalate from decade to decade. A NATO war game conducted in 1955 in central Europe projected only a restricted use of small-scale nuclear weapons as a second line of defense in case of a Russian tank and infantry advance. The estimated casualties were put at more than 1.5 million people in the first two days of the campaign. In 1980 a study concluded that an attack by the United States and the Soviet Union on each other's military targets alone, and limited to the deployment of nuclear artillery shells and bombs, would result in 5 to 6 million civilians dead and about 400,000 military casualties, leaving behind more than one million civilians suffering from radiation disease (McNamara, *Disaster,* 33f.). All-out nuclear attack by one superpower on the other would produce losses so great as to turn the territories of the largest nations into graveyards. Already in 1970, an expert estimated that in case of total nuclear attack by the United States, 100 million Russians would die if no evacuation to civil defense shelters had occurred; but even if there was time for evacuation, 10 million Russian casualties would still result (von Weizsäcker, *The Politics of Peril,* 169f.).

Until the end of the 1980s, the accumulation of fantastic arsenals in atomic weapons has continued unabated since 1946. While the United States was far ahead of the Soviet Union for many years, by the late 1980s a virtual parity in atomic stockpiles of the two superpowers was reached. In 1987 the number of nuclear weapons stored in the United States for use by its operational strategic forces was given as 12,874; the number of comparable weapons in the Soviet Union did not lag far behind. In addition, it is estimated that four other nuclear powers possess significant nuclear capabilities: the United Kingdom (534 nuclear weapons), France (473), China (perhaps 350), and Israel (undeclared, but estimated at 100–200). Altogether, this adds up to a present global nuclear stockpile that packs the power of at least one million Hiroshima-size bombs, capable of setting off a deadly energy 2,667 times as great as the total explosive force employed in World War II (Sivard, *Expenditures,* 16). Only very recently, in December 1987, was a step taken which gives some hope for an eventual reversal of the nuclear buildup. This occurred when President Reagan and Secretary Gorbachev signed the treaty on intermediate-range nuclear missiles, agreeing to destroy or dismantle one class of nuclear weapons altogether and to seek future accords aiming at far more substantial cutbacks in offensive nuclear arms. The additional steps in the same direction, taken since December 1987, are worthy of full support and give rise to renewed vigor in addressing the huge problems and dangers that remain.

The presence of nuclear deterrence has unquestionably contributed, perhaps more than any other factor, to the fact that the major military powers in the world have not waged direct war with each other since the end of World War II. But the fear of nuclear catastrophe has provided only a highly precarious balance that cannot be trusted to be an effective measure ensuring abiding peace. Several factors demand attention and must be considered.

a. Since 1945, the nuclear threat has not prevented the outbreak of a great number of wars fought with conventional weapons. While the territory of the superpowers and their strong industrialized allies has remained free of the ravages of war, military confrontation has shifted to the developing and underdeveloped nations. Some of these wars are fought with tremendous losses and savage brutality. They are fed through a booming international arms trade in which governments and private interests are equally involved. The six nations with the largest military budgets in the world accounted for 80 percent of the international arms trade, with the United States and the Soviet Union leading the field by a large margin. The imports of arms were, in great measure, responsible for the fact that in 1987 alone 22 wars were being fought, in each of which more than 1,000 deaths were estimated (Sivard, *Expenditures,* 10f. and 28).

b. The creeping proliferation of nuclear capabilities threatens to destabilize the balance of terror established between the superpowers. Although the Nuclear Non-Proliferation Treaty of 1968 had by 1987 been signed by 137 nations not possessing nuclear weapons, some important and populous nations (e.g., India and Pakistan) have so far refused to sign. Iraq's potential for development and use of nuclear arms, together with biological weapons, contributed to the outbreak of the war in the Persian Gulf and demonstrated that lessened tensions between the superpowers are not enough to prevent a devastating military campaign against a rival aspiring to join the club of those who possess atomic weaponry. In addition, nuclear reactors for the peaceful production of atomic energy are operating today in many countries on all continents. These power plants yield as a by-product plutonium, which could be used for the production of nuclear weapons at any time a government so decided. It is estimated that the amount of plutonium available through commercial reprocessing in power plants would be sufficient, by the year 2000, to enable the production of 49,000 nuclear weapons (Sivard, *Expenditures,* 1985, 19). There is an enormous risk that the possession of nuclear arms will spread significantly in the decades ahead. This capability will be available to countries that might fall into the hands of fanatics and desperadoes who could kindle the fire leading to a nuclear holocaust.

c. The possibility of technical failure and of miscalculation exists, which could trigger nuclear exchanges. It is reported that in 1979 and 1980 in the United States, and in 1984 in the Soviet Union, computer failures led to war alerts in the command posts of the strategic forces (Sivard, *Expenditures,* 20). Although, so far, rational human decisions have prevailed over technical mistakes, this may not always be the case. The constantly increasing technical sophistication of nuclear weaponry leads to larger dependence on more and more sophisticated computer systems, reducing the range reserved for human decisions. Particularly ominous, in this respect, is the development of the Strategic Defense Initiative ("Star Wars"), which relies on computer systems of a complexity that virtually eliminates the control of human decision makers (McNamara, *Disaster,* 169f.).

In conclusion, it must be stated that the introduction of nuclear weaponry has produced a dilemma that defies traditional approaches to questions of peace and war. In planning for nuclear confrontations, shifting U.S. strategies have not succeeded in providing an acceptable form of deterrence. Concepts of "massive retaliation," "mutual assured destruction" (MAD), "flexible response," and now the aim of fashioning an effective defensive shield against nuclear attack, have so far failed to produce a reliable balance of power, leading instead to ever new escalations in the arms race. It is certain that the Strategic Defense Initiative will be no exception to this series of failures, especially not if it should become technically successful. In the unlikely event, as many experts insist, of Star Wars' ability to provide a sufficiently tight protective shield, it is foolish to expect, in the long run, anything else from Soviet leadership but the redoubling of their efforts to defeat this defensive system. Thus nothing can be expected except a new round in the arms race involving expenditures more ruinous for both sides than ever before.

The dilemma remains. Scientific and technological advances have produced war capabilities that constantly threaten to destroy their inventors together with the entire civilization on which these advances have been built. The search for peace in the atomic age is beset with an endemic danger that military strategies by themselves cannot possibly remove. "The great bombs fulfill their purpose of protecting peace and freedom only if they are never dropped. They also do not fulfill their purpose if everybody knows that they will never be dropped. Precisely for that reason, there exists the danger that, one day, they will be dropped" (C. F. von Weizsäcker, quoted in Altner, *Überlebenskrise,* 48; my trans.).

2. Economics of War and Peace

The persistent efforts by President Gorbachev in recent years to reach agreements with the United States in the reduction of nuclear arms, and in slowing down the arms race, are motivated, at least in part, by the recognition that the economy of the Soviet Union cannot continue to bear the burden of the exorbitant expenditures caused by the fixation on developing an ever more costly arsenal of nuclear weaponry. Estimates put the amounts spent for military purposes in the USSR from 1960 to 1987 at $4.6 trillion, which contributes substantially to the fact that, in comparison with 142 other countries, the USSR ranks only twenty-third on a scale measuring the economic and social benefits available to the population (Sivard, *Expenditures,* 5). Total military expenditures between 1960 and 1987 in the world amounted to the fantastic sum of $15.2 trillion and comparative figures reveal that, while the world gross national product rose only slightly between 1974 and 1987, the global military expenditures doubled in the same period of time.

The increasing cost of the military buildup in the world is by no means exclusively attributable to the race in developing atomic weaponry by the superpowers. Expenses incurred through military development in countries of the Third World were in 1988 seven times as large as in 1960, and it gives pause for thought to realize that monies spent for the military effort were then 2,900 times as large as the expenses incurred in international peacekeeping efforts (Sivard, 5).

Nonetheless, the anxiety of military strategists concerning the balance in the possession of nuclear deterrents remains a major cause for continual funding of excessively expensive research, development, and production of nuclear arms. The nervousness exhibited by planning staffs has time and again led to the assumption of a "gap" in one form of preparedness or another, and the perceived existence of such a gap has led invariably to grotesque expenditures which, after some time, were found to be based on miscalculations. Robert McNamara, Secretary of Defense for seven years in the Kennedy and Johnson administrations, gives revealing insights into misconceptions of the planning staff which fueled the fever to commit huge budgets to research and development. In 1960, when John F. Kennedy campaigned for the presidency, he spoke of concern about a "missile gap" that was assumed to threaten the security of the United States. The expressed concern was based on intelligence estimates from the Air Force. But when McNamara took office he investigated the information that had led to the assumption of a serious deficiency in U.S. missiles. It was found that there was indeed a gap but it favored the United States by a large margin (McNamara, *Disaster,* 43f.). Since the alleged "bomber gap" of the 1950s, and the "missile gap" of the 1960s, six more perceived gaps have been given considerable publicity, but all of them were subsequently found to have been based on faulty sources and miscalculations (Sivard, 9). I do not know if anyone has ever attempted to calculate the sums of money appropriated and expended on the basis of false information and of faulty calculations leading to assumed "gaps" that threaten the military security of the United States, but the amounts would appear to be staggering.

This is not to say that the cost of military preparedness is constantly rising exclusively on account of a security psychosis that seems to obstruct rational judgments. Weapons get increasingly more complicated, and consequently also costlier. This is true not only for atomic armaments but for "conventional" weapons as well. A bomber built in World War II cost a great deal less than its counterpart today. Figures are available which demonstrate that the costs of the weapons industry have risen out of proportion with the general rise in costs. The average increase in the cost of goods and services in the United States between 1945 and 1987 was 6.5 percent, but the price paid for weaponry in 1987 was 105 times larger than in 1945 (Sivard, 15).

I am in no position to calculate the impact of the expenditures incurred in the arms race on the global and national economies, but it stands to reason that the evidence showing the far greater growth of military-related expenditures in comparison to the rate of growth of the global, and U.S., national gross product argues for the drain on national economies due to the cost of the arms race. The production and distribution of goods and services, commitment to education and health care, and attention to cultural developments—these are the losers in the competition for available public and private funds. This seems to be particularly the case in countries of the Third World, where expenditures for weapons imports and for the conduct of wars contribute substantially to the impoverishment of their people, and where the resulting poverty feeds renewed rebellion and revolutionary wars. But the superpowers are not exempt from this vicious cycle. Their competing ideologies claim to hold the key to a future of true human liberty and happiness. But their headlong rush to erect a wall of threats undermines the economic means to build a life of freedom. Thus the extravagant defense of freedom endangers that freedom itself. This is true both of the United States and of the Soviet Union, their different concepts of the nature of human freedom notwithstanding. A reality has emerged before our eyes in which competing concepts of human freedom are not allowed to demonstrate the truth of their claim, either to their citizens, for their benefit, or to the world at large. The procurement of a shield of protection around both systems drains away so much economic strength that the freedoms themselves suffer greatly.

3. Nature in the Nuclear Age

Limited and full-scale nuclear war would not only cause horrifying human casualties, it would also be disastrous to the natural environment. A nuclear exchange of one third of the nuclear arsenals stored in the United States and in the Soviet Union would result in the instantaneous deaths of an estimated 1.1 billion people in the Northern Hemisphere, with another billion doomed to die a short time after the explosions (Miller, *Environment,* E14). But the effect of such a blast on the balance and resources of nature would be no less devastating.

A blast of the magnitude mentioned above would contaminate all surface water supply in the Northern Hemisphere through radiation and the leakage of toxic materials into lakes and rivers. A large number of experts have roughly agreed that the huge amount of dust and soot hurled into the atmosphere and stratosphere by the blast would settle in an enormous dark cloud preventing, at first, 96 percent of the sunlight from reaching most of the Northern Hemisphere, and thereafter blocking, for up to two months, 50 percent of the sun's rays from reaching the earth. The probable result is estimated to be a reduction in temperature to -23 degrees Celsius (-10 degrees Fahrenheit) for about one quarter of a year, sufficient to change most of the northern half of the globe into a mass of ice and bone-chilling cold. The effects of this catastrophe rival the vision of any apocalyptic seer. The remains of human population, already deprived of most of the resources and aids to which it was accustomed, would need to find shelter from colossal storms caused by the temperature changes on the surface of the earth. Livestock and wildlife would suffer as severely as the human population and would probably, in large measure, die out. Crops and the soil itself would be contaminated by radioactive fallout. Forests and grasslands would already have been largely destroyed by fires raging over vast areas of land. Even a small nuclear blast involving less than 1 percent of the reserves now stored in the nuclear arsenals would, it is said by those experts, produce a nuclear winter in the Northern Hemisphere with temperatures sinking to -20 degrees Celsius (-4 degrees Fahrenheit) for over two months.

In addition, a paradoxical reversal of the nuclear winter would also take place. A full-scale nuclear war would cause a reduction in the atmospheric layer of ozone of some 30 to 70 percent over the Northern Hemisphere. The ozone layer protects the surface of the earth by filtering out about 99 percent of the dangerous ultraviolet radiation emanating from the sun. It is calculated that a regeneration of the atmosphere's layer of ozone would take from 2 to 20 years. Consequently, after the effects of a nuclear winter had worn off, opposite effects caused by exposure to harmful sun rays would set in. The consequences for fundamental changes in the climate of the earth would be beyond calculation. (The information contained in the last two paragraphs is for the most part from Miller, *Environment,* 80–81 and E14–15.)

In this chapter we have concentrated almost exclusively on the menace of nuclear war. But it is necessary to pay at least some attention to nonmilitary effects of modern technology on our environment. Not only a nuclear blast can damage the ozone layer in the atmosphere. The exhaust of supersonic planes and the chemicals released through aerosol spray cans and leaking refrigerators and air conditioners can also adversely affect the ozone protection. It is possible that some early pessimistic assessments of this danger need to be revised, but attention to possible dangers to the environment remains necessary.

More serious, perhaps, are the difficulties posed by the energy needs of the world. Proven oil reserves in the world, together with reserves likely to be found, will—if the present rate of increase in consumption persists—last only for 18 to 30 years. Coal reserves would last much longer, but they could also be exhausted in a period short enough to require immediate planning; given a 4 percent annual increase in consumption and a total switch to coal as energy supply, coal reserves would last only for 100 years. Planning for energy to be supplied by nuclear reactors and solar light therefore becomes mandatory; the possibility of nuclear fusion appears to be still too controversial to permit definite planning. Nuclear reactors are used all over the world as suppliers of energy. But they pose a double danger to the environment that cannot yet be discounted. Nuclear waste is potentially a powerful pollutant of earth and air, and no ultimately satisfactory solution for storage has yet been found. So far, great amounts of highly radioactive nuclear waste are deposited in provisional storage and, as long as this condition lasts, the menace of contamination remains. Also, the danger from malfunction of nuclear reactors remains real. The accidents at Three Mile Island and, especially, at Chernobyl have made it clear that technical failures in the reactors, whether or not caused by human error, have the potential to cause great damage to human, animal, and plant life as well as to the whole environment (on this paragraph, see von Weizsäcker, *Peril*, 10–34).

It seems that the conclusion is inevitable: Modern science has managed to exploit nature, enabling the human race to marshal its forces in ways not imaginable a mere fifty years ago. But this mastery has brought with it dangers to human existence, and indeed to our earth as we know it, of a magnitude not anticipated two generations before us. The human master mind has created its own enslavement, and potentially its extinction. Ways out of this threat can only be found if a form of science is devised for the future that is guided and governed by the necessity to be caretaker of nature, and therefore to be limited by what, in the language of theology, is called human responsibility in answer to the world's creation by God.

Even the welfare of our earth calls out today: It is a time for peace.

Select Bibliography

Altner, G. *Die Überlebenskrise in der Gegenwart: Ansätze zum Dialog mit der Natur in Naturwissenschaft und Theologie.* Darmstadt: Wissenschaftliche Buchgesellschaft, 1987.

McNamara, Robert S. *Blundering Into Disaster: Surviving the First Century of the Nuclear Age.* New York: Pantheon Books, 1986.

Miller, G. Tyler, Jr. *Living in the Environment: An Introduction to Environmental Science.* 4th edition. Belmont, Calif.: Wadsworth Publishing Co., 1985.

Sivard, Ruth L. *World Military and Social Expenditures 1987–88.* Washington, D.C.: World Priorities, 1988. (A series of annual publications, begun in 1951. References in chapter 1 are from the 1987–88 issue, unless otherwise indicated.)

Wallis, Jim, ed. *Waging Peace: A Handbook for the Struggle Against Nuclear Arms.* San Francisco: Harper & Row, 1982.

Weizsäcker, Carl Friedrich von. *The Politics of Peril: Economics, Society and the Prevention of War.* New York: Seabury Press, 1978.

2

Biblical Words
of Peace

We are on the way to letting the New Testament speak on the matter of peace. But it is necessary to recognize that making one's way toward the New Testament along the road of Old Testament and Jewish traditions is not merely an exercise in the history of a word; the journey becomes, and remains, a part of the destination. The heart of the matter itself is at stake if we include the Old Testament in the search for the reality named "peace" in the New Testament. We begin the biblical part of this book, therefore, with the question: What are biblical words of peace?

1. Shalom

It is beyond dispute that the only Hebrew word basic for our search is the word *shalom* (*šalom*). It was translated in the Septuagint by the Greek noun *eirene* (*eirēnē*), expressing peace, in so overwhelming a majority of cases that we can disregard the fact, for purposes of New Testament studies, that there are Hebrew equivalents other than *shalom* for what we mean by peace (*'emunah, mesarim, menuḥah*).

The noun *shalom* occurs some 235 times in the Masoretic text of the Old Testament; the count in standard dictionaries varies slightly. Its range of meaning is extraordinarily wide. The word is used in the common language of the day, but it appears also in worship and in law. Its net spreads over communal and individual life, and it is at home in the areas of political concerns as well as in that of protophilosophical discourse in wisdom literature. Moreover, Israel's language about God is given some of its distinctive force by the word *shalom*. In many of its uses the word carries, for our feeling of language, a flexibility and adaptability that defy a translator's desire to find a precise English equivalent. It is not only understandable, then, but required that English Bible translations, if they render the Hebrew *shalom,* adopt many English words that give the reader no clue of the original. To cite a few examples from the New Revised Standard Version (NRSV): Psalm 38:3, "There is no *shalom* in my bones," is translated with the phrase "There is no health in my bones"; the question "What is his *shalom?"* in Genesis 29:6 becomes "Is it well with him?"; and "the prosperity of the wicked" in Psalm 73:3 is a rendition of the Hebrew *"shalom* of the wicked."

The General Use of Shalom

The English word "well-being" provides, perhaps, the most satisfactory attempt in translation to cover the sweep of the Hebrew *shalom* in a general way. This is not to claim that "well-being" represents the meaning of the root *šlm*. In fact, the meaning of the root is not established beyond dispute; even after repeated and intensive investigations, the proposals to define the basic meaning still vary from "totality," "intactness" (Walter Eisenbeis and many others) to "compensation" (Gillis Gerlemann). "Well-being" is simply intended to render an acceptable general equivalent to *shalom* as it appears to be used in many different contexts.

In roughly 10 percent of its usage in the Old Testament, *shalom* appears in greetings. Two people meeting each other offer the wish *"Shalom* be with you," and in parting from each other they say "Go in *shalom."* (Thus Joseph, on meeting his brothers again, Gen. 43:23, interpreted by NRSV with the translation "Rest assured"; on the departure: Achish to David, 1 Sam. 29:7). The greeting can be modified into the form of the inquiry "How is his (her) *shalom?"* (Thus Jacob asking about the condition of Laban, Gen. 29:6.) In these cases, the greeting or the inquiry have in mind the general well-being of a person. As a part of everyday speech, they must have been used in a very conventional way, implying no more subtlety or depth than our phrase "How are you?"

Not only is the good condition of people expressed by *shalom*. Jeremiah asks about Jerusalem, "Who will turn aside to ask about your welfare (*shalom*)?" (Jer. 15:5), and the same prophet, in his letter to the exiles in Babylon, urges them to care for the welfare of the city in which they are detained: "Seek the welfare of the city where I have sent you into exile, and pray to the Lord on its behalf, for in its welfare you will find your welfare" (Jer. 29:7; *shalom* three times). The good condition of animals is also *shalom*. Joseph is sent by Jacob to his brothers to find out "if it is well with your brothers and with the flock" (Gen. 37:14; *shalom* both times). In a very telling sentence, David is reported to have asked Uriah "how Joab and the people fared, and how the war was going" (2 Sam. 11:7). Joab, the people, and the war are all alike questioned about their *shalom*. It is obvious, in this case, that *shalom* cannot possibly mean "peace" in the sense of a condition without war. David is interested in the good fortune of his field commander, his troops, and the military operation in which they are engaged. In this passage their *shalom* comes very close to indicating their success in the field.

In some contexts, *shalom* encourages translations that deviate no less than 2 Samuel 11:7 from our concept of peace. Jeremiah suffers from denunciations against him: "All my close friends (men of my *shalom*), are watching for me to stumble" (Jer. 20:10). The women of the royal household in Jerusalem, who are being led away into captivity, complain about having been deceived by their "trusted friends" (Jer. 38:22, "men of your *shalom*"). If it is the notion of friendly relations which can be captured by *shalom* in these Jeremiah verses, then the word can, at times, emphasize the idea of security and harmony. Again Jeremiah is asked by God how he will cope with the thickets of the Jordan if he falls down even on "safe land" (land of *shalom,* Jer. 12:5). Harmonious relations between rulers and peoples are signified by *shalom* (between Solomon and Hiram, 1 Kings 5:12 [5:26 Heb.]), and even the death of a person can be said to happen "in *shalom"* if it is the conclusion of a full and satisfying life rather than a violent, unnatural death (good old age, Gen. 15:15; to die not by the sword = to die in *shalom,* Jer. 34:4f.).

We may conclude, then, that *shalom* speaks very generally of a favorable condition, of the well-being or welfare, of persons and circumstances. In many contexts, the word appears to carry greater specificity, recommending translations like success, friendship, harmony, and security. This expansiveness of connotations, however, makes it easily comprehensible that *shalom* may signify healthy political, commercial, and diplomatic relations as well. Thus the term comes close to, or even coincides with, our word "peace" in its relation to public and international life. Since this aspect of the matter lies closer to the issues we will be exploring later, it becomes necessary to proceed now with attention to more detail.

Political and Military Uses of Shalom

The examples cited for various meanings of *shalom* are highly selective and could be supported by many more references. But at the point we have now reached, an effort will be made to be more comprehensive.

Ecclesiastes 3:8 states, there is "a time for war, and a time for peace (*shalom*)," and in Leviticus 26:6 the security of the land, with its population free of fear that the sword will ravage its territory, is summed up in the sentence "I will grant peace (*shalom*) in the land." In sentences like these, the immediate context makes it clear that *shalom* means freedom from the reality and the threat of war. The offer of *shalom* to a city in Deuteronomy 20:10, prior to the commencement of hostilities, means the offer of avoiding military conflict, as the alternative between war and peacemaking in 20:12 confirms. The defeated Sisera, in fear for his life on Israelite territory, flees into the land of the Kenites because there was peace (*shalom*) between Canaanites and Kenites at this time (Judg. 4:17). The Ammonites demand restoration of their land without recourse to war (in *shalom,* Judg. 11:13). The tribe of Benjamin, threatened with extinction because of a violation of amphictyonic law, is finally offered reconciliation by a proclamation of peace (*shalom,* Judg. 21:13). After the restoration (through military force) of Israelite land from the Philistines, the sentence is added: "There was peace (*shalom*) also between Israel and the Amorites" (1 Sam. 7:14). War and peace are juxtaposed as opposites in 1 Kings 2:5 and 20:18; Solomon rejoices in peace on every side (*shalom;* NRSV "rest"), untrammeled by either enemies or misfortune (1 Kings 5:4); and Hezekiah, confronted with the specter of a military disaster that will result in the deportation of his own sons, consoles himself with the prospect that at least during his lifetime he will have "peace (*shalom*) and security" (2 Kings 20:19 and Isa. 39:8). Solomon is contrasted with the bloodthirsty David as a "man of peace" (1 Chron. 22:9). Psalm 120:6f. breaks out in the lament, "Too long have I had my dwelling among those who hate peace (*shalom*). I am for peace (*shalom*); but when I speak, they are for war."

We should, however, not draw far-reaching conclusions from those sentences to the effect that Old Testament passages, at least here and there, oppose war on principle. A glance at the wider context of two of the previously quoted statements can clarify this. The sentence, Yahweh "will grant peace in the land" (Lev. 26:6) expresses not only a desirable state of affairs but also an affinity between Yahweh's presence and blessing with peace. Nonetheless, the immediate continuation speaks of the way in which this peace is either prepared or secured: "You shall chase your enemies, and they shall fall before you by the sword. Five of you shall give chase to a hundred, and a hundred of you shall give chase to ten thousand; your enemies shall fall before you by the sword" (Lev. 26:7f.). By the same token, the offer of peace before the attack against a city in Deuteronomy 20:10 is no renunciation of the use of arms if the offer is refused. In that case, the siege of the city is to begin and "when the Lord your God gives it into your hand, you shall put all its males to the sword" (Deut. 20:12f.). We can thus far only say that the word *shalom* assumes, in certain passages, the meaning of peaceful and healthy conditions between peoples. However, this does not imply the renunciation of martial violence in the pursuit of this peace in accordance with the principles of nonviolent resistance.

Shalom in Israel's Faith

We have, so far, considered some uses of the word *shalom* in which the setting appears, to our understanding, quite secular. Whether they were so to the authors of the Old Testament may be questioned. The neat separation of a "secular" from a "sacred" domain is, after all, of very modern vintage, and one may suspect that ancient Israelites would not have comprehended it. There are, however, many contexts in the Old Testament in which the word *shalom* is explicitly drawn into the vortex of Israel's faith in Yahweh. To passages of this kind we can now direct our attention.

Closely related to greetings is the blessing; in both, *shalom* is the good which is desired for or imparted to the recipients. At the end of two psalms of pilgrimage, a blessing is invoked on the Israelite community as a whole: "Peace (*shalom*) be upon Israel" (Pss. 125:5; 128:6). In cultically solemn form this blessing is entrusted to the Aaronite priesthood:

> The Lord bless you and keep you;
> The Lord make his face to shine upon you,
>   and be gracious to you;
> The Lord lift up his countenance upon you,
>   and give you peace (*shalom*). (Num. 6:24–26)

It has been observed that codes of law in the ancient Near East end with regularity in statements about blessing on those who conform to the code's regulation, and curse on those who disregard it. Collections of laws in the Old Testament maintain this pattern. We may once more return to Leviticus 26:6 with its promise of peace in the land. The promise is part of a much longer statement on blessings that concludes the Holiness Code (Leviticus 17–26) and that is followed by the announcement of curses on those who are disobedient. The opening section on the blessings (Lev. 26:3–13) stipulates the condition, namely, conduct in agreement with the laws contained in the code, and then proceeds to describe the contents of the blessing: There will be an abundance of rain to make the land fruitful, there will be security for its inhabitants, and even wild animals will not be able to disturb the safety of the land. In the center of this list of blessings we find the sentence "I will grant peace in the land" (v. 6). Whether *shalom* is here intended to be one link in a chain of correlated divine gifts, or whether it concentrates all the other goods into a single and central concept, it is manifest that *shalom* is linked together with obedience to the law, with the promise of fertility of nature, and the expectation of safety from disturbances caused by human enemies or by dangerous beasts. The passage is so paradigmatic that it may be quoted in full:

> If you follow my statutes and keep my commandments and observe them faithfully, I will give you your rains in their season, and the land shall yield its produce, and the trees of

the field shall yield their fruit. Your threshing shall overtake the vintage, and the vintage shall overtake the sowing; you shall eat your bread to the full, and live securely in your land. And I will grant peace in the land, and you shall lie down, and no one shall make you afraid; I will remove dangerous animals from the land, and no sword shall go through your land. You shall give chase to your enemies, and they shall fall before you by the sword. Five of you shall give chase to a hundred, and a hundred of you shall give chase to ten thousand; your enemies shall fall before you by the sword. I will look with favor upon you and make you fruitful and multiply you; and I will maintain my covenant with you. You shall eat old grain long stored, and you shall have to clear out the old to make way for the new. I will place my dwelling in your midst, and I shall not abhor you. And I will walk among you, and will be your God, and you shall be my people. I am the Lord your God who brought you out of the land of Egypt, to be their slaves no more; I have broken the bars of your yoke and made you walk erect. (Lev. 26:3–13)

Shalom is unthinkable without obedience to Yahweh's law. It is Israel's responsibility to live and act in positive response to the instructions that God has promulgated, and in clinging to this law resides Israel's welfare. Faithfulness to the law and righteousness are, therefore, indissolubly united with peace:

> Steadfast love and faithfulness will meet;
> righteousness and peace (*shalom*) will kiss each other.
> Faithfulness will spring up from the ground,
> and righteousness will look down from the sky. (Ps. 85:10f.)

"Great peace (*shalom*) have those who love your law; nothing can make them stumble" (Ps. 119:165). *Shalom* can be pursued and this pursuit is identical with departure from evil: "Depart from evil, and do good; seek peace (*shalom*), and pursue it" (Ps. 34:14). Evil can be set as the direct opposite of *shalom*. This evil (*ra'*) is understood as disregard to Yahweh's order for life and, therefore, the transgressor has no part in *shalom*.

> Mark the blameless, and behold the upright,
> for there is posterity for the peaceable (*shalom*).
> But transgressors shall be altogether destroyed;
> the posterity of the wicked shall be cut off. (Ps. 37:37f.)

There is no peace (*shalom*), says the Lord, for the wicked.
(Isa. 48:22)

There is no peace (*shalom*), says my God, for the wicked.
(Isa. 57:21)

Deceit is in the mind of those who plan evil,
    but those who counsel peace (*shalom*) have joy. (Prov. 12:20)

In wisdom literature, the love for the law is modified by the love of wisdom in which *shalom* is attained. Wisdom's "ways are ways of pleasantness, and all her paths are peace (*shalom*)" (Prov. 3:17). Therefore the admonition is given:

My child, do not forget my teaching,
    but let your heart keep my commandments;
for length of days and years of life
    and abundant welfare (*shalom*) they will give you. (Prov. 3:1f.)

Shalom and the King

The care for the good order of life was entrusted, in particular, to the king. It seems likely that the Davidic monarchy in Jerusalem, building on older local traditions of Canaanite origin and incorporating generally held ideas about kingship in the ancient Near East, developed an ideology in which the king was both the origin and the guarantor of the *shalom* of his people by virtue of his endowment with Yahweh's powers. The range of meaning for *shalom* in this context is extraordinarily wide. It stretches from the king's care for justice, particularly his responsibility to the poor and needy, to the vision of a universal dominion over the entire world and the riches of a life of nature in which incessant fertility of the land is provided.

In an old psalm, the royal dominion of Yahweh over other gods and his command of the forces of nature, described in partial accommodation of traditional Canaanite concepts, is made the basis for the blessing: "May the Lord give strength to his people! May the Lord bless his people with peace (*shalom*)!" (Ps. 29:11). *Shalom* is here the condition of nature under the lordship of Yahweh, who, sitting enthroned as king over the waters of chaos (Ps. 29:10), breaks the powers of a wild nature which, left to its own devices, would destroy all possibilities of orderly and protected human life. In some analogy to this picture of King Yahweh enthroned above gods and nature, the kings in Jerusalem were projected into an idea of royal power and responsibility that far surpasses any historical realization. Especially in Psalm 72, the magnificent mantle of this kingship is spread out, and the king is presented as the offspring and guardian of *shalom*. He is responsible for administering Yahweh's justice and faithfulness on earth, which is synonymous with *shalom:*

Give the king your justice, O God,
   and your righteousness to a king's son. (v. 1)

In his days may righteousness flourish
   and peace (*shalom*) abound, until the moon is no more. (v. 7)

In his administration of justice the care of the disadvantaged is made the obligation of the king:

May he judge . . . your poor with justice. (v. 2)

May he defend the cause of the poor of the people,
   give deliverance to the needy,
   and crush the oppressor. (v. 4)

For he delivers the needy when they call,
   the poor and those who have no helper.
He has pity on the weak and the needy,
   and saves the lives of the needy.
From oppression and violence he redeems their life;
   and precious is their blood in his sight. (vs. 12–14)

Under this royal rule nature will deliver its abundant blessing:

May the mountains yield prosperity (*shalom!*) for the people,
   and the hills righteousness! (Ps. 72:3, NRSV alt.).

Indeed, his government is like an enduring provision of the fruit-giving rains whose continuance can be invoked:

May he be like rain that falls on the mown grass,
   like showers that water the earth. (v. 6)

May there be abundance of grain in the land;
   may it wave on the tops of the mountains;
   may its fruit be like Lebanon;
   and may people blossom in the cities
   like the grass of the field. (v. 16)

The *shalom* whose pledge is the king's just rule is coupled with the hope of a long life for the king:

May he live while the sun endures,
    and as long as the moon, throughout all generations. (v. 5)

Long may he live! (v. 15)

May his name endure forever,
    his fame continue as long as the sun. (v. 17)

Within the radius of the king's *shalom* lies, finally, the idea of a worldwide governance by the royal house in Jerusalem and the acquisition of great wealth:

> May he have dominion from sea to sea,
>   and from the River to the ends of the earth.
> May his foes bow down before him,
>   and his enemies lick the dust.
> May the kings of Tarshish and of the isles
>   render him tribute,
> may the kings of Sheba and Seba
>   bring gifts.
> May all kings fall down before him,
>   all nations give him service. (vs. 8–11)

The canvas of *shalom* under Yahweh's vicegerent glows in all colors, and we must notice that the expectation of military victory over enemies and the subjection of hostile governments under Davidic supremacy are here seen not as a contradiction, but as the consequence and manifestation of *shalom*.

The psalms mentioned above reflect a cultic practice in which the exceedingly high estimation of the Davidic dynasty as agent of Yahweh's world government was perpetuated from one generation to another without regard to the actual accomplishment of a living king in Jerusalem. But prophetic voices arose which concentrated elements of the cultic picture of the king into a single royal individual who would in truth be Yahweh's chosen anointed one (Messiah). The word *shalom* is associated with the most important of these prophetic statements. In Isaiah 9:1–7 an heir of David is announced who is to begin an era of peace (*shalom,* 9:7). This is captured in one of the four names he is to be given at his coronation, the name Prince of Peace (*shalom,* 9:6). This era of peace has not been initiated without military force, as evidenced by the burning of soldiers' boots and blood-soaked clothes on the battlefield after the victory (9:5), and it will be a time of peace that is, again, linked to the triumph of justice and righteousness in the future king's government (9:7). Much more radical is the transformation of the conditions in the messianic vision of Isaiah 11:1–9. The peace among animals (11:6f.) is added to the older hope of protection of human life from harm by dangerous animals (11:8); the constant emphasis of the king's dedication to justice is repeated with great force (11:3–5); and the inauguration of messianic rule is achieved by the inspiration of the king with Yahweh's own spirit (11:2). Although the word *shalom* is not used in Isaiah 11:1–9, the whole picture is a forceful image of the peace in the messianic government. Much more earth-bound is the language of the same hope in Micah 5:2–6 [1–5 Heb.]. Perhaps this ruler, who is to be the incarnation of what has been genuine kingship from the beginning of time (5:2), is in this passage entitled "He is our peace," *zeh šalom* (5:5 [5:4 Heb.]), but it is evident that this king's peace is a pacification which is carried out by the use of the sword against the Assyrian enemy (5:5f.). The traditional royal symbol of the shepherd is used in Ezekiel's two announcements of a Davidic king who will establish a "covenant of peace" (*shalom* in Ezek. 34:25 and 37:26). This covenant of peace is linked to the security of the land, fruitfulness of the land, cessation of the threat from outside enemies, and the absence of danger from wild animals (Ezek. 34:25–31 and 37:24–28). Finally (Zech. 9:9f.), a messianic king is introduced who, in contrast to riders on war horses, will be seated on an ass, and whose government from one end of the earth to the other will result in the abolition of the instruments of war.

Prophetic Concern for Shalom

Even at its best times, and with its worthiest representatives, the Judean monarchy in Jerusalem could not bring to realization the lofty claims held up by this ideal of the king. The destruction of the northern kingdom by the Assyrians in the last third of the eighth century B.C., and the downfall of the Judean monarchy under Babylonian blows in the first

decades of the sixth century B.C., could not but call into
question the vision of the king as Yahweh's agent and the
shalom linked to his rule. In fact, it is certain that the
historical events preceding the several phases of the Babylonian takeover in Judea, the destruction of Solomon's temple,
and the final deportation into Babylonia of the ruling class in
Jerusalem were associated with sharp conflicts about the
validity of Yahweh's promise of *shalom*. The policy of
resistance against the invading Babylonians was supported
by a group of prophets who sought to strengthen the determination and confidence of a government that was not about to
capitulate to the enemy's onrush. On the opposite side stood
prophets who insisted that reliance on the promise of *shalom*
was ungrounded because the time of God was not a time of
well-being but a time of judgment. The struggle has left its
clearest literary traces in the book of Jeremiah, which makes
it also clear, however, that neither Jeremiah nor his major
opponent Hananiah (Jeremiah 28) were isolated figures. The
slogan of the group of prophets backing the official policy of
military resistance to Babylon is captured in Jeremiah's
saying, "Ah, Lord God! Here are the prophets saying to them,
'You shall not see the sword, nor shall you have famine, but I
will give you true peace (*shalom*) in this place'" (Jer. 14:13).
These prophets are certain that the presence of Yahweh with
king and temple is not only reliable forever but implies a
guarantee of the welfare of the nation which, even against
great odds, can be counted on to produce a historically
manifest preservation: "They keep saying to those who
despise the word of the Lord, 'It shall be well with you
(*shalom* will be with you)'" (Jer. 23:17). But the word from
Yahweh that Jeremiah hears is the reverse of this conviction:
"Upon all the bare heights in the desert spoilers have come;
for the sword of the Lord devours from one end of the land to
the other; no one shall be safe (have *shalom*)" (Jer. 12:12).
Therefore, false prophets and priests "have treated the
wound of my people carelessly, saying, 'Peace, peace,' when
there is no peace" (Jer. 6:14 and 8:11). Jeremiah has heard
that Yahweh's time for Jerusalem is not *shalom* but disaster
and military defeat, and the weapons of the invaders are not
simply the tools of foreign enemies but the sword of God.
Jerusalem's *shalom* is taken away by the source itself (Jer.
16:5) and consequently there is no peace to be found but the
cry of terror and panic (Jer. 30:5). We may assume that the

false prophets of the time knew as well as Jeremiah that the love of God's law, the requirement of justice in the land, and the life guided by devotion to Yahweh alone were integral components for a condition of true peace. But unlike them, Jeremiah heard a verdict of Yahweh on king, priests, and people that disclosed a rottenness to the core in which *shalom* was already lost.

The course of events discredited Jeremiah's opponents, and the later collections of prophetic memories eliminated them from any consideration for inclusion in the canon of scripture. But soon the time would change. During the Babylonian captivity, when many, perhaps a majority, of Judeans lived in despair over the loss of homeland, independence, and the center of their worship, a prophet arose who announced that the time of judgment was over and a period was about to begin whose glory would outshine even the most treasured moments of Israel's past. We do not know the prophet's name and we have become accustomed to calling him, dryly, the second Isaiah (Isaiah 40–55). In this unknown prophet's words, the word *shalom* gains new meaning. *Shalom* now stands in a context in which liberation from the Babylonian yoke is expected in a new exodus in which the liberated will be brought home triumphantly, accompanied by marvels of nature that will put Moses' leadership in the first exodus into the shadow. The wilderness through which the new exodus must proceed will change into a landscape filled with lakes and springs in which all kinds of trees flourish (Isa. 41:18–19), whole rivers will flow through the desert, and armies will be put to rest in such a fashion that the former things at the time of Moses are not worth consideration, so startlingly novel is that which is to come (Isa. 43:16–19). In language deliberately reminiscent of concepts used to describe Yahweh's creation of the world, the glorious future deliverance is said to be no less than a new creation of God (Isa. 42:5–9; 44:24; 51:9–11). It is time, then, for great joy, and the *shalom* of this new time is instilled with its glory. Joy and *shalom* now belong together (Isa. 55:12). The messenger who announces the coming back of the liberated to Jerusalem has a message in which the good, salvation, and peace are bundled, to make them virtual synonyms of each other (Isa. 52:7). The old connection of *shalom* and justice is maintained (Isa. 54:12f.), but added to it is the anticipation of a divine act of deliverance so special that the old period of disintegration and decay is turned into a new era, an era of life whose peace was brought about by deliverance, even salvation from a disaster whose causes and effects could be removed only by an act of Yahweh analogous to his word of creation.

The language of Deutero-Isaiah has helped to prepare the way for patterns of thought and speech that later became characteristic of apocalyptic: the concept of deliverance requiring an act of God comparable only to a new creation, and the highly picturesque language that cloaks historical events in poetic imagery. The expected *shalom* is affected by this new intensity of language. *Shalom* is now well on its way to becoming a reality dependent on a new creation, an eschatological expectation, and it is embedded in a linguistic context that employs metaphors conjuring up miraculous rejuvenation as the order of new things.

Still later pictures of the peace of a new age in the Old Testament follow the same tendency. The prophet Haggai marshaled his energies for encouraging the people to rebuild the ruined temple in Jerusalem; and in the hope for this new temple, as expressed in his words, are plainly eschatological overtones (Hag. 2:6–9). The new temple will be a place of *shalom* (Hag. 2:9; NRSV "prosperity") into which so much silver and gold will be poured that its splendor will surpass the Solomonic building. But this will not come to pass until there is a shaking by God of heaven, earth, sea, and dry land, which is to say the entire universe, whose old condition has to be supplanted first by a new cosmic order. Similar, but less influenced by concepts of a new age, is the hope of *shalom* associated with the second temple in Zechariah 8:9–13.

We have come to the end of this survey of the meaning of *shalom* in the Old Testament. Its conceptual range is extremely wide. The word played a definite role in everyday language, in diplomatic and political frames of reference, in the vocabulary of worship, in the language of the royal court and its ideology, in prophetic speech, and in the sayings of wisdom teachers. In all these settings the word assumed characteristic nuances of connotation, combined with definite associations to other important terms that color its specific sense. But this is not the end of the history of the word in our Bible. It entered, through the Septuagint, the world of the Greek language and became, partly through this entry, a very important term for the New Testament.

2. Eirene

In the Septuagint

After the Babylonian exile, large parts of Judaism remained permanently in foreign countries outside Palestine. There they adopted the language of the host nation as their own. Especially in Egypt, after the Hellenization following the conquests of Alexander the Great, the Jewish diaspora no longer retained Hebrew or Aramaic as their mother tongue, and the necessity arose to translate the Hebrew scriptures into Greek for use in worship and in the schools of the synagogue. This process of translation led to the formation of a standard Alexandrian translation of the "Old Testament," the Septuagint (LXX), whose complicated growth and whose differences from the Masoretic Text with regard to the limits of canonical authority do not need to detain us.

As the authoritative collection of scripture, the LXX became the "Bible" for Hellenistic Judaism and, to a large degree, of the emerging Christian communities. The importance of its impact on the formation of language and thought on the New Testament can, therefore, hardly be overestimated. The translation of the Hebrew word *shalom* into the Greek term *eirēnē* (*eirene*) is one single illustration of a process that, within the larger framework of common Hellenistic Greek, produced a new form of the Greek language with a spirit all its own.

We saw, in the preceding section, how wide a margin of meaning is to be considered when the Hebrew *shalom* is translated into a Western language. In principle it would have been possible for translators to render the word, according to its different contexts, with a good dozen different Greek equivalents. This, however, was decidedly not the procedure adopted by the translators of the LXX. They rendered *shalom* in the vast majority of cases with *eirene,* so much so that one can say—exceptions notwithstanding—that *eirene* stands for Hebrew *shalom* in the LXX.

It is true that there are exceptions. In some two dozen instances, *shalom* is expressed with a different Greek phrase. A few illustrations of this procedure may serve as examples. In Jacob's vow at Bethel, the wish is expressed that he may come back to his father's house "in *shalom*" (Gen. 28:21), which LXX translates with *meta sōtērias* (*sōtēria* in classical

Greek can carry the meaning of "happy return"); the question "Is it well with him?" (Gen. 29:6; Hebrew: What is his *shalom?*) is rendered with a verb referring to physical health (LXX: "Is he healthy?"); when Moses and Jethro meet, each asks "after the other's welfare" (Ex. 18:7; Hebrew: about his *shalom*), LXX senses the fact that this is a formal greeting and translates accordingly with the Greek verb for "greet"; and in Isaiah 55:12 the phrase "You shall go out in joy, and be led back in peace (*shalom*)" is put into the words "You shall go out in gladness (*euphrosynē*) and you will be taught in joy (*chara*)."

Instances of the reverse procedure are even more isolated. In less than twenty cases LXX has used the word *eirene* to translate a term other than *shalom*. The evidence is so scanty that it is justified, for our purposes, to omit it altogether.

The prevalence of the noun *eirene* as translation for Hebrew *shalom* is astounding in view of the much narrower meaning of the Greek word. *Eirene,* in the history of the Greek language down to the origin of the LXX, means predominantly a condition free from war, a time at which wars have ceased. Closely associated with this narrow signification is the use of the word with the sense of "peace treaty," or a condition of quietness and an amicable attitude. It goes without saying that this restricted range of connotation covers a section of what can be envisaged by the Hebrew *shalom,* while it is incapable, in its traditional usage, of conveying the richness of the Hebrew word.

In view of this evidence, interpreters have drawn diametrically opposite conclusions from the fact that LXX translates *shalom* virtually as though it was synonymous with the Greek *eirene.* It has been said that this translation severely restricted the true meaning of the Hebrew texts so that a wealth of associations and connotations remained unintelligible for readers of the Old Testament in Greek, with a consequent loss of the many concrete aspects of *shalom* referring to questions of law, economics, and education. Conversely, the claim is made by others that the LXX greatly enriches the original meaning of *eirene* in Greek so that a wide stream of Hebrew thought and feeling entered into the common language of Hellenistic culture, producing, in effect, a new form of Greek distinct from others.

It appears difficult to settle this argument with general considerations. It is to be expected that a dozen readers of the

LXX in Alexandria around the time of Christ would be likely to read a dozen different nuances whenever they chanced upon the word *eirene.* Depending on their education, and on their familiarity, or lack of it, with large sections of the Greek "Old Testament," they would be inclined to associate more "Greek" or more "Hebrew" overtones in their reading. On balance, however, it appears that the position is relatively closer to the truth which sees in the LXX rendition of *shalom* with *eirene* a significant and far-reaching enrichment of Greek by the power of the Old Testament language. First, there is the fact that *eirene* in LXX occurs in the same contexts as it does in the Hebrew version. It is the strength of the context, the settings given in narratives, the association with similar words in hymnic and didactic passages, which determine the meaning of *eirene* as much as that of *shalom.* Second, Hellenistic Greek had, quite apart from the LXX, begun to associate the consequences of peace, as the absence of war, with the word *eirene* itself.

Philemon, one of the principal writers of Attic comedy around 300 B.C., wrote: "peace brings weddings, festivals, relatives, children, friends, wealth, health, corn, wine, and oil." This sentence does, of course, not impart to *eirene* the same depth and range as the Hebrew *shalom;* but it does show that Hellenistic *eirene* was capable of associations that prepare the ground for an expansion of meanings in that direction. Lastly, the New Testament is the most outstanding single collection of texts which is demonstrably dependent on the LXX and gives us definite clues to how the Septuagint was understood by some who were the heirs of its linguistic work. In the New Testament, however, it is quite manifest that *eirene* is used in meanings far transcending the traditional narrow connotation in pre-Hellenistic Greek, preserving important aspects of the range of significations embodied in *shalom.* To this aspect of the matter we can now direct our attention.

In the New Testament

A tone of joy and triumph permeates much of the New Testament, and its frequent mention of peace is one of the reasons for it. The life story of Jesus can be summarized in the phrase "good news of peace" (Acts 10:36, RSV). Christ's work is the achievement and declaration of peace; he is in person "our peace" (Eph. 2:14). Through this work, God can be known and believed as the "God of peace" (Rom. 15:33; 16:20; 1 Cor. 14:33; 2 Cor. 13:11; Phil. 4:9; 1 Thess. 5:23; 2 Thess. 3:16; Heb. 13:20).

The remarkable frequency of the phrase "the God of peace" alone suggests that in the word "peace" some writers of the New Testament, especially the apostle Paul, found an appropriate vehicle to concentrate the whole content of the Christian gospel. In the gospel of Jesus Christ something unprecedented, something utterly unexpected, something of ultimate validity had appeared in the world, and one of the best ways to speak of this cheerful news was its summation into the word *eirene*.

But the unexpected and unprecedented nature of this making and declaration of peace is everywhere in the New Testament connected, meaningfully and essentially connected, to a prior history to which it belongs as its climax. The New Testament, in spite of the amazing and disturbing novelty of its "gospel of peace," places itself within the history of Yahweh's dealings with Israel; it understands its own proclamation of peace as the surprising, but truly fitting, culmination of Yahweh's gift of *shalom*. On the plane of language, and this is the only aspect which concerns us at this point, we should then expect that the New Testament use of *eirene*, with or without the mediation of the LXX, shares vital aspects of the Old Testament word *shalom*.

This is indeed the case. The typical setting for the use of *shalom*, the association with other leading ideas, and the great comprehensiveness and flexibility of the word in Old Testament traditions, are all preserved in the New Testament. That does not mean to imply that the New Testament's idea of *eirene* is simply a carbon copy of an assortment of Old Testament uses of *shalom*. On the contrary, the word *eirene* in the New Testament has received a content that reshapes and reorients the notion of *shalom* in ways that no Old Testament theology could distill it as a necessary, or demonstrable, consequence. But in the new the old is kept alive, and without the old *shalom* the new *eirene* could not be what it is.

As in the Old Testament, and in daily Jewish practice, peace is offered in the Christian community in greetings and at the time of departure. The seventy disciples in Luke 10 are instructed by Jesus to enter a house, during their mission, with the traditional greeting "Peace to this house!" (10:5), a phrase accurately understood by Matthew to be a salutation ("as you enter the house, greet it"; Matt. 10:12). There is a great deal more behind this salutation than being a simple greeting (see chapter 3); but with regard to its form the greeting is commonplace. The farewell wish invoking peace is equally an everyday practice, even if there is, again, more than the traditional formulation involved when some Christian prophets are sent off from Antioch "in peace" (Acts 15:33).

Greeting and farewell have their literary counterparts in the opening and closing salutations in New Testament letters. The greeting "Grace to you and peace" (Rom. 1:7) is almost constant in New Testament epistles. Less frequent is the closing wish "Peace to all of you who are in Christ" (1 Peter 5:14), or a similar expression. Sometimes the conferral of peace is put not only at the end of a letter but at the conclusion of a major section; the unit Romans 14:1–15:32 is ended with the sentence "The God of peace be with all of you. Amen" (Rom. 15:33).

Typical LXX phrases are adopted in expressions like keeping or making peace (*eirēneuein*), as in Mark 9:50 ("Be at peace with one another"), or pursuing peace as in 1 Peter 3:11 ("Seek peace and pursue it").

Beyond those formal agreements, however, the New Testament employs *eirene* with a wideness of connotations that indicate the decisive influence of Old Testament statements about *shalom.*

Personal discord is at stake when, in Stephen's speech, Moses is said to have made an effort to reconcile the quarreling parties "toward peace" (Acts 7:26; omitted as redundant by NRSV). Political conflict is in view when a delegation of citizens from Tyre and Sidon appear before king Herod asking for peace (Acts 12:20); here the negotiations for peace do not aim at the cessation of warfare but at the elimination of political tensions. In Acts 24:2f. an even wider horizon of political reality is addressed. The Roman governor Felix is praised as the man through whom "we have long enjoyed peace," a peace entailing the introduction of administrative reforms. This appears to appeal rather definitely to Roman pride in the achievements of the "Pax Romana" (see chapter 5), conferring on *eirene* the meaning of security under the protective shield of Roman government.

The connotation of physical well-being and welfare is

meant in James 2:15–17: "If a brother or sister is naked and lacks daily food, and one of you says to them, 'Go in peace, keep warm and eat your fill,' and yet you do not supply their bodily needs, what is the good of that?" In respect to its form, the phrase "Go in peace" is nothing more than the traditional wish at the time of departure. But the context of this wish determines *eirene* as a condition in which the essentials of clothing and food are provided.

In a few verses in the Gospel, *eirene* appears again as the customary farewell wish, but the stories in which this wish is expressed confer on the word "peace" far-reaching theological implications. The woman, identified as "a sinner," who intrudes into the banquet at a Pharisee's house, is assured by Jesus, "Your sins are forgiven," and then dismissed with the words, "Your faith has saved you; go in peace" (Luke 7:48, 50). Very similar is the incident involving a woman who, after suffering from a flow of blood for twelve years, is healed of her disease and sent away with the words, "Daughter, your faith has made you well (lit.: has saved you); go in peace, and be healed of your disease" (Mark 5:34; cf. Luke 8:48). The context of the greeting, and the presence in both cases of the word "salvation," give *eirene* in these narratives a meaning in which peace is not directly identified but is placed into the immediate proximity of forgiveness of sins and restoration of health. In view of Old Testament usage which connects *shalom* with health and with salvation, this use of *eirene* cannot come as a surprise. It may be added in this context that in the mind of the author of Acts, the "gospel of peace" (10:36, lit.) is the same as "the message of this salvation" (13:26), again joining peace and salvation closely together.

In individual books in the New Testament, the specific range of meanings for *eirene* changes considerably. Thus, for Paul, peace is the new condition of those who live in Christ, whose hostility to God is done away with, and this peace is particularly linked to the apostle's teaching about the righteousness of God. The sentence "Since we are justified by faith, we have peace with God through our Lord Jesus Christ" (Rom. 5:1) cannot be divorced from the other: "The kingdom of God is not food and drink but righteousness and peace and joy in the Holy Spirit" (Rom. 14:17). Of course, Paul's thought about God's righteousness is a distinctively Christian, highly individual and subtle achievement; but it is also not without connections to the strong tradition emerging from the Old Testament which had, in some contexts, virtually identified righteousness and peace.

It is not necessary at this point to probe further, since the New Testament's understanding of peace will engage us throughout the succeeding chapters. But some conclusions in view of contemporary work for peace can already be drawn even at this preliminary stage of our search.

3. Some Conclusions

First, it is striking to observe the extremely diverse meanings that are part of the nature of biblical words for peace. Peace, in both the Old and the New Testament, is a condition reaching into almost any aspect of human life, communally or individually considered. It is at stake in basic issues of material welfare; it comes to life in physical health; it is expressed in justice and good order; it cannot thrive except in a climate of serious social concern; it provides a home for success and prosperity; it becomes synonymous with salvation; and it is also necessarily linked to harmony and good understanding in international relations. Sometimes this, sometimes another aspect of the richness of meanings predominates in different biblical books or passages, and not all of them are at all times of equal importance. But one cannot avoid the conclusion that the many meanings belong together; they are all branches growing from a single tree. That implies that none of the single areas envisaged by biblical words of peace can receive theologically appropriate consideration without careful attention to all the others. The search for peace in the sense of care for the avoidance of military conflict, for instance, is at once relativized and strengthened. It is relativized in that peacemaking, with regard to the causes of military conflict, cannot succeed without simultaneous attention to processes of just law, to economic fairness, and to social responsibility. It is at the same time strengthened, because the outbreak of war negates the wholeness of peace no matter what favorable conditions of good justice, economic health, or social equity may be sought through the conflict.

Second, it is apparent, especially in the Old Testament, that different social groups share in the obligation to find and preserve peace. There is the responsibility of the king to care for the *shalom* of his people; the priests in charge of the worship in the land are agents for the flourishing of *shalom;*

the teachers of wisdom are instrumental in their teaching to advance *shalom* through the schools, and the several groups called upon to administer the law are involved in securing *shalom*. Of course, none of the social organisms that were alive at one time of the Old Testament or the other, nor any social structure that we might discover in the New Testament, can provide a blueprint for the life of the church today, let alone for modern social organizations in the life of a nation. But whatever changes in social grouping have come to pass in the course of time, one very general conclusion seems to be possible. The Christian church will best be able to fulfill its task in the search for peace if it insists on calling all existing social organisms to responsibility for peace. The church will have to set convincing examples for that first of all within and for itself. Its worship must project constantly and centrally a love of peace; its government and administrative agencies have to pursue peace as a foremost concern; and its educational programs are obliged to elevate the subject of peace to a position of primary urgency. Only if this is achieved will the church have the right and the power to exert its influence also on secular social structures, in an effort to strengthen those centers and forces of public life which are most beneficial for the pursuit of peace in all its ramifications.

Select Bibliography

Durham, John I. *"Šālôm and the Presence of God."* In *Proclamation and Presence: Old Testament Essays in Honour of Gwynne Henton Davies,* ed. John I. Durham and J. R. Porter, 272–293. Richmond: John Knox Press, 1970. (Emphasizes that *shalom* is the gift of God which is received only as a consequence of the presence of God.)

Eisenbeis, Walter. *Die Wurzel šlm im Alten Testament.* Berlin: Walter de Gruyter, 1969. (The most comprehensive etymological study available.)

Foerster, Werner. *"eirēnē etc."* *Theological Dictionary of the New Testament,* vol. II, ed. G. Kittel, trans. G. W. Bromiley, 400–402, 406–420. Grand Rapids: Wm. B. Eerdmans Publishing Co., 1964.

Gerlemann, Gillis. "šlm genug haben," *Theologisches Handwörterbuch zum Alten Testament,* ed. E. Jenni and C. Westermann, vol. II, 919–935. Munich: Chr. Kaiser, 1976.

Gowan, Donald E. *Shalom: A Study of the Biblical Concept of Peace.* Pittsburgh: Creative Edge, 1984. (One of the rare studies devoted to Old and New Testament together. An excellent guide for adult Christian education courses.)

Rad, Gerhard von. "Šālôm in the Old Testament," *Theological Dictionary of the New Testament,* vol. II, ed. G. Kittel, trans. G. W. Bromiley, 402–406. Grand Rapids: Wm. B. Eerdmans Publishing Co., 1964.

Schmid, Hans Heinrich. *Šālôm: "Frieden" im Alten Orient und im Alten Testament.* Stuttgart: Katholisches Bibelwerk, 1971. (An excellent and comprehensive study, taking the general ideas in the ancient Near East into closer consideration.)

White, Hugh C. *Shalom in the Old Testament.* Philadelphia: United Church Press, 1973. (Brief sketch of the history of meanings of *shalom,* predicated on sociopsychological theories.)

3

The Peacemaker

The Gospel of Matthew preserves two sayings of Jesus about peace that appear to contradict each other:

> Blessed are the peacemakers, for they will be called children of God. (5:9)

> Do not think that I have come to bring peace to the earth; I have not come to bring peace, but a sword. (10:34)

The conflict between these two sayings reaches deep. It signals the tension between opposite ends of one and the same thing, the kingship of God, and this tension must not be quickly and cheaply released, otherwise the subject itself becomes very seriously distorted. It is worth our while to look at both sayings in some detail to set the stage.

1. Peace and Sword

The seventh and eighth blessing in Matthew's form of the Beatitudes show strong verbal and thematic affinities to his wording of Jesus' command to love enemies. "Blessed are the peacemakers, for they will be called *children of God*. Blessed are those who are *persecuted* for righteousness' sake, for theirs is the kingdom of heaven" (5:9–10) is analogous to "Love your enemies and pray for those who *persecute* you, so that you may be *children of your Father* in heaven" (5:44–45a).

The similarity between these sentences gains weight when their Lukan form is also compared. The seventh and eighth beatitudes in Matthew have no parallel in Luke, but the injunction to love enemies receives strong emphasis, without use of the word "persecute," in Luke 6:27–28: "But I say to you that listen, Love your enemies, do good to those who hate you, bless those who curse you, pray for those who abuse you." Form- and tradition-critical studies of Matthew can add two observations that are solid enough to be considered virtually common opinion: The eighth beatitude (5:10) is a composition of the evangelist, who sought to give a perfect symmetry, in two strophes, to the first eight blessings; and the theme of persecution is of considerable importance to the First Gospel. In consideration of this evidence, it can be stated that the affinity between 5:9–10 and 5:44–45a is intentional with Matthew. He, or the tradition preceding him, has changed the wording of a saying of Jesus on love toward enemies and has added a blessing in which a thematic relation between peacemaking, persecution, and love for the enemy is suggested.

Sayings in Matthew 10 leave no doubt that the persecution originates with judicial and governmental forces, not with opposition from within the Christian community of Matthew's acquaintance. The sentence "When they persecute you in one town, flee to the next" (10:23) stands in the context of the experience that Christian missionaries will be brought before councils and synagogues, governors and kings (10:17f.), and the cause of this persecution is the announcement of peace through the Christian mission (10:12f.).

The "greeting" to the house which the missionaries enter (Matt. 10:12) is more explicitly preserved in Luke's parallel version of this sentence by the phrase, "Whatever house you enter, first say, 'Peace to this house!'" (Luke 10:5). The announcement of the immediacy of the kingdom of heaven (Matt. 10:7) is synonymous with the offer of peace, an offer which, however, arouses the extreme hostility of the official representatives of the judiciary and political administration in whose territory the Christian mission is conducted.

This leads to some preliminary conclusions about the blessing on the peacemakers in Matthew's beatitudes. The making of peace is an essential aspect of the dawning of the kingdom of heaven. In announcing this coming, the Christian missionaries impart to those whose houses they enter that peace which is the very essence and power of God's rule over the world. This active and strenuous personal involvement for the achievement of peace is an effort in which the ever-present line of division between friends and enemies is erased. Love of the enemy, even the enemy who arrests and engages in hostile proceedings before courts of law, is the manner of making peace under the auspices of the kingdom of heaven. But this peacemaking, which—as long as it remains true to its own nature—wipes out all boundaries, evokes in actual fact hatred, rejection, and hostility. It meets a world of responses which is by no means ready to accept this offer of peace, but insists that it is not yet time to yield to the coming of the kingdom of heaven, and hence to the arrival of universal peace. And, therefore, the actual reply of many of those who wield the power is the sword. The Christian mission, in Matthew's understanding, does not produce all-embracing harmony. On the contrary, divisions will arise even within families, among friends and neighbors, between those who are prepared to accept the offer of peace and those who are convinced that the time for peace has not arrived.

It is in the context of these divisions that Matthew has placed Jesus' saying, "Do not think that I have come to bring peace to the earth; I have not come to bring peace, but a sword" (10:34). The word is set in the situation brought about by the Christian mission, which divides families into hostile camps (10:21, 35f.). There are, however, indications which would suggest that the saying originally had even farther-reaching implications. With regard to its form, Matthew 10:34 belongs to a group of sayings in the Synoptic Gospels in which Jesus puts the purpose of his life into a single sentence, beginning with the words "I have come." "I have come to call not the righteous but sinners" (Mark 2:17; Matt. 9:13; Luke 5:32); "I came to bring fire to the earth" (Luke 12:49); "The Son of man has come [=I have come] to seek out and to save the lost" (Luke 19:10). In sentences like these, to which others could be added, the unique authority of Jesus is cast into a single statement that puts into a nutshell the meaning of his entire mission. The saying about the bringing of the sword belongs, through its form, to this type of self-declaration. It is therefore likely that the statement in Matthew 10:34 belongs originally, not to a situation produced by the Christian mission, but to those cryptic words in which Jesus speaks about the purpose of his own work as the agent of the coming kingdom of God. He is, as this agent, an envoy not of peace but of conflict to the point of death.

Thus, a chasm opens up before us. We have to take seriously, on the one hand, the blessing of the peacemakers who are children of that God whose coming into power spells peace, and, on the other hand, an understanding of the mission of Jesus in a word of self-disclosure in which peace is denied. The chasm does not present us with an irreconcilable contradiction. But in order to gauge its dimensions, we will have to make the effort to come to grips with both sides of the issue. And so we will turn, first, to the aspect of the sword.

2. "I Have . . . Come to Bring . . . a Sword"

The survey on biblical words of peace in chapter 2 touched on the emergence of a hope in the Old Testament that at a decisive climax in history a king, the anointed one, would arise who would initiate peace and rule in peace. This messianic hope is, wherever it appears, connected with a struggle leading ultimately to the victory of Yahweh and his people. In fact, the expectation of an eventual coming of a universal peace to all nations on earth is predicated on the condition that Yahweh will be known and served as the only true God everywhere in the world.

> In the center of the Old Testament's hope lies not the vision of a neutral peace in the world in which all nations, as they are, live peaceably side by side. Rather, in the center of the hope lies the faith in Yahweh's power, the faith that Yahweh will ultimately prevail—be it by a voluntary submission of the nations under him, be it by his victory over his enemies manifest to all. The Old Testament is concerned primarily not with peace among people, but with the lordship of God. (H. H. Schmid, *"Šalôm,"* 90; my translation)

These features of the messianic hope continue in Jewish writings closer to New Testament times. The expectation of a messiah assumes, at this period, very diverse forms which makes it impossible to systematize them into a common "messianology." But among many other manifestations, Jewish messianic hope retains the picture of the messiah as king of peace. The final kingdom of peace is initiated either by a victory through force of arms over all pagan people, or by the submission of all foreign nations to Israel's God. The consequence of this struggle and the ultimate victory is the universal abandonment of idolatry and the recognition of Yahweh's rule and law as the only dominion guaranteeing peace. Statements about the messiah as the king of peace do not abound in Jewish literature of that period, but some examples may be mentioned which attest to the survival, at this time, of the Old Testament hope of a messianic peace-maker.

The Sibylline Oracles contain some short passages that evidence the existence, in the Jewish communities of Egypt, of a messianic figure whose task is the elimination of the curse of warfare. Book III alludes to a hope that God will send a "king from the sun" who will "stop the entire world from evil war" but this bringing of peace is conditioned by the king's killing of opponents and the imposition of loyalty oaths on others (III, 652–654). In Book V, a savior figure from heaven is expected who could be identical with the "king sent from God" (V, 108). If that is so, Book V also testifies to the vision of a Messiah of peace in whose reign a city of God with its holy temple will be reestablished (V, 420–427), and in whose reign "terrible things no longer happen to wretched mortals" but murder and the din of battle will cease (V, 429, 431). In this passage also it is made entirely clear that the messianic (?) dominion of peace is consequent to a destruction of peoples and their rulers who have rejected God's law (V, 414–419).

In two chapters of the second Baruch, a messiah of peace is introduced who has come to restore the conditions of para-dise to the earth (*2 Baruch* 29 and 73). When this "anointed one" will be revealed, he will sit down "in eternal peace on the throne of his kingdom" (73:1). This final peace is de-scribed in language that reflects a great deal of the wealth of the word *shalom*. There will be a banquet in the garden of Eden at which the flesh of the ancient monsters Behemoth and Leviathan will be eaten, and the earth will become marvelously fruitful (29:4–6). Even manna, given during Israel's sojourn in the wilderness as an emergency ration, will become a daily food from heaven (29:8). *Shalom* in full compass will then arrive on earth: Health will descend like the dew, joy will encompass the earth, wild beasts will no longer threaten and will become subject even to a child, and women will no longer have to endure the pain when they bear their children (73:2–7). But even here, the dominion of the messiah of peace is initiated by the destruction through force of the enemies of the messiah's reign; the description of his kingdom is preceded by the sentence, "All those, now, who have ruled over you or have known you, will be delivered up to the sword" (72:6).

The only passage in Jewish literature of the New Testament era in which the reign of a messiah of peace is not associated with a specific mention of the destruction of enemies is found in the *Testament of Levi* 18. In this chapter a priest-king (18:1 and 3) is portrayed who will restore the light of the knowledge of God to the whole inhabited earth, and in whose reign "there shall be peace in all the earth" (18:4). Then the heavens will be opened and the gates of paradise unlocked, and this priestly messiah will have the power to "remove the sword that has threatened since Adam" (18:10). No martial conflict with human enemies is mentioned, but the priest-king of the end time will struggle victoriously against the antagonist of God in heaven and his host: "Beliar shall be bound by him, and he (i.e., the priest-king) shall grant to his children the authority to trample on wicked spirits" (18:12). Thus, even in *Testament of Levi* 18, the arrival of a messiah of peace without a preceding or accompanying struggle is inconceivable.

Synoptic texts in the New Testament, speaking of the proclamation and of the enactment by Jesus of the approaching kingdom of God, share this conviction without reservation. It is true that they do not simply adopt Jewish presuppositions about the coming of a messiah of peace; strong modifications, even reversals of convictions, are taking place. But that does not alter the fact that the Synoptic Gospels cannot conceive of Jesus as the agent of God's kingdom without cognizance of a fight against elements which, in fact, prevent the manifestation of the kingdom of God.

A convenient starting point is given in a passage preserved, with considerable differences, by all the Synoptics: Matthew 12:22–30; Mark 3:20–27; Luke 11:14–23. This passage shows a certain resemblance to Testament of Levi 18, and it would appear to provide the basis for a fuller understanding of Jesus' word in Matthew 10:34, "I have not come to bring peace, but a sword." The three Synoptic passages report about an accusation against Jesus by opponents who claim that he casts out demons with the help of Satan (or Beelzebul). As part of Jesus' defense against this charge,

Matthew and Luke add a parabolic sentence that is important for the present argument. This parable in a nutshell is, according to widespread agreement, best preserved by Luke. It reads (in the translation by J. A. Fitzmyer in his Anchor Bible Commentary volume):

> When a powerful man fully armed stands guard over his courtyard, his belongings are safe and sound. But when a more powerful man attacks and overpowers him, he carries away all the weapons on which he had relied and divides up his booty. (Luke 11:21f.)

The language of armed aggression is used throughout this saying. One party is fully armed, but an attack is made by one even more powerful, and after the attack has succeeded the weapons and booty are won. The context of the little parable identifies the actors in the armed encounter. The powerful man is Satan, and the more powerful attacker is Jesus, who takes the spoils from the vanquished devil. The encounter between the two is cast in language belonging to armed human conflict, and the similarity to Matt. 10:34 is increased when it is noticed that the translation quoted renders with "safe and sound" an original Greek that says literally "in peace." We get, then, a close analogy between Matthew 10:34 and Luke 11:21f., which can be schematized:

Matt. 10:34: not peace, but sword
Luke 11:21–22: (Satan has) not peace, but is attacked and defeated.

This leads us to the original reference for the declaration "I have not come to bring peace, but a sword" in Matthew 10:34. Against its redactional context in Matthew 10, the sentence originally does not refer to the persecution by human oppressors. The enemy is superhuman; the peace that is meant is the undisturbed authority of Satan over the affairs of the world, which authority Jesus is destroying; and the sword refers to the battle for the inauguration of God's rule in the end time. The saying exhibits, therefore, an altogether essential and necessary association of Jesus with the "sword." The work of his life is predicated on his victorious wielding of this sword, and his person is comprehended as the legitimate warrior of God.

In Luke 10:17–20 a saying of Jesus is preserved which talks

of the fall of Satan from heaven; "I watched Satan fall from heaven like a flash of lightning. See, I have given you authority to tread on snakes and scorpions, and over all the power of the enemy; and nothing will hurt you" (10:18–19). The saying is set in the context of the disciples' return from their mission (10:17), upon which they rejoice in the power to cast out demons in Jesus' name. The vision of Satan falling from heaven belongs, in this context, to the experience that the emissaries of God's kingdom are able to overcome the power of those superhuman forces that bind their human victims to a life of misery. But there are reasons to conclude that the word about Satan's fall from heaven does not originally belong to this context. Immediately before his report of the disciples' return (10:17) Luke gives another saying of Jesus stating a terrible judgment on Capernaum (10:15): "And you, Capernaum, will you be exalted to heaven? No, you will be brought down to Hades." Both the condemnation of the town of Capernaum (10:15) and the vision of Satan's fall (10:18) use a reference to Isaiah 14:12–15; "How you are fallen from heaven, O Day Star, son of Dawn! . . . You said in your heart, 'I will ascend to heaven.' . . . But you are brought down to Sheol, to the depths of the Pit.' The Isaiah oracle applies to the king of Babylon, but it had been used in Jewish tradition as a prediction of the expulsion of Satan from heaven: Satan belongs to God's court of heavenly beings, but his arrogance will, in the end, be answered by his removal from the heavenly court and his fall from heaven. Since both Luke 10:15 and 10:18 adopt this concept of Satan's expulsion, it is reasonable to assume that the two verses belonged together at some time of the pre-Lukan tradition. Luke placed 10:16–17 between the words on Capernaum and on Satan's fall to produce a sequence of verses in which the authority of the disciples is attributed to Jesus' granting to them the healing powers of God's kingdom. Taken as a separate saying, however, the vision of the fall of Satan from heaven expresses the triumph of Jesus over Satan. This triumph, and the consequent expulsion of Satan from heaven, is put in the language of warfare in Revelation 12:7–10: "And war broke out in heaven." In the course of this war the archangel Michael and his angels battle victoriously against Satan (the dragon), who, as a result of his defeat, is thrown down from heaven: "The great dragon was thrown down, that ancient serpent, who is called the Devil and Satan, the deceiver of the whole world." This fall of Satan from heaven is the inauguration of God's kingdom: "Now have come the salvation and the power and the kingdom of our God and the authority of his Messiah, for the accuser of our comrades has been thrown down, who accuses them day and night before our God" (Rev. 12:10). Revelation 12:7–10 reflects very early Christian concepts about the risen Christ as the victor in the eschatological war against Satan and his forces. In this drama, the fall of Satan from heaven signals his defeat in a heavenly battle and the establishment of God's rule in Christ. Jesus' vision of Satan's fall in Luke 10:18 is clothed in words stemming from the same apocalyptic imagery. Therefore it depicts him, as in the little parable in Luke 11:21–22, as God's warrior whose purpose is Satan's destruction as a power in heaven and on earth. His mission, in the fight against God's opponent, is the wielding of the sword (Matt. 10:34).

There is yet another piece of tradition, retained by Matthew, which belongs to the same cluster of ideas. Matthew 11:1–19 deals with the position of John the Baptist in relation to Jesus' work. John is given an eminent place of honor; he is the greatest human being ever born—until a radical change occurs in the conditions of the world through Jesus' words and acts, in which the kingdom of heaven is beginning to revolutionize history (11:11). But the Baptist's activity already borders on the arrival of the kingdom of heaven, which from this time forward is met with violent resistance. "From the days of John the Baptist until now the kingdom of heaven has suffered violence, and the violent take it by force" (11:12). The translation of this verse poses difficulties; adopted here is a rendition which assumes that three Greek words employed in the verse (*biazō, biastēs, harpazō*) all refer to the same idea of a hostile action. In the context of the verse, it is beyond question that the violence committed refers to the incarceration of John, and the resistance against his work. But John's fate is seen as a special case of what is generally to be expected to happen to the kingdom of heaven.

If this understanding of Matthew 11:12 is correct, there emerges a web of correlated ideas that make up a highly dramatic picture. Luke 11:21f. had in view a conquest of Satan's territory and possessions through the victorious in-

invasion of one armed with the power of God, and Luke 10:18 looked at a forceful deposition of Satan from a place of privilege before God which he had occupied until this time. There is no hint in these sayings that Satan's defeat is only partial; his overthrow appears final. Matthew 11:12, however, talks about a counterattack against the kingdom of heaven and an attempt to retake lost territory. The counterattack is, in this saying, not attributed to Satan but to human opponents who launch an offensive to curb the increasing effectiveness of the kingdom of heaven. But it is likely that Matthew 11:12 breathes the same spirit of vivid, apocalyptic imagery as do the previously discussed Lukan verses. Thus the actions of the "violent" are hardly perpetrated without the presence of a Satan who—in apocalyptic terms—directs the wills and deeds of his subjects from beyond the observable stage of human history. The ideas clash: There is a defeat of Satan here, on the one hand, described in language of an apocalyptic recasting of the notion of Yahweh as warrior, and there is, on the other hand, a counteroffensive of the forces conspiring against the victory of the kingdom of heaven. This tension must not be eliminated. It expresses the dialectic between the arrival of a complete rule of God and, with it, the inauguration of the ultimate peace in the world, and the continued, and even intensified, determined resistance to this dawn of a new age. But it must be noted that both sides of the dialectic are expressed in terms of violent, warlike encounters that are set in motion by Jesus' coming: He has indeed come to bring the sword!

3. The Peacemaker

The coming of Jesus involves a struggle in which the victory over an enemy is necessary. Seen from this angle his symbol is, and remains, the sword not the dove. But there is another angle from which his life is viewed in the Gospels. He is the peacemaker, and the task of bringing peace to earth is so essential to the accomplishment of his mission that a neglect of this aspect would lead to a complete misconstrual of Jesus' person and work. This is the aspect of the issue which is now before us. It will be treated, first of all, without regard to the other side of the matter, signaled by the word "sword." Only in the end will the attempt be made to correlate the two poles of the apparent contradiction (chapter 4, conclusions).

Framework of the Lukan Writings

In the Lukan writings in the New Testament, Luke's Gospel and Acts, the word "peace" comes close to becoming a theological term that captures the whole meaning of the Christ event (see Willard M. Swartley in the Select Bibliography). This can be seen, initially, in the opening sentence of Peter's address placed in the framework of the acceptance of Cornelius, the first Gentile, into the Christian community (Acts 10). Peter's speech (10:34–43) is not typical of a sermon aimed at a Gentile audience; rather, its content suggests an origin in the preaching and instruction presented to the early Christian community. Much of the content of the address is a thumbnail sketch of our fully developed Gospels (10:37–41), and although a few details of this mini-Gospel are reminiscent of material characteristic of Luke's Gospel, it can still be claimed that the summation of the main stations of Jesus' life in Peter's sermon provides an outline preserved by all the Synoptics. This summary of the gospel is introduced with the phrase, "God sent the word to the children of Israel by proclaiming the good news of peace" (10:36). This sentence is incomplete in the original, and its reconstruction is not altogether certain. What is certain is the fact that, in the adoption of Isaiah 52:7, good news (gospel) and peace are placed into close proximity and that a sketch amounting to an outline of our complete Gospels can be supplied with the heading "The announcement of the good news of peace." The whole story of Jesus is thereby made a declaration of peace.

The same intent can be discerned in the Gospel of Luke itself. In the Christmas narrative (Luke 2:1–20), and in the Lukan redaction of the account of Jesus' entry into Jerusalem (or rather into the temple, in Luke's view), there is found a hymnic praise of God which in form and content is so clearly similar that the Gospel's readers are designed to be led from one story to the other. The shepherds of the Christmas story are surprised by the appearance of "the angel of the Lord," who meets their terror at the sight of God's glory with assurance: The angel has come as a messenger of "good news (gospel) of great joy" (2:10) because of the birth of a savior in the city of David, namely, Christ the Lord (2:11). Immediately thereafter, an angelic chorus puts into hymnic praise the meaning, the importance, and the essence of this birth as it is seen from heaven, which is to say from the vantage point of true and ultimate reality (2:14; parentheses added):

> "Glory to God in the highest heaven,
>   and on earth peace (among those whom he favors)!"

Luke's version of Jesus' entry into Jerusalem follows, in general, the Markan account (19:28–40). But in his narrative, Mark's unspecified "many" who pay homage to Jesus (Mark 11:8) become "the whole multitude of the disciples" who, in sentences greatly augmented by Luke (19:37–38), "began to praise God joyfully with a loud voice for all the deeds of power that they had seen," saying:

> "Blessed is the king
> who comes in the name of the Lord!
> Peace in heaven,
>   and glory in the highest heaven"

The correspondence between Luke 2:14 and the second half of 19:38 is unmistakable. If one disregards the explanatory phrase (lit., "among the people of his pleasure") in 2:14, two hymnic ascriptions of praise remain whose forms are the same. Each consists of two lines. In each the words "glory" and "peace" are the subjects of one line, and in each there is a reversal of the word order between line 1 and line 2. In 2:14, line 1 states first the subject ("glory"), then the place ("in the highest"), while line 2 inverts the order, naming the place first ("on earth") and then the subject ("peace"). In 19:38b, the arrangement is the opposite: line 1 gives first the location and then the subject, and line 2 again inverts the order by having the subject precede the place. The position of these hymnic statements in the Gospel, the dominance of the words "glory" and "peace," and the analogous artistry of the architecture of the phrases make the two hymnic praises guideposts in the composition of the Gospel of Luke as a whole.

This observation invites further considerations. The first hymn of praise is sung at the very beginning of the story of Jesus' life by celestial beings who have insight into what is not manifest on the plane of earthly history. A very inconspicuous and ordinary birth is declared to be the most momentous event when the heavens open and the hidden truth of this birth is announced from above as it is known by God. The birth of this child is in accordance with the glory God possesses high above the inglorious state of the earth, but it is also the moment when the peace corresponding to God's glory in heaven takes hold on earth to transform this earth into a land of peace. The second hymn of praise is offered by human voices at the time when the "king" has completed his work in the exercise of his royal office and is about to enter Jerusalem and the temple. The multitude of disciples cannot command the insight of heavenly beings, but they can become an antiphon to the angels' praise because they have seen with their own eyes Jesus' deeds of power which have happened on earth, and in which the glory and peace of heaven became visible to them.

Yet, in spite of the formal and thematic correspondence between the praise of the angels and of the disciples, there is also a telling difference. The antiphon of the disciples falls short of the angels' praise. The angels had seen, in Jesus' birth, an event that confirms God's glory in heaven and spreads God's peace on earth. But the disciples, in retrospect of Jesus' works and in entering the king's city, can ascribe glory and peace only to the realm above, "in heaven peace, and glory in the highest heaven" (Luke 19:38, lit.). To their perception it is not yet truthful to echo the angels' choir word for word. It is clear to them that God's glory and peace were manifest in Jesus' life among them. But to declare "peace on earth" remains for them premature. What is the reason for this incongruity, for this persistence in reservations? The answer is given by the evangelist in placing, immediately after the disciples' homage, a scene in which Jesus, looking at the city, laments over the condition and the fate of Jerusalem (Luke 19:41–44). Again, the passage is peculiar to Luke, as are the two hymnic praises of angels and disciples. The contrast could not be greater between the scene of the disciples' jubilation and Jesus' mourning. The disciples rejoice and engage in praise with loud voices—Jesus weeps and envisions Jerusalem's disaster. But, once more, in Jesus' lament over the city the word "peace" plays a decisive part: "If you, even you, had only recognized on this day the things that make for peace! But now they are hidden from your eyes" (19:42). Jesus' tears for Jerusalem are caused by the knowledge that his offer of peace is rejected by the leadership of the people, who even now demand that the disciples' praise be stopped (19:39; also only in Luke).

The peace on earth announced by the angels had indeed been initiated by the work of the man whose birth the angels greeted. But it had not conquered the world. As for the city whose name dedicates it to peace, and which by rights should receive God's peacemaker as the legitimate heir of the history of kings associated with it, this city will not only cast aside what would make for its peace, it will even kill the one through whom that peace is presented. The dark shadow of this rejection of peace in Jerusalem already falls on the disciples' praise of God's glory and peace. Stepping forward into the time of Jesus' passion in Jerusalem, the peace could still be ascribed to heaven, but it could not yet be claimed for the earth.

Looking back on Acts 10:36, and on the chorus of angels and disciples in Luke's Christmas story and his version of the entry into Jerusalem, some conclusions can be drawn. In the Lukan writings, the whole ministry of Jesus, including his death, resurrection, and continuing history in his community, can be summed up by calling it the good news of peace. From his birth on, he is designated from above to realize peace on earth, a peace seen and praised by the Christian community, but yet in grave jeopardy because of its rejection by powerful and influential groups who manage, in the end, to get rid of the troublesome intruder through whom God's peace threatened to break out all over the world. The body of Luke's Gospel, from Jesus' birth to his entry into Jerusalem, is to be understood as a manifestation of God's glory and peace in Jesus' work and word; but the account of the "good news of peace" is punctuated by the passion events, which make it clear that the universal acceptance of the power and terms of this peace have not yet happened on earth. In this sense, it can be claimed that Luke used the idea of peace as an organizing concept for his presentation of the life of Jesus and his community, and that he considered peace to be one term that could comprehensively capture the essence of "gospel" and of the resistance against it.

In this survey of the connection between "gospel" and "peace" in the Lukan writings, no attempt was made to specify the meaning of *eirene*. A set of questions can no longer be left unasked: What, in the Lukan passages discussed, is the specific sense of "peace"? Is Luke alone among the Synoptic Gospels with his thematic coordination of gospel and peace? Do the other Synoptics have further, and perhaps differing, contributions to make to the topic of peace in their writings?

The reader may be reminded that already in chapter 2 reference was made to Jesus' use of traditional farewell phrases employing the word "peace," and it was further suggested that peace in those passages was connected to health and healing, and to the power to forgive sins (Mark 5:34; Luke 7:50; 8:48). These few connections may, initially, serve as heuristic signs that—in logical expansion of the Old Testament tradition—*eirene* in the gospels may be found in narratives and sayings concerned with healings and forgiveness.

The Son of David

The messianic title most widely in use in several Jewish groups, at the time close to Jesus and the emerging Gospel tradition, was the phrase "Son of David." Detailed investigations of the use of this title in the New Testament have discovered that the Synoptics attributed a somewhat different importance and meaning to the expression, and that the application of the title to Jesus is made in the great majority of cases within the framework of healing stories (see especially C. Burger, *Jesus als Davidssohn*). Since, of all the Synoptics, Matthew contains the largest number of instances in which Jesus is identified with the "Son of David," and since this evangelist also exhibits the keenest interest in the title, we shall, in this section, concentrate on the first Gospel.

Aside from the infancy narratives in Matthew 1 and 2, which presuppose interest in the Davidic line as Jesus' ancestry, the first Gospel contains seven sections in which the title Son of David appears. In one instance (22:41–46), a discussion between Pharisees and Jesus is devoted to christological controversies about the relationship between a messianic claim built on belonging to a line of descent coming from David and the *kyrios* title employed by the Christian community. The other six sections in Matthew are all associated with healing stories.

9:27-31   Two blind men cry out to Jesus, "Have mercy on us, Son of David!" Their eyes are opened, they are asked not to divulge the news, but they promptly spread Jesus' fame.

12:22-24   A blind and dumb demoniac has his speech and sight restored by Jesus. Amazed witnesses ask the question, "Can this be the Son of David?," a question answered by Pharisees by charging that Jesus heals in the power of the prince of demons.

15:21-28   A Canaanite woman requests Jesus' help for her possessed daughter with the cry, "Have mercy on me, Lord, Son of David." After resistance by Jesus ("I was sent only to the lost sheep of the house of Israel," v. 24) the daughter is healed.

20:29-34   Two blind men cry out to Jesus, "Have mercy on us, Son of David." Their sight is restored.

21:1-11, 14-16   Entry into Jerusalem at which Jesus is greeted with the shout, "Hosanna to the Son of David!" When Jesus heals blind and lame people in the temple, children repeat the shout, "Hosanna to the Son of David."

For our purpose, the two sections Matthew 21:1-11 and 14-16 are of importance. They are also given special weight by the evangelist through the use of the fulfillment quotation from the Old Testament, characteristic for Matthew. Some details in this passage demand our attention.

Matthew's account of Jesus' entry into Jerusalem is dominated by the fulfillment motif: "This took place to fulfill what had been spoken through the prophet, saying, 'Tell the daughter of Zion, Look, your king is coming to you, humble, and mounted on a donkey, and on a colt, the foal of a donkey'" (21:4-5). The Old Testament quotation adopts Zechariah 9:9, perhaps combined with a short phrase from Isaiah 62:11. The Zechariah quote is given according to the LXX, which, in contrast to the Masoretic text, distinguishes the ass and her foal. The insertion of the quote from Zechariah 9:9 defines Jesus expressly as king, in accordance with the prophetic hope of a messiah, and the homage paid to him by the crowd echoes it in the words "Hosanna to the Son of David" (v. 9).

The Zechariah quotation serves to tell what kind of king he is who is now entering his own city, and it functions at the same time to describe the character of this "Son of David." He is said to be humble (*praüs*). It is the third and last time that the word *praüs* is used in Matthew's Gospel; it was employed in the blessing of the meek (*praüs*) (5:5) and Jesus' self-designation "I am gentle (*praüs*) and humble in heart" (11:29). A precise meaning of the word *praüs* is difficult to determine. In the LXX it most often translates a Hebrew word that is nearly equivalent to "poor," and it came to be used in later Jewish texts in the sense of "mild" and "friendly." The contexts in Matthew's Gospel, however, seem to point in a direction in which the concern for the downtrodden and discouraged is emphasized. The first three beatitudes group together the "poor in heart," the "mourners," and the "*praeis,*" indicating that those who lack confidence and who suffer from grief are in company with those who stand at their side in gentleness and friendliness. In 11:29, the *praüs* Jesus is the man who cares for those "whose work is hard, whose load is heavy" (11:28, NEB). Matthew 21:5 is perhaps not over-interpreted if it is noticed that Matthew did not quote Zechariah 9:9 fully. He left the words "triumphant and victorious" out, and since it can be observed throughout his Gospel that the fulfillment quotations are phrased with great care, this omission is hardly due to coincidence. If that is so, Matthew wants, in his characterization of the king Jesus, studiously to avoid the use of adjectives that could give rise to the misunderstanding that he might be another potentate who is about to subdue his enemies with military force. The king Jesus who enters his city, and by the same token the "Son of David," is introduced as the ruler who is consumed with the care of his most needy subjects and whose dominion is entirely dedicated to the relief of those who are in dire circumstances.

The story of Jesus' entry into Jerusalem is connected, in Matthew's account, to the scene in which healings take place in the temple and the children continue the shout "Hosanna to the Son of David!" (21:14–16). Both of these details are found in Matthew alone. They are in line with the evangelist's emphasis in the other "Son of David" passages whose essentials can now be summarized.

It is very striking to note that Matthew has, five out of

seven times in his Gospel, combined the current messianic title "Son of David" with narratives concerned with healings. This combination of motifs is unknown to Jewish messianic expectations in the era when the New Testament emerged. As varied as the hope for a messiah was, it did not include the idea of the coming king as either a miracle worker or a healer. On the other hand, as we saw before, some Jewish texts do attest to the hope that a future messianic figure would bring about a restoration of paradise, in which a victory over satanic forces would occur (*Test. Levi* 18:12) and in which all manner of evil, including illness and death, would be banished from earth (*2 Baruch* 73:2–3). In those texts, the overcoming of satanic power and of the curse of illness and dying are expressly connected with the establishment of an ultimate peace, and the Messiah is anticipated there as the king who reigns in a realm of peace. Although the "Son of David" sections in Matthew do not expressly state that the person of Jesus is as David's son, the bringer of peace, the combination of the healer with the claim to the messianic office suggests a horizon of understanding similar to the visions in *Testament of Levi* and *2 Baruch*. As the king who rules his people by restoring their health, Matthew's Jesus is the peacemaker who has broken the death grip of that force which had usurped the power of God in the earth.

Peace and Kingdom of Heaven

In connection with the sending of disciples on a mission, Matthew and Luke preserve a saying in which the word "peace" is of central importance.

> Whatever house you enter, first say, "Peace to this house!" And if anyone is there who shares in peace, your peace will rest on that person; but if not, it will return to you. (Luke 10:5–6)

The version of the same saying in Matthew seems to show signs of a longer process of reworking in its adaptation to particular steps that reflect missionary practice and experience:

> Whatever town or village you enter, find out who in it is worthy, and stay there until you leave. As you enter the house, greet it. If the house is worthy, let your peace come upon it;

but if it is not worthy, let your peace return to you. (Matt. 10:11–13)

Among the several differences between the two versions, we note only three that have a bearing on the meaning of peace in the saying. First, in the Lukan form the missionaries are enjoined to say "Peace to this house." This is changed to the instruction to greet the house in Matthew. This difference is, however, more apparent than real because the customary salutation upon entering a house, in a Jewish-Christian community, for which Matthew is written, would in any case be the wish of peace. We may assume that Matthew's readership knew, without further explanation, that the salutation was identical with the greeting "peace [be] with you." More weighty is another difference. The words in Luke suggest the conviction that the greeting with peace will result either in a resting of peace on the house or a return of the peace to the disciples who offered it; the indicative form of the verbs makes this a statement of fact. In Matthew, the verbs "come upon" and "return" are put in the third-person imperative, carrying the implication of wish or expectation. Third, Matthew's "worthy house" is, in Luke's version, determined by the head of the household who is a "child of peace." In the Lukan form, there is a correspondence between the gift of peace through the disciples' mission, and the acceptance of it by the "child of peace": The offer of peace will disclose what its recipient is, and only those who are already predisposed for peace will receive the gift of peace.

There is no question that the presuppositions of the saying are more forcefully stated by Luke. The greeting with peace is not simply a salutation in our sense of the word; it is the offer of a powerful reality to be conferred upon the recipient. The greeting "Peace to this house" is imbued with the strength of peace itself, and this strength will do its work, either by imparting its reality to those who are prepared for peace, in whom the fruit of peace will grow, or by returning ineffectively to the givers, thereby disclosing that the intended recipients are not of peace. The very offer of peace, therefore, has the power to separate "children of peace" from "children of strife," and the word that imparts peace is effective, in either case, by revealing what is the nature of those who are met by the announcement of peace.

The greeting with peace is, however, in both Gospels not

conceived as a magical force. Rather, the peace offered is, in Matthew and in Luke, connected to the preaching of God's kingdom and to the healing of the sick (Matt. 10:7-8; Luke 10:9). Concerning this connection, it would seem again that the Lukan order is more illuminating than Matthew's. There is a close formal parallel between the peace saying in Luke 10:5-6 and the healing of the sick with the announcement of the kingdom of God in Luke 10:8-11. In each unit, we can observe four steps that correspond with each other.

Luke 10:5-6	Luke 10:8-11
Step 1: Entering of a house	Entering of a town
Step 2: Reception by a child of peace	Reception by those who feed the missionaries
Step 3: Impartation of the peace to the child of peace	Healing of the sick and announcement that the kingdom of God is near
Step 4: Rejection of peace	Rejection of the offer of the kingdom

Although the details of the four steps in vs. 8-11 are more elaborately developed, a basic progression of thought in four steps is observable in both units. They can be reduced to a simple fourfold scheme, identical in both: entry, reception, effect for salvation, effect for curse. If this scheme is realized, the different content of the wording in step 3 becomes an indication that the gift of peace is an alternate way of speaking about healing and the closing in of God's kingdom. In other words, the peace offered by the missionaries is the same as the proclamation of the arrival of the kingdom of God with its resultant effect of healing. Peace, in these sayings, is not a desirable condition of life that is attainable through good and decent efforts by anyone at any time; it is identical with the breakthrough of God's dominion in the word and work of Jesus, and in his servants who bring healing into a world ravaged by sickness.

In Matthew 10:7-8 and 11-13 the congruence of peace and the kingdom of heaven with its resultant healing is not so clearly suggested as in Luke. An intimate connection between them is, however, presupposed by Matthew as well. In turning our attention now to the first Gospel, we start with the assumption that, for Matthew, the preaching of the immediacy of the kingdom of heaven and its healing powers are the actual content of the peace which is brought by the twelve, and with them by the wandering charismatics of Matthew's church.

In the section on the Son of David in this chapter, we observed that this messianic title was so strongly associated with healing stories that we had to conclude: Healing is, for Matthew, the predominant messianic work (11:2–5), and this impression is confirmed by the emphasis on healing stories in this Gospel. The further association of the healing narratives with the "humble" king led us to the assumption that we were at the threshold of a description of the messianic king of peace as one whose dedication to the lowliest of his subjects and to the healing of their infirmities made him the fulfillment of ancient and recent hopes for a king after God's own heart. The analysis of the sayings in Matthew 10:11–13 and Luke 10:5–6 confirmed this assumption and led us to the conclusion that the peace brought by the missionaries is an alternate word for kingdom of heaven (Matthew), or kingdom of God (Luke), and the power of healing set free by it. This requires, with regard to the first Gospel, some further elaboration.

In 4:23 and 9:35, Matthew weaves into the texture of his narrative two redactional summaries that are virtually identical. Reduced to their essential parts, the two summaries say,

> Jesus went about . . .
> teaching in their synagogues
> and proclaiming the good news of the kingdom
> and curing every disease and every sickness.

The two summaries provide a bracket around chapters 5–9 in which 5–7 is given as an example of the teaching, and 8–9 as a collection of narratives illustrating the healing power of the one who has come to announce the nearness of the kingdom of heaven. The phrase "gospel of the kingdom" is peculiar to Matthew. It integrates both the teaching and the healing of Jesus into a dominating concept on which they both depend: His teaching unfolds the instruction that is derived from the kingdom's imminence, and the works of healing tell of the results of the kingdom's presence (12:28).

The concept of God's kingdom that had developed in Jewish worship and teaching was one in which the world of human history, at large, was seen to be determined by allegiances and influences inimical to the God of Israel because it was bound by idolatry; and the conduct of human life appropriate to the rule of Israel's God was enshrined in the very particular commandments of the law of Moses. Therefore the actual rule of God was realized in heaven, but on earth it was displaced by powers that had supplanted the true and living God and installed in his place a set of pseudo gods who were in charge of affairs on earth. The results of this takeover of illegitimate rulers were devastating. In terms of our subject of peace, the outcome of general human subservience to pseudo gods was experienced as the destruction of the *shalom* of the world; first of all in human history, but also in the realm of nature and in the order of the universe. The bondage to the idols, and therefore the loss of the true God's kingdom on earth, was within human history broken only at some particular points, as in the life of Abraham, of Moses, of David, and in the existence of a single people on earth who would renounce idolatry and, by taking the "yoke of the kingdom" upon themselves, would make the true God king on earth again. But the repossession of all of human history by the God of Abraham and Moses was an object of hope in an ultimate and final triumph of this God over all pseudo-divine challenges, and only in this ultimate victory could the *shalom* of the world be restored. The announcement of the imminent arrival of the kingdom of God by John the Baptist, and by Jesus, anticipates this radical change in the power constellations of history which will wrench human life from the clutches of Satan and restore it to its only legitimate master.

In the Gospel of Matthew, the healing Jesus is presented as the messianic authority who brings peace by granting release from every form of infirmity and sickness. It must be kept in mind, however, that this peacemaking is set in the framework of the message about the impending coming of the kingdom of heaven. In that framework, the healing stories are much more than cheerful news about the personal recovery of this person or another due to the marvelous power of a healer who has become a personal benefactor. In conjunction with the preaching of the kingdom, the healing narratives are flares in the night announcing the coming of a day whose light will enlighten the earth at large, down to its last crevice and corner. Matthew has brought out this universal element in Jesus' healings by emphasizing that Jesus healed *every* disease and *every* sickness (4:23; 8:16; 9:35; 10:1; 12:15; 14:35f.). The insistence on the all-inclusive power of the healer is not an enthusiastic hyperbole that exaggerates, beyond all reason, the historical effectiveness of Jesus in his lifetime, but the reflex of the expectation of the inbreaking kingdom of heaven on the healing narratives. This kingdom has not yet come, and it is already present. It has not yet come because it belongs to the kingdom's essence that it is to be universally in power, displacing every competing loyalty and dependency, and so creating a new form of reality that can be apprehended only as a new heaven and a new earth. But it is also already present, in Matthew's Gospel, in the healing act of the messiah of peace, and in the acts of his disciples (10:1), in which an ultimate and universal victory of the true God of all history is prefigured and pre-sent.

Matthew's concept of Jesus as the messianic bringer of peace in his healings, is, however, not yet complete. Less direct and less explicit is a connection of the concept of peace with other aspects of Jesus' teaching and activity. The word "peace" is not employed in these contexts, but associations are built into the Gospel which suggest that the gift of peace, in the power of the kingdom of heaven, reaches farther than the healing stories would by themselves suggest.

A starting point is provided by the continuation of the summation of Jesus' activity in Matthew 9:35, which was mentioned above. The summary sentence in 9:35 not only provides a bracket for all materials in Matthew 5–9, it also paves the way for the following instruction to the Twelve on their wandering mission in Matthew 10. The bridge between the summation of Jesus' work (9:35) and the sending of the disciples (10:1) begins with these words: "When he saw the crowds, he had compassion for them, because they were harassed and helpless, like sheep without a shepherd" (9:36). The remark about Jesus' compassion for the crowds and the comparison to sheep without a shepherd is, in somewhat simpler form but with similar wording, found at the beginning of Mark's account of the feeding of the five thousand (Mark 6:34). Matthew adopted and slightly elaborated the sentence in Mark 6:34 and placed it together with a summary statement on Jesus' work that puts in a nutshell the totality of Jesus' mission. Only an abbreviated form of Mark 6:34, omitting the comparison with sheep and shepherd, was retained by Matthew at the start of his version of the feeding story (14:14). This is, however, enlarged by a reference to healings that took place at the spot where the miraculous feeding was about to begin. Is there any explanation for this editorial procedure on the part of Matthew?

We cannot attempt an answer to this question until we have given some attention to the comparison with shepherd and sheep (Matt. 10:36). The student of the history of the word *shalom* will immediately be reminded that the shepherd image is one of the most frequently employed symbols for a king in the entire ancient Near East, and that the Israelite hope for a messianic figure who would establish peace is combined more than once in the Old Testament with the picture of the shepherd. Ezekiel 34 and 37 especially come to mind, where a Davidic messiah is presented as the faithful shepherd who will initiate a covenant of peace (34:23, 25; 37:24, 26). Indeed, Matthew 10:36 may allude to Ezekiel 34:5, but this is not certain. The saying "people are like sheep without a shepherd" was not uncommon, and it does refer to leaders other than kings in Numbers 27:17 (Moses and Joshua). But in the context of Matthew's Gospel as a whole, we have here an explicit allusion to a messianic passage in the Old Testament in which a future king is said to shepherd his sheep and usher in a time of peace. In the story of the magi, the birthplace of Jesus is commented upon by high priests and scribes with the words, "And you, Bethlehem, in the land of Judah, are by no means least among the rulers of Judah; for from you shall come a ruler who is to shepherd my people Israel" (2:6). The verse causes considerable difficulties because its first half does not agree with either the LXX or the Masoretic text. But enough remains clear to permit us definite conclusions. Matthew 2:6 is a combined quotation of Micah 5:2 and 4 [5:1 and 3, LXX] and 2 Samuel 5:2 ("It is you who shall be shepherd of my people Israel," spoken of David). The combination of quotes achieves the identification of an heir of the Davidic line with the messianic shepherd-king whose reign produces peace (Micah 5:5); although one needs to notice that the peace in the Micah passage is a pacification of Assyria, which will suffer military defeat and which will in the future be ruled by the sword. Matthew's intention in weaving this combination of Old Testament quotes into Jesus' infancy story is plain enough: The child born in Bethlehem is the true heir of the messianic hope, and as messiah he will be the shepherd-king beginning the long-expected era of peace. Having already been introduced to the shepherd-king, the peacemaker, in the story of the magi, the careful reader of the summary of Jesus' work in 9:35–36 cannot fail to identify the sheep-shepherd motif with the shepherd-king of peace in 2:6.

This enables us to answer the question what purpose Matthew had in mind in lifting Mark's introduction to his first feeding narrative (6:34) out of this context and positioning it into a summary statement (Matt. 9:36). Matthew saw the messianic peacemaker in the man who had compassion on the crowds because they were harassed and helpless, like sheep without a shepherd. Since it was associated with a theme of such principal importance, Matthew considered that the sentence was not given due importance if it served merely as an introduction to an individual story, no matter how miraculous its content. For him, it captured the nature of Jesus' entire life, and consequently he placed it in a summary statement that, in retrospect, interprets all of Matthew 5–9 and, in anticipation, guides the reader through the single sections that lie ahead in the Gospel.

The clearest connections between the compassionate shepherd-king who initiates peace in the summary of 9:36 is traceable to the beginnings of both feeding stories in Matthew; in each narrative Jesus' compassion on the crowds is stressed (14:14; 15:32). The feeding stories are therefore primarily understood as royal acts in which the king cares for the elementary needs of his subjects, protecting them from the danger of starvation. But the miraculous element of the stories must not be rationalized away. It belongs to the epiphany of the king, who inaugurates the new world of peace, to set free the wonderful powers of heaven that are at his disposal, so that a desolate and arid land becomes the scene of a meal for multitudes who are preserved from hunger.

When Jesus is seen as the messianic bringer of peace in the feeding stories, the range of meanings of peace is extended beyond the healing narratives. Peace is now the condition of a protected and nourished life under the care of the inaugurator of the kingdom of heaven. Peace includes the availability of nourishment that sustains the body, and the serious lack of food is a condition of life in which peace is denied those who have to go hungry. The ironic question in the letter of James captures this aspect of peace with particular poignancy: "If a brother or sister is naked and lacks daily food, and one of you says to them, 'Go in peace, keep warm and eat your fill,' and yet you do not supply their bodily needs, what is the good of that?" (James 2:15–16).

The association of themes in Matthew requires one further step. The shepherd-king who brings peace to his people is driven by compassion for the multitude (9:35; 14:14; 15:32), and the king who regards the lowly (21:5) grants peace to those who carry heavy burdens (11:28–29). This implies that the achievement of peace for the messiah Jesus is the result of an internal disposition. The authority of Jesus to heal, to protect, and to provide is linked to a life that is directed toward the concerns, disappointments, and pains of people whose well-being is threatened or lost. Compassion is more than pity. In compassion, the helper participates in the ills of the other to such a degree that the marrow of the helper's existence is affected by the other's plight.

It is most significant that in two places in his Gospel Matthew has inserted explanatory Old Testament quotations in the context of healing narratives. The account of the healing of Peter's mother-in-law is climaxed by the comment in 8:17, "This was to fulfill what had been spoken through the prophet Isaiah, 'He took our infirmities and bore our diseases'" (or, perhaps better, "He took away our infirmities and removed our diseases"), and one of the summary accounts of healings is followed by a long quotation based mainly on Isaiah 42:1–4 that contains the sentence, "He will not break a bruised reed or quench a smoldering wick until he brings justice to victory" (12:20). We have noticed that the restoration of the peace of the kingdom of heaven is, for Matthew, first and foremost the healing of every sickness. But the Old Testament quotations make the point that these healings are not meant as spectacular showpieces, or as the exercise of a magic power in the healer. They ground Jesus' authority to heal in his will to be affected by the sufferers, and the determination to serve those whose life is marred by brokenness. In light of this, it is certainly no coincidence that the praise of the healing king is echoed by the children—who, to the society of their time, belonged to the ones with little status—and is rejected by leaders in authority, who are offended by the children's voices (21:14–16).

This leads to one last expansion of the theme of peace and the kingdom of heaven in Matthew's Gospel. In Matthew 18 we find a collection of sayings, combined with two parables, which are composed in a way suggesting a brief compendium for the order within a Christian community. Presbyterians might consider it a *Book of Order* in a nutshell. But this ordering of the life of the community is entirely dominated by the concern for the "child" and the "little ones."

The chapter opens and closes with the interests of the kingdom of heaven: Its opening question asks, "Who is the greatest in the kingdom of heaven?" (18:1), and its closing parable explains behavior appropriate to the kingdom of heaven (18:23). Within this bracket, the initial question about greatness is answered by Jesus' putting a child in the midst of his disciples. The greatest in God's dominion is the person who lives before God as a child. The child is dependent on the care, protection, and guidance of those who are more powerful and more experienced, and this dependency is the mark of true greatness under God's parental care.

If the child provides a true image for faith in God's protection, it follows that the "little ones" cannot be treated with disdain or neglect. If one of the less important and gifted members of the community is given offense leading to sin, a corruption within the community has occurred which is so momentous that the issue of eternal destiny is at stake (18:6–9). The little ones are protected because their angels see the face of God and their Father in heaven wills their preservation (18:10–14). An offense suffered by one member in the community through another must be dealt with in accordance with the care that is owed even to the offending person. All means possible must be employed to strive for reconciliation (18:15–20). Forgiveness is the litmus test of the community's vitality in the order set by the kingdom of heaven, and the chapter closes with a parable in which the obligation to forgive is declared to be the condition for receiving God's pardon (18:21–35).

The combination of themes in Matthew 18 is remarkable; the composition moves from concern for the less highly regarded members of the community to the problem of sins committed by one member against the other. This combination would seem to be meaningful in a community in which greatness was predominantly determined by the issue of living in obedience to the law of God. The whole tenor of Matthew's Gospel confirms this assumption: doing the will of God is greatness, and disregarding it reduces a person to a position of being the least in the kingdom of heaven (5:19). But the content of the law of God is restated authoritatively by Jesus, the messenger and inaugurator of the kingdom, who has come to embrace in his life the broken and despised, the sick and the helpless, the sinners and the backsliders. Compassion for the little ones is the hallmark of the king of peace, and the power to forgive sins is therefore included in his office of ushering in the peace of God. The blessing of a person who has received from him the forgiveness of God in the words "Go in peace" (Luke 7:50) is not found in Matthew's Gospel; it is, nevertheless, for this evangelist, also a crucial aspect of the peace brought by the king of peace.

Select Bibliography

Betz, Otto. "Jesu heiliger Krieg." *Novum Testamentum 2* (1957): 116–137.

Brandenburger, Egon. *Frieden im Neuen Testament: Grundlinien urchristlichen Friedensverständnisses.* Gütersloh: Gütersloher Verlagshaus Gerd Mohn, 1973. (Indispensable, based on reconstruction of two bases of primitive Christian concepts of peace: one apocalyptic, the other hymnic.)

Burger, Christoph. *Jesus als Davidssohn: Eine traditionsgeschichtliche Untersuchung.* Göttingen: Vandenhoeck & Ruprecht, 1970.

Cassidy, Richard J. *Jesus, Politics, and Society: A Study of Luke's Gospel.* Maryknoll, N.Y.: Orbis Books, 1978. (Luke's portrait of Jesus as determined advocate of the underprivileged makes him in his staunch passive resistance a real threat to Rome.)

Gibbs, James M. "Purpose and Pattern in Matthew's Use of the Title 'Son of David.'" *New Testament Studies* 10 (1963/64): 446–464.

Fitzmyer, Joseph A. *The Gospel According to Luke.* Anchor Bible 28–28A. 2 vols. Garden City, N.Y.: Doubleday, 1985.

Ford, J. Massyngberde. *My Enemy Is My Guest: Jesus and Violence in Luke.* Maryknoll, N.Y.: Orbis Books, 1984. (Distinguishes the war-prone attitude in the infancy section from the medium position of John the Baptist, and from the nonviolent Jesus in the body of Luke's Gospel.)

Schmid, Hans Heinrich. *Šālôm: "Frieden" im Alten Orient und im Alten Testament.* Stuttgart: Katholisches Bibelwerk, 1971.

Schnackenburg, Rudolf. "Die Seligpreisung der Friedensstifter (Mt

5, 9) im mattäischen Kontext," *Biblische Zeitschrift,* n.s. 26 (1982): 161–178.

Swartley, Willard M. "Politics and Peace (*Eirēnē*) in Luke's Gospel." In *Political Issues in Luke-Acts,* ed. Philip Scharper and John Eagleson. Maryknoll, N.Y.: Orbis Books, 1984. (Shows Luke's special emphasis on peace with a pervasive stress on social, economic, and political justice.)

4

The Opposition
to Peace
in the Gospel
of Matthew

Looking back at the last chapter, we can say that a picture has emerged in which peace is so firmly associated with the gospel that it represents one aspect of the good news in its totality. Jesus is described in the Synoptic Gospels as the herald and inaugurator of God's governance in the world through which the peace of a new earth is ushered in. It is, then, no exaggeration to say that the entire activity of Jesus, in word and deed, is the making of peace; and that the life of his community is given direction by his blessing on the peacemakers.

The Gospels are, however, not fairy tales in which a paradise restored is offered without regard to competing and hostile realities. They tell not only of a victory over Satan, but also of the continuing effects of bondage to Satanic power. Their messianic king does not proceed from one victory to another without running into the most determined opposition, an opposition that succeeds in eliminating Jesus, the troublesome intruder, by passing the verdict of a court upon him—one that brands him as a blasphemous seducer—and by executing the death penalty on him. The peace of the Gospels is clearly an embattled peace. We shall, therefore, proceed by looking at the question: What becomes of the peace of the good news, and to those who bring it, in the confrontation with its opposition? We shall do so by concentrating on the Gospel of Matthew, which, with deliberate reflection and consistency, represents one response to our question.

1. The Peace of the Gospel and the Wars of Revolution

This section requires the allocation of the Gospel of Matthew within the constellation of events and places that provide the most likely background for its composition. Necessarily, such allocation remains hypothetical, but its major points appear to be sufficiently probable to serve as references for the interpretation of Matthew with which this section is concerned. No attempt will be made here to give any evidence for the soundness of these assumptions; instead, the reader is referred to the discussion of the issue by Ulrich Luz and Eduard Schweizer in works listed in the bibliography at the end of this chapter.

It is assumed, then, that the first Gospel was written by a Jewish-Christian for Jewish-Christian communities that had suffered separation from their parent Judaism. This separation is endured with a keen sense of abiding loyalty to the Old Testament and to Jewish traditions, and it is combined with the certainty that the gate is now open to claim the whole world as rightful inheritors of the promises made by the God of Israel. The agony of separation is still intensely felt, and the wounds it has caused are still bleeding. The alienation from Judaism is experienced in the clash with a form of Jewish life dominated by pharisaism, and this, together with a cluster of other observations, leads to the conclusion that Matthew belongs in a historical setting that is determined by the reconstruction of Jewish culture through pharisaic leadership in the aftermath of the catastrophic loss of the war with Rome in the years 66–74. Quite a number of additional observations encourage the further assumption that the Gospel of Matthew originated in a Syrian city sometime within the last two decades of the first century, hardly much after the year 90. What is particularly important for our search is the placement of the Gospel in the time that still quakes in the aftershocks of the disastrous attempt to liberate Jewish life from alien domination by the force of arms.

Jesus' speech on the final and triumphant arrival of the Son of man from heaven, and of the dissolution of the present order of the world (Matthew 24), makes mention of the necessity of wars prior to the coming of the end. "You will hear of wars and rumors of wars; see that you are not alarmed; for this must take place, but the end is not yet" (24:6). These words are often quoted in our time. In books and pamphlets, over the radio and on the television screen, they are used to justify the notion of the inevitability of war because of the divine order of history which has preordained warfare to precede the arrival of the end of our old world. Contemporary events are identified with isolated apocalyptic sayings in the Bible, the menacing configuration of superpowers is, not so subtly, split up into camps of the righteous here and camps of the godless atheists there; and with slight of hand, Jesus' saying that wars must take place is turned into an imperative demanding the continuation of military readiness as a divine ordinance. In reality, this type of reasoning turns the intention of Matthew 24:6 into its opposite: The saying is lodged in a solemnly stressed warning against false messiahs and prophets who, out of religious conviction, incite to revolutionary war to gain freedom for God's people.

Of all the Synoptics, Matthew's apocalyptic discourse, in chapter 24, is most frequently laced with allusions and references to the revolutionary spirit that was responsible for the outbreak of the Jewish war against Rome in A.D. 66. Matthew made considerable changes in the form of the discourse that he had available in Mark 13. Only two facets of his editorial rearrangement and rephrasing are important to the present inquiry. Matthew removed the section Mark 13:9–13 almost entirely from his account of Jesus' discourse on the end time and placed it with the instructions for the wandering missionaries in Matthew 10:17–21. The result of this is that the warnings concerning the impending oppression, and even persecution, by governmental agencies, and the warnings concerning divisions in the families, are no longer seen as consequences of the apocalyptic woes but as the result of the community's mission. Of the smaller changes Matthew has made, only a few are noted here because they have an immediate bearing on our theme. At the beginning of the discourse, Jesus warns against deceivers coming in his name who say, in Mark's version, "I am he" (13:5). This is given greater specificity by Matthew, who writes, "I am the Messiah!" (24:5): Matthew is concerned that the claim inherent in the statement "I am he" is unambiguously identified as a messianic claim. Mark does, at a later point in the speech, also warn against deceivers who appear as claimants to messianic dignity together with false prophets (13:21–22), and Matthew follows his lead here almost verbatim (24:23–24). But Matthew has added an oracle, without parallel in Mark, that speaks of the arising of many false prophets who will deceive a lot of people (24:11). Apparently, in the combination of pseudo messiahs and pseudo prophets, Matthew is particularly wary of the false prophets, who are somehow seen to be in league with messianic pretenders. Mark had not identified the location where the false Christ would have to be expected; those who speak of his coming will only say "look here" or "look there" (13:21). But Matthew is at this point more precise. People announcing him will say not only "he is here or there" (24:23), but quite specifically, "he is in the wilderness" or "he is in the inner room" (24:26; without parallel in Mark).

From these observations we can draw some conclusions. Matthew knows of wars, of the clash between nations and kingdoms which, together with famines and earthquakes, will be the beginning of a period of suffering (24:6–8). This is connected to the experience of hatred and persecution suffered by the community (24:9), and to the specter of apostasy and betrayal in the community itself because of the appearance of false prophets who succeed in deceiving many (24:10–11). Both aspects of the trouble are brought into close connection to the war, mentioned immediately before, by an emphatic "then," or "at that time," which opens the sentences in 24:9 and 10 (again without parallel in Mark). Matthew is concerned that the arrival of messianic pretenders, mentioned before the statement about the outbreak of war (24:5 and 6–7), is clearly understood as a messianic claim. He shares with Mark the combination of pseudo messiahs and pseudo prophets, but he adds special emphasis to the pseudo prophets who play a key role in damaging the community. The wilderness, as one locale from which the deceiving messiahs are to be expected, is additionally identified by the first evangelist.

Together with material that Matthew shares with Mark, we can isolate a cluster of ideas that is correlated because it belongs to an ideology which provided the motivation for the revolutionaries' war against Rome in A.D. 66–74. This cluster of ideas may be broken down into four points:

a. *The appearance of pseudo Christs.*

24:5 "Many will come in my name, saying, 'I am the Messiah!' " Followed immediately by the mention of wars.

24:24 Together with false prophets: "False messiahs and false prophets will appear." They are credited with "great signs and omens."

b. *The arrival of pseudo prophets.*

24:11 "Many false prophets will arise."

24:24 Together with false Christs; see (a).

c. *Deceptions will occur.*

24:4 "Beware that no one leads you astray," subjects unidentified.

24:5 Messianic pretenders "will lead many astray."

24:11 False prophets "will arise and lead many astray."

24:24 False messiahs and false prophets, performing "great signs and omens," act "to lead astray, if possible, even the elect."

d. *The exodus and its miracles.*

24:24 False messiahs and prophets will appear "and produce great signs and omens."

24:26 The false messiah is announced: "Look! He is in the wilderness."

It is immediately evident that the ideas are interconnected. The messiahs and prophets can be mentioned separately (vs. 5 and 11), but they are also combined (v. 24); both messianic and prophetic pretenders are united in the effort to lead people astray (vs. 5, 11, 24); both groups perform great miracles (v. 24); and there is also, as will be seen presently, a connection between messianic and prophetic claims, the appearance in the wilderness, and the performance of miracles (vs. 24 and 26).

The Jewish insurgents against the power of Rome who, in the year 66, began open warfare with the military forces of the empire, show traits that resemble the picture in Matthew 24 very strikingly. Our best source by far for the events of the Jewish war is the Jewish historian Josephus, who was personally involved in the struggle. From his pen we possess two extensive descriptions of the Jewish-Roman war, one written around A.D. 80 entitled *The Jewish War* (*JW*), and one written twenty years later in the closing books of his *Jewish Antiquities* (*Ant.*). Valuable additional evidence is found in Josephus's autobiography (*Vita*).

From Josephus's writings we collect, first of all, without much critical comment, some statements showing the close affinity of the Jewish revolutionaries with the four points observed in Matthew 24. We shall then have to proceed, however, to some evaluation of the affinity, which will require caution.

Messianic Pretenders According to Josephus

Josephus nowhere in his extensive accounts of the Jewish-Roman war uses the word "pseudo Christ" (*pseudochristos*). But he describes a number of leaders in the Jewish revolt who made claims to kingship, and the wording of the passages suggests, at least in some cases, messianic aspirations.

Already seventy years before the outbreak of the war, Josephus mentions some figures who made claims to be kings in the transition period after the death of Herod the Great in 4 B.C. He says that at this time the country was "a prey to disorder, and the opportunity induced numbers of persons to aspire to kingship (*basileia*)." (*JW* II, 55; similar to the summary in *Ant.* XVII, 285, "Anyone might make himself king.") The list of names given by Josephus is identical in *JW* II, 55–65 and in *Ant.* XVII, 271–285; they are a certain Judas, son of Ezekias, who successfully attacks the royal palace in Sepphoris; Simon, a former slave of Herod, who leads a band of brigands gutting the royal palace in Jericho; and the shepherd Athrongaeus, who together with his four brothers manages to tyrannize the country for a long time. It can be observed that in the *Antiquities* Josephus was less reluctant to mention the claims to royal office by these men than he was when he wrote the *Jewish War*. The account in *JW* says nothing of such claims by Judas, while the parallel account in *Ant.* states that he "had ambition for royal rank" (XVII, 272). Of Simon, *JW* says only that he "assumed the diadem himself" (II, 57), but *Ant.* adds that he was also proclaimed king by his troops (XVII, 274). Athrongaeus is characterized as having handled leadership like a king and having "donned the diadem" in *JW* II, 61–62; yet in the account of *Ant.,* his kingship is emphasized four times in the short passages (XVII, 278–284). It is reasonable to conjecture that Josephus was disposed, in the late work, to allow the facts of many claims to kingship in the confusion of the year 4 B.C. to come out more clearly. He was then less constrained by the caution to hide from Roman eyes, as much as possible, the vigor of Jewish aspirations for their own king. Though none of Josephus's statements can prove messianic aspirations, nevertheless we can say with confidence that the time was ripe in Judaism when a period of great political uncertainty could produce claimants to kingship based on support other than their belonging to the line of ancestry deriving from David.

During the war, some figures appeared on the scene who, like their predecessors in 4 B.C., may have pursued messianic aspirations. In the summer of A.D. 66, a certain Menahem replenished his arms from the armory of the fortress Masada and moved into Jerusalem. Menahem's entry into the holy city is described by Josephus as the return "like a veritable king" (*JW* II, 434) after which Menahem "became the leader of the revolution." The next day, the high priest and his brother were killed because of their advocacy of restraint in the conduct of the war, Menahem became an "insufferable tyrant" who "believes himself without a rival" and appears "clad in royal robes" (*JW* II, 442, 444). This Menahem was the son or grandson of Judas the Galilean, whom Josephus credits with being the founder of a sect of Judaism bent on revolt against Rome, who refused to pay tribute to the Romans and who drew practical political conclusions from the first commandment of the Decalogue amounting to rejection, on principle, of any and all forms of subservience to a foreign power (*JW* II, 118). It appears likely that Menahem's short accession to absolute power, after the elimination of the high priest, and his continuation of the ideas of his father (or grandfather), had messianic implications. But, once more, we cannot be certain; what Josephus reports does not in itself constitute unambiguous messianic pretensions.

The same is true of Simon bar Giora. One of many brigand leaders in the early stages of the war, he was set upon by troops of the high priest and fled to the sicarii (dagger men) on Masada, whose confidence he gained. After separating himself again from the sicarii, he conducted successful forays in the countryside. Finally he was militarily strong enough to move into Jerusalem, where he became the main commander of Jewish troops during Titus's siege of the city in A.D. 70. He was taken prisoner, paraded before the Roman crowd at Titus's triumph in Rome, and executed in the Roman Forum. Some details in Josephus's narratives about Simon have led scholars to conjecture that Simon had messianic ideas. His followers are said to have been "subservient to his command as to a king" (*JW* IV, 510). He carried out a program of release of slaves that might have been understood as the inauguration of a messianic year of liberation in accordance with Isaiah 61:1–2 (*JW* IV, 508), and he showed the kind of bodily strength and courage in battle that can be interpreted as indicators of a messianic claim based on the old Israelite tradition of the mighty warrior of God (IV, 503–504). But none of that is incontrovertible evidence; all the traits Josephus mentions allow for different explanations.

We can summarize, then, by saying that the revolutionary zeal among opponents of the Roman rule in Palestine produced a good number of individual leaders who assumed royal prerogatives, both long before and during the war, and that the possibility cannot be discounted that some or all of them were indeed messianic figures. However, corroborating evidence from other sides would be required in order to see in the "messianic" leaders of the revolutionaries persons who can provide an actual background upon which to place the warnings in Matthew 24 against false messiahs.

Prophets in Josephus

Josephus knows of a number of prophetic figures who appeared close enough, or during, the Jewish-Roman war to merit consideration. There are five Josephan passages which require attention.

During the administration in Judea of the procurator Fadus (A.D. 44–48), about twenty years prior to the war, "a certain impostor named Theudas persuaded the majority of the masses to take up their possessions and to follow him to the Jordan River. He stated that he was a prophet and that at his command the river would be parted and would provide them an easy passage" (*Ant.* XX, 97–98a). Theudas is, for Josephus, clearly a prophet and a miracle worker. His promise to part the Jordan for passage to the followers is a sign that makes him either a second Moses (Exodus 14) or a second Joshua (Josh. 3:14–17). He claims a leadership role that would set in motion again the event that led to Israel's liberation from Egypt, or the entry into the promised land. Josephus mentions no call to arms in Theudas's message, but the fact that he and his followers were immediately met by

Roman cavalry and either killed or taken prisoner (*Ant.* XX, 98) makes it clear that at least the Romans understood Theudas's proclamation not as an innocent expression of Jewish religion, but as a political demonstration aimed at the achievement of liberation from Rome.

Under the procuratorship of Felix (52–60), two incidents took place which Josephus narrates in somewhat different form in *JW* II, 258–263 and in *Ant.* XX, 167–172. The first is the appearance of a group of impostors and deceivers who are further described as acting "under the pretense of divine inspiration fostering revolutionary changes" (so *JW* II, 259; the clause is not found in *Ant.* XX, 167). The continuations of Josephus's report then vary only slightly. He says in *JW* II, 259 that "they persuaded the multitude to act like madmen, and led them out into the desert under the belief that God would there give them tokens of deliverance." In *Ant.* XX, 167–168, the account reads: "The impostors and deceivers called upon the mob to follow them into the desert. For they said that they would show them unmistakable marvels and signs that would be wrought in harmony with God's design." The "impostors and deceivers" are prophets, since they claim to act under divine inspiration, and their message is linked to the accomplishment of a revolt. As in the case of Theudas before, they promise the reenactment of signs and omens of Israel's wilderness time under Moses [*terata kai sēmeia* in *Ant.* XX, 168, as in Matt. 24:24], the wonders being signs of freedom. The meaning of this prophetic stirring was not lost on the Romans, as Josephus's continuation shows: "Against them Felix, regarding this as but the preliminary to insurrection, sent a body of cavalry and heavy-armed infantry, and put a large number to the sword" (*JW* II, 260).

Still under Felix there occurred the rise of an Egyptian Jew whom Josephus calls specifically a false prophet (*JW* II, 261; *pseudoprophētēs,* as in Matt. 24:24). He moved with a band of some thirty thousand followers from the desert to the Mount of Olives, a traditional place in Jewish expectation for the arrival of the messiah. He planned to take Jerusalem by force, to overpower the Roman garrison, and "to set up himself as a tyrant of the people" (*JW* II, 262). In view of this description, it can hardly be doubted that the phrase "tyrant of the people" is a deliberate misnomer on the part of Josephus hiding the fact that the Egyptian arrived with specific messianic pretensions. Possibly that throws some light on the evidence, discussed before, that several figures claiming royal stature were also presented as "tyrants" by the historian (Menahem, *JW* II, 442; Simon bar Giora, *JW* IV, 508), suggesting that the term "tyrant" may be a cover word for the title "messiah." Josephus's account of the Egyptian prophet in the *Antiquities* adds the information that "he wished to demonstrate from there (i.e., the Mount of Olives) that at his command Jerusalem's walls would fall down" (*Ant.* XX, 170), an unmistakable reenactment of Joshua's march seven times around Jericho that brought the city's walls tumbling down (Josh. 6:15–21). In the Egyptian Jew we meet, therefore, a claimant to both prophetic and messianic powers who has set out to take Jerusalem by the power of divine intervention as at the period of Israel's taking possession of its promised land.

Shortly thereafter, under the procurator Festus (60–62), brief mention is made of another unnamed impostor. "Festus also sent a force of cavalry and infantry against the dupes of a certain impostor who had promised them salvation and rest from troubles, if they chose to follow him into the wilderness. The force that Festus dispatched destroyed both the deceiver himself and those who had followed him" (*Ant.* XX, 188). The passage confirms the ongoing activity of charismatic individuals who persuade people to trust in their leadership when acts of deliverance, as in Israel's wilderness period, will usher in a glorious future of salvation and rest, politically conceived. It may be worth noting that either the word "salvation" or the word "rest" could well have been captured, in the original setting, by the word *shalom*.

Josephus on Deceivers

In Matthew 24, the warning against false Christs and false prophets is repeated four times with great emphasis. Josephus also is greatly concerned about the danger posed by deceivers and impostors who publish false prophecies designed to arouse the hope of people for miraculous divine intervention. Much of the evidence has already been mentioned in the section on the prophets, and it is sufficient to draw together the evidence already presented. Josephus repeatedly declares prophets advocating armed insurrection to be impostors and deceivers. Theudas and the unnamed Egyptian, the group under Felix and the individual under the administration of Festus, all share the historian's judgment: they are deceivers under the mantle of divine inspiration.

Although Josephus does not label the royal or messianic leaders as impostors, like the prophets, there is no question that he sees the prophets as important allies to the tyrants. He tells us that a false prophet proclaimed, while the temple was already burning, that God would show "signs of salvation" in the temple court, and he adds the comment: "Numerous prophets, indeed, were at this period suborned by the tyrants to delude the people." This leads him to conclude: "When the deceiver actually pictures release from prevailing horrors, then the sufferer wholly abandons himself to expectation" (*JW* VI, 285–287). The alliance between prophetic impostors and revolutionary leaders bent on war is equally manifest in Josephus's comment immediately following his description of the Egyptian, when "the impostors and brigands, banding together, incited numbers to revolt" (*JW* II, 264). To Josephus, the false prophets are the more dangerous and, therefore, the real deceivers. Introducing them in *JW* II, 258, he writes, "There arose another body of villains, with purer hands but more impious intentions, who no less than the assassins ruined the peace of the city."

The Miracles of the Exodus in Josephus

The discussion above of pro-revolutionary prophets gave occasion to mention an almost consistent connection between these charismatic supporters of the war and their expectation that the miracles of the time of Israel's exodus from Egypt, of the period in the desert, and of the occupation of their land, would be repeated. Without citing the passages again, a summation yields us this picture: Under both Felix and Festus, groups of prophets emerge who wish to lead the people into the wilderness, where they are enticed to hope for "signs and wonders," for "signs of salvation." These signs are often no more clearly specified than they are in Matthew 24:24, except that the promised parting of the Jordan by Theudas, and his intended march around Jerusalem, to bring down the city's walls, refer unmistakably to the wonders performed by charismatic leaders at the time of Israel's liberation from Egypt and the settlement in the land of promise.

The wilderness is not always the location where the acts of

deliverance are expected to happen. The term functions like a code word among others, which stands for acts of divine intervention through miraculous events which belong to the time of Israel's beginnings, which brought about the nation's deliverance from deadly dangers and established its freedom. The enthusiasts claiming illumination by God understand their own time, the time of the Jewish-Roman war, to be a period at which the great events that brought the nation into existence will be reenacted. The conclusion is therefore inevitable that the revolutionaries with their prophets were gripped by the hope that their time would become the witness of God's establishment of his universal rule in the world, or, in terms of Jesus' preaching, the coming of the kingdom of God.

Looking back at this section, the essential points can be summarized as follows. Matthew 24 has, among several other changes, altered the form of Jesus' apocalyptic discourse found in Mark 13 by stressing the importance of messianic claims, by adding weight to the danger posed by false prophets, and by weaving into the discourse a saying that identifies the desert as the place from which many will expect the messiah to arise. This combines to produce a picture in which the outbreak of war among nations is linked to the emergence of messianic and prophetic claims by people who expect the wilderness as the place where a renewal of great signs and wonders will take place as in the time of Israel's origin. But this whole concatenation of ideas—war, messiah, prophet, wilderness, miracles—is viewed as a great temptation, which must be resisted. The very same combination of motifs is traceable in Josephus's account of charismatic prophets and exceptional royal figures—perhaps messianic pretenders—who promise the return of the great age of Israel's foundation with all its signs and wonders. A good case can be made that this concurrence of motifs is already fully at work in Mark 13, but it is certainly more emphasized in Matthew 24 and can therefore be considered one guide, among others, for the understanding of the chapter as a whole.

2. The No to the Sword

We return, once more, to Matthew 24. Immediately after the warning to beware of false messiahs (v. 5), the outbreak of wars and the conflict between nations and kingdoms was announced (vs. 6–7). In Matthew, this is followed by a section that contains words found only in this Gospel (except for v. 9; see Mark 13:9a and 13a; also Matt. 24:13 is identical with Mark 13:13b):

9   Then they will hand you over to be tortured and will put you to death, and you will be hated by all nations because of my name.
10   Then many will fall away, and they will betray one another and hate one another.
11   And many false prophets will arise and lead many astray.
12   And because of the increase of lawlessness, the love of many will grow cold.
13   But the one who endures to the end will be saved.
14   And this good news of the kingdom will be proclaimed throughout the world, as a testimony to all nations; and then the end will come. (Matt. 24:9–14)

Verses 10–14 in this special Matthean section expect troubles to arise within the Christian community. They are caused by false prophets who gain a hearing in the community and undermine its unity. We assume now that, in analogy to Josephus's false prophets, these charismatics are advocates of a claim to exclusive and abiding privileges granted by Israel's God. They are convinced that the hour of the final war for liberation has struck, and that their struggle for the decisive Jewish victory marks the end of the old time ushering in the new age at which, through the Jewish victory, God's people will make their God the only ruler over the earth.

These prophets are a temptation to the Jewish-Christian community in Syria within which Matthew writes his Gospel, because charismatic prophets are known and honored there (10:41; 23:34). The false prophets, fomenting revolution and nationalistic privileges, enter the Christian community "in sheep's clothing, but inwardly [they] are ravenous wolves" (7:15). They can display an appearance that makes them almost indistinguishable from the true Christian prophets. They can say, "Lord, Lord, did we not prophesy in your name, and cast out demons in your name, and do many deeds of power in your name?" (7:22). They are Christian charismatics and exorcists, but they will cause dissension and conflict in the community, instilling hatred and betrayal in its midst. Matthew's most serious charge against them is that their activity causes love to grow cold. What is meant by this love is not a general disposition to friendliness toward others, but the specific form of love expected in the Christian community as it is expressed in the Sermon on the Mount: "I say to you, love your enemies and pray for those who persecute you" (5:44). This love has grown cold under the operations of the false prophets, who have slipped back into the old habit of dividing the world into camps of friends and foes, and into the posture of insisting that the world can be saved only by fighting for the cause of God's special people against its enemies. But if the pseudo prophets are convinced of the need violently to force the kingdom of heaven into appearing, Matthew counters that they misconstrue the signs of the time. For the end will not be forced by their rebellion, but it will be prepared by the spreading of the gospel: "This good news of the kingdom will be proclaimed throughout the world, as a testimony to all the nations; and then the end will come" (24:14). The phrase "this good news (gospel) of the kingdom" concentrates Jesus' entire teaching and acting into a single term that is virtually synonymous with the first Gospel itself. This gospel is to be preached to all nations (28:19). It is the gospel of the king of peace who blesses all peacemakers (5:9), in that it is bound to that interpretation of Israel's law by Jesus in which the command to love enemies calls forth a truly new era. In this era the compulsion to divide the human race into the good and the bad is replaced by the provocation of the kingdom of heaven, the new world, which trusts God's grace to be sufficient for the just and the unjust (5:45).

This proposal for understanding the false prophets in Matthew 24, and perhaps throughout the first Gospel, is based on the assumption that in the Syrian-Jewish population, around the year 90, a spirit of revolution and armed resistance was still alive enough to cause trouble even some twenty years after the collapse of the immense effort to resist Rome by force of arms. There is, to my knowledge, no historical evidence available that could prove the continued virulence of this kind of spirit in the region where Matthew was most likely written. But there is evidence that the defeat by Rome and the destruction of Jerusalem had not extinguished the fires of revolution in other areas of the Jewish diaspora. After the end of the war, Josephus tells us, a group of some surviving sicarii fled into Alexandria in Egypt, and "again embarked on revolutionary schemes, and sought to induce many of their hosts to assert their independence," holding high their banner of their God's exclusive lordship, and not shrinking from murder of fellow Jews who would not be subjected to their views (*JW* II, 410–411). The very dream of a move into the wilderness, complete with a display of signs and apparitions, was propagated by a certain Jonathan the weaver. He had a different group of surviving sicarii at his disposal and, after having been taken prisoner, contrived a scheme to bring Catullus, Roman governor of Libya, to his side. This caused such a commotion that Catullus derived from it the excuse to kill some three thousand wealthy Jews in the province (*JW* VII, 437–446). Revolutionary spirits are not extirpated by military defeats, and, in the case of the Jewish revolutionary fever after A.D. 74, we have the additional fact that a definite and explicit messianic claim, by Bar Kokhba, could, some sixty years after the attempted termination of the revolutionaries, produce yet another full-fledged Jewish war of liberation, whose effects on the life of Judaism were even more severe than the first defeat under Titus. In the Bar Kokhba revolt we also come across the interesting fact that the Christian confession of the messiah Jesus clashed with the messianic claim of Bar Kokhba himself. The Christian writer Justin Martyr asserts, "In the recent Jewish war, Bar Kokhba, the leader of the Jewish uprising, ordered that only the Christians should be subjected to dreadful torments, unless they renounced and blasphemed Jesus Christ" (*1 Apol.* 31). As in Matthew 24, the conflict of Christ and counter-Christ is produced by the will to engage Rome in a war for independence. In view of these reports from the period after the first Jewish war with Rome, it does not seem farfetched to assume that the Jewish population of the diaspora could, at many places, rekindle the flames of enthusiastic hope for the restoration of a free Jewish nation. The apocalyptic temperature was raised and could be brought again, at any moment, to the pitch of a raging fever.

A scene in Matthew's account of Jesus' arrest carries the same denial of the zealotic war ideology for salvation. Together with all the other evangelists, Matthew reports the attempt of a disciple to offer resistance at Jesus' arrest by drawing the sword (Matt. 26:51; Mark 14:47; Luke 22:50; of Peter in John 18:10) and cutting off the right ear of one in the arresting party. Matthew comments on the incident with Jesus' words, which are not found elsewhere: "Put your sword back into its place; for all who take the sword will perish by the sword. Do you think that I cannot appeal to my Father, and he will at once send me more than twelve legions of angels? But how then would the scriptures be fulfilled . . . ?" (26:52–54).

The reference to the help of legions of angels in this instruction must be taken quite seriously. It is a characteristic of many of the narratives involving wars of Yahweh in the Old Testament that the host of heaven fights in support of Israel, and apocalyptic thought at the time of the New Testament had revived this idea, whose impact is evident in the book of Revelation. The Son of God indeed has the power to ask God for protection by a host of angels who are conceived as warriors on behalf of the just. Now, as never before in the Gospel's narrative, would be the time to call upon the "great signs and omens" with which God intervenes to ensure the freedom of his just servant. But this possibility is rejected by Jesus as the devil's suggestion; for self-preservation without God's word and divine protection against a deadly fall were rejected in Jesus' resistance of the tempter (4:1–7). Once more—as once in the beginning so now at the end—Jesus does not yield to the temptation to preserve his life by resisting evil with evil's own armor. If anything in Matthew's Gospel, this scene at the arrest is the authentic interpretation of the sentence in the Sermon on the Mount, "Do not resist an evildoer" (Matt. 5:39). Had he resisted there, he would have ceased to be the one toward whom scripture was tending in speaking of the eternal "must" with which God has willed to justify the righteous who is subjected to the cruelties of his enemies.

We are ready to return to the beginning of this chapter. We noticed there that the apocalyptic discourse in Matthew 24 is aware of a necessity that wars would be fought involving kingdoms and nations in mortal conflict. We also noticed a tendency to understand this necessity as an acknowledgment that wars are inevitable, sometimes even a trend to make these sayings serve as a justification to encourage a readiness for war against nations led by atheist governments. Against this it must be stressed with the greatest insistence that those who construe a divine obligation for armed resistance to a foreign, and pagan, oppressor are, in Matthew 24, the false messiahs and lying prophets who deceive with the hallucination of miracles from heaven. The Christ of the gospel of peace has no part in this deception. The divine "must," under whose guidance he lives, involves the refusal to employ "arms for peace." To be true to what he is as the Son of God, he must suffer the onslaught of his enemies unto death; and so must his believers, who are warned not to let their love—the love of the enemy—grow cold, seduced by the appeals of false prophets (24:11–12).

Select Bibliography

Barnett, P. W. "The Jewish Sign Prophets—A.D. 40–70: Their Intentions and Origin." *New Testament Studies* 27 (1980–81): 679–697.

Brandon, S. G. F. *Jesus and the Zealots: A Study of the Political Factor in Primitive Christianity.* New York: Charles Scribner's Sons, 1967. (Thesis: Although not a zealot, Jesus pursued patriotic goals later eliminated by the evangelists for apologetic reasons.)

Cullmann, Oscar. *Jesus and the Revolutionaries.* New York: Harper & Row, 1970.

Edwards, George R. *Jesus and the Politics of Violence.* New York: Harper & Row, 1972. (A thorough rebuttal of the thesis of S. G. F. Brandon, with extensive comments on the contemporary problem.)

Hare, D. R. A. *The Theme of Jewish Persecution of Christians in the Gospel According to St. Matthew.* Cambridge: Cambridge University Press, 1967.

Hengel, Martin. *Die Zeloten.* Leiden: E. J. Brill, 1961. (Pays much attention to the theological element of the revolution against Rome.)

———. *Victory Over Violence: Jesus and the Revolutionists,* trans. Robin Scroggs. Philadelphia: Fortress Press, 1973.

Horsley, R. A. "Ancient Jewish Banditry and the Revolt Against Rome." *Catholic Biblical Quarterly* 43 (1981): 409–432.

Luz, Ulrich. *Matthew 1–7: A Commentary,* trans. W. C. Linss, 79–95. Minneapolis: Augsburg, 1989.

Rhoads, D. M. *Israel in Revolution: 6–74 C.E.: A Political History*

Based on the Writings of Josephus, Philadelphia: Fortress Press, 1976.

Schweizer, Eduard. "Matthew's Church," in *The Interpretation of Matthew,* ed. G. Stanton, 129–155. Philadelphia: Fortress Press; London: SPCK, 1983.

Smith, M. "Zealots and Sicarii, Their Origins and Relations." *Harvard Theological Review* 64 (1971): 1–19.

5

The Book of Acts
and the Pax Romana

The word *eirene* is used seven times in the book of Acts. Even a cursory glimpse at the verses involved will show that, in most cases, the word covers areas of meaning quite different from those in the Synoptic Gospels.

7:26   Moses meets quarreling Israelites in Egypt and seeks to reconcile them "to peace." "Peace" seems to indicate a reconciliation among conflicting parties; the conflict lies on the human level.

9:31   After the persecution of the Jerusalem church (8:1) and the removal of the threat from Saul through his conversion, the church throughout Judea, Galilee, and Samaria has "peace." Freedom from oppression and a measure of safety are here in mind.

10:36   This verse was discussed earlier, in chapter 3. The word of God sent to Israel is "the good news of peace by Jesus Christ."

12:20   A delegation from the cities of Tyre and Sidon appears before Herod asking "for peace." *Eirene* is here applied to the field of politics and of the administration of cities and kingdoms.

15:33   The congregation in Antioch sends a delegation from Jerusalem back "in peace." This may be no more than a traditional farewell but it may also, in view of its connection with the council in Jerusalem, imply the preservation of the unity of the emerging church.

16:36   The Philippian jailor, ordered by the magistrates, releases Paul to freedom and to go "in peace." Paul initiates a protest based on his Roman citizenship. The relation of "peace" to issues of Roman law and police procedures is obvious.

24:2   A certain Tertullus, in the service of the Jerusalem hierarchy, addresses the Roman governor with the diplomatic flourish, "Because of you we have long enjoyed peace." The context leaves no doubt that *eirene* is connected to Roman law and Roman administration.

Surveying these passages, one finds it immediately striking that the word "peace" has in Acts made some long strides in the direction of human relationships and even of very mundane matters that are the concerns of kings and governors, city officials and the police. In two cases (16:36; 24:2) the word cannot be severed from Roman justice and government; and in 12:20, it is indirectly involved also because the relative independence of a Jewish king is predicated on the functioning of the superior Roman order. Since awareness of the political reality manifested in the administration of Roman justice and the exercise of Roman power is a characteristic of Luke's Gospel and of Acts, it is necessary for us to move first to a consideration of the issue of peace as it was understood and practiced in the Roman empire in the period initiated by Julius Caesar and Octavianus Augustus.

1. The Pax Romana

Luke is alone among the evangelists in placing the story of Jesus into the larger framework of history. He wants his readers to understand that the events about which he is writing were not confined to some remote corner of the Roman empire (Acts 26:26), and that they can stand up to historical inquiry (Luke 1:1–4). The beginnings of the two major figures in Luke's Gospel, Jesus and John the Baptist, are coordinated with the history of the empire. A census carried out by the Roman governor of Syria, at the edict of Augustus, sets the forces in motion that bring Jesus' parents to Bethlehem, where the messiah is to be born (Luke 2:1, 4):

divine destiny and historical circumstance combine to effect the birth of Jesus, and the historical difficulties attached for the modern historian to the census of Quirinius are, with regard to Luke's intention, beside the point. Even more meticulous is the note putting the activity of John the Baptist into the framework of what was, to readers of Luke's time, world history (Luke 3:1–2). There we are informed about the emperor of the time, the Roman governor of Judea, the three Jewish heads of state in their respective regions, and the Jewish high priests: a note fit for record keeping in a historical archive. Evidence of this type could easily be multiplied, but it is not required for our present purposes. Luke wants to bind the life on earth of Jesus of Nazareth and the life of his growing community—both taken together are, for Luke, the history of Jesus Christ!—into Greco-Roman society and Roman law and justice, because it is God's will that the purpose of Israel now be historically realized in the mission to the ends of the earth of a community in which both Jew and Gentile have the right to live together in peace. The concrete world of the Roman empire, its concrete forms of Hellenistic and Roman culture, its actual societal and political conditions, all these have become a focus of interest for Luke because they are the field in which the Christian mission plants its seeds. That holds true also for the subject of peace. The concept of peace in the book of Acts is engaged in silent dialogue with the ideal of the Roman Peace (Pax Romana). Acts does not mention this ideal by name. But it can be demonstrated that Luke is not only familiar with Roman law and interested in its administration; he is also conversant with specifics of Roman pride, with the atmospheric factor of the Roman mood of self-evaluation, and he is secure enough to give it its due. The inference is unavoidable: Luke knew about the Roman sentiment regarding its supreme achievement—it is no exaggeration to say, its world mission—namely, the spreading of the Roman Peace over the entire civilized world.

For the Roman mind, peace is always indissolubly connected with law and justice. This is already indicated by the etymology of the word *pax* (peace), which is related to the verb *pacisci* (to make a treaty). A peace without law and order is, to the Latin understanding, inconceivable. Peace is a binding agreement between peoples or nations, and it is the object of wars to bring it about. It is the goal of all military confrontation, which aims at the imposition of the laws of peace by the victor upon the defeated (*leges pacis imponere,* or *dare*).

This marriage of a legal mode of thought with the concept of peace continued in full force at the time of the breakdown of the republican order of state and the inception of the rule of the Roman emperors. With Julius Caesar, the constant feud of powerful coalitions of the republican parties, the incessant civil wars, and the consequent weakening of the Roman body politic, came to an end. Caesar was hailed by many as the savior from a political system which was producing self-destruction, and it was, to the Roman mind, no contradiction in terms that this eminent warrior called himself the "peacemaker." It is, to the reader of the New Testament, of more than passing interest that Antonius, in his laudation of Caesar, is said, in the Greek of the historian Dio Cassius, to have praised him as *eirēnopoios* (peacemaker), with the very word used in Jesus' blessing on the peacemakers in Matthew 5:9 (Dio Cassius, *Roman History,* XLIV, 49, 2). After Caesar's murder in 44 B.C., his work was carried to completion in the long reign of Augustus as *princeps* (27 B.C.–A.D. 14). Augustus succeeded in uniting the consolidation of power in his person with the continuance of essential elements of the republican constitution.

Under Augustus the reality of the Pax Romana, and the enthusiasm for it, reached its zenith. Already in Caesar's time, *pax* was deified in the Roman provinces, and Augustus established her cult as goddess in Rome as well by erecting the altar of the Pax Augusta (ca. 14 B.C.). A politically motivated decision, therefore, led to the deification and the introduction of a cult of "Peace" in Rome as symbol of the emperor's will to achieve the pacification of the whole empire under the might of the sword of the legions and the universal domination of the laws of Rome. As early as A.D. 4 official prayers for the deity Pax are known (*Feriale Cumanum*), and the cult continued unabated through the first century A.D., as evidenced by the building of Vespasian's temple of peace in A.D. 75 (one year after the end of the murderous Jewish war!).

Augustus's policy of pacification was largely successful. He was able, for only the third time in the annals of Roman history until then, to close the doors of the temple of Janus in 29 B.C. as a sign of peace throughout the empire. Typically

Roman in its coordination of peace, law, and good order is the evaluation of the peace established in Augustus's principate by the historian Velleius Paterculus, who writes about 30 A.D.:

> The civil wars were ended after twenty years, foreign wars suppressed, peace restored, the frenzy of arms everywhere lulled to rest; validity was restored to the laws, authority to the courts, and dignity to the senate. . . . Agriculture returned to the fields, respect to religion, to people freedom from anxiety, and to each citizen his property rights were now assured. (*History of Rome* II, 89)

Velleius's enthusiasm about the Pax Romana continues in his verdict on the rule of Tiberius (A.D. 14–37):

> Justice, equity, and industry, long buried in oblivion, have been restored to the state. . . . Right is now honored, evil is punished; the humble man respects the great but does not fear him, and the great has precedence over the lowly but does not despise him. The Augustan peace, which has spread to the regions of the east and of the west and to the bounds of the north and of the south, preserves every corner of the world safe from the fear of brigandage. (*History of Rome* II, 126)

Of course, this security and respect for law have not been achieved without the guardianship of the Roman sword. Velleius states that he would have to devote a whole life to history writing if he were "to tell of the wars waged under his [Augustus's] command, of the pacification of the world by his victories" (II, 89). Hopes were kindled for a destiny of Rome to rule in peace through a dominion that would forever extend over the whole world. Poets of the Augustan era voice this trust in Roman destiny. Virgil announces, through an oracle of Jupiter, what lies in store for the Romans: "For these I set neither bounds nor periods of empire; dominion without end have I bestowed" (*Aeneid* I, 278f.). It is Augustus who is to bring back the golden age of peace to the world, including the farthest regions of the east:

> This, this is he, whom thou so oft hearest promised to thee, Augustus Caesar, son of a god, who shall again set up the

Golden age amid the fields where Saturn once reigned, and
shall spread his empire past Garamant and Indian. (*Aeneid*
VI, 791–794)

Other nations may have produced better artists, advocates, or
astronomers, but:

Remember thou, O Roman, to rule the nations with thy
sway—these shall be thine arts—to crown peace with law, to
spare the humbled, and to tame in war the proud. (*Aeneid* VI,
851–853)

Practically at the same time as Virgil, Horace praises the
peace Augustus brought in an ode:

Thy age, O Caesar (Augustus), has restored to farms their
plenteous crops . . . , has closed Quirinus' fane empty of war
[a reference to the closing of the doors of the Janus temple];
has put a check on licence, passing righteous bonds; has
banished crime and called back home the ancient ways
whereby the Latin name and might of Italy waxed great, and
the fame and majesty of our dominion were spread from the
sun's western bed to his arising. While Caesar guards the state,
not civil rage, nor violence, nor wrath that forges swords,
embroiling hapless towns, shall banish peace (*otium*). *Carmi-
na* IV, Ode XV)

The achievements of the Pax Romana were in fact remarkable, and while they were not equalled by Augustus's successors, they remained more than mere Roman state ideology
throughout the first century A.D. Wars in the provinces were
reduced, the safety of commerce by land and by sea was far
greater than ever before, and the Roman administration of
the empire provided the shield of a common law while
allowing a measure of independence to the subjected peoples.
The availability of Roman citizenship to non-Romans spread
a measure of partnership to every nation in the empire, and
the gradual growth of a universal Greco-Roman culture began
to bind together vastly different populations from Parthia in
the east, to Spain in the west, and from northern Africa in the
south to Britain in the north. Yet it was not hidden to keener
eyes among Roman observers that the Pax Romana had not
succeeded in bringing back the golden age. There was justifia-
ble doubt whether the blessings of the Roman peace were

such to the subjugated. After all, the Pax Romana was attained and preserved by the edge of the Roman sword, and desires for independence and liberty among nations in the provinces were eradicated with ruthless consequence. The historian Tacitus was not deaf to the legitimate outcries of the victims of Roman "pacification." Describing the conquest of Britain by Agricola, his father-in-law, he puts these words into the mouth of a British chieftain, Calgacus, who exhorts his troops:

> Today the uttermost parts of Britain are laid bare; there are no other tribes to come; nothing but sea and cliffs and these more deadly Romans whose arrogance you shun in vain by obedience and self-restraint. Harriers of the world, now that earth fails their all-devastating hands, they probe even the sea. . . . To plunder, butcher, steal, these things they misname empire: they make a desolation and they call it peace. (*Agricola* 30)

In spite of critical insights like these, and in spite of a continuing erosion of the reality of the Pax Romana in the course of the first three centuries A.D., an ideology about the peacemaking power of the empire remained in force until its end. Only a few years before the sack of Rome by the Visigoths under Alaric in A.D. 410, Claudian can still praise the consul Stilicho in words more ideological than were heard at the time of the blooming of the Roman peace under Augustus:

> 'Tis she (Rome) alone who has received the conquered into her bosom and like a mother, not an empress, protected the human race with a common name, summoning those whom she has defeated to share her citizenship and drawing together distant races with bounds of affection. To her rule of peace we owe it that the world is our home, that we can live where we please. . . . Thanks to her we are all one people. Nor will there ever be a limit to the empire of Rome, for luxury and its attendant vices, and pride with its sequent hate, have brought to ruin all kingdoms else. (*On Stilicho's Consulship* III, 150–161)

2. Peace and the Administration of Roman Law in Acts

Twice in the book of Acts (16:36 and 24:2) the word "peace" is used in the context of the apostle Paul's encounter with Roman governmental authorities. We turn our attention first to the latter of these verses, where the meaning of the word is unambiguous.

Acts 21:17–26:32 relates Paul's last visit to Jerusalem, the attempts against his life by leading Jewish factions in the city, his arrest and protective custody through Roman authorities, and the events leading to his appeal to have his case decided by Caesar, resulting in the voyage to Rome. This unit of Acts is dominated by a long series of court proceedings before Jewish and Roman judges of highest rank, and by the speeches set within this framework. The culmination of the trial is reached when, for the last time, a powerful Jewish delegation consisting of the high priest and members of the *gerousia* are invited by the Roman governor Felix to plead their case against Paul in Caesarea, where the apostle is held in prison (24:1).

The spokesman for the Jewish delegation is a certain Tertullus, an advocate familiar with the Jewish and Roman law who presents the charge against Paul (24:2–8). Tertullus begins his plea with the customary flattering praise for the achievement of Felix: "When Paul had been summoned, Tertullus began to accuse him, saying: 'Your Excellency, because of you we have long enjoyed peace, and reforms have been made for this people because of your foresight. We welcome this in every way and everywhere with utmost gratitude.'" (vs. 2–3). This piece of diplomatic flourish does not agree with the judgments of Josephus (*Ant.* XX, 141–144) and Tacitus (*Histories* V, 9; *Annals* XII, 54) on Felix, both of whom severely censure his personal conduct and his handling of the affairs of his province. But that does not diminish the value of Tertullus's opening statement. As the ensuing accusation (vs. 5–8), the opening is very carefully worded in its appeal to the expectations of the time. A Roman governor is representative of the imperial claim to spread the Pax Romana to all nations within the empire's boundaries, and this rule of peace is brought about through the enactment of reforms for the benefit of the dependent peoples. These reforms, which Augustus had first initiated, had now, under his successors, become the hallmark of the blessings of the Roman peace everywhere.

The opening of Tertullus's plea binds Felix to the ideal of Roman administration. It makes him responsible for the realization of the most cherished claim of Roman rule, which is the extension of the Pax Romana in the area of his responsibility. The word *eirene* has, then, in this context very concrete political implications. It entails the duties of a state official, it is brought about by administrative measures, and it envisions the enjoyment of a secure life for whole populations under reliable and just laws.

In contrast to 24:2, Acts 16:36 has, to most commentators, no political overtones at all. After the magistrates have given orders through police that the jailor set Paul and Silas free from prison, the jailor delivers the message and closes with the words, "Go in peace." This phrase is generally understood to be no more than the traditional parting wish among people in the Near East, but it is sometimes remarked that the jailor had in the course of the events in the Philippian prison become a member of the Christian community. The farewell greeting is reminiscent of Jesus' dismissal of healed and forgiven persons in Luke's Gospel (7:50; 8:48), and its use by Luke in the words of the jailor may be meant to characterize him as a Christian.

But this understanding of the jailor's words runs into difficulties. Philippi had been a Roman colony since 31 B.C., it had been granted privileges enjoyed by Italian cities, and its life was organized under the exclusive administration of Roman officials. The warden of the prison in Philippi was certainly a Roman, and in the mouth of a Roman the use of the Semitic wish of *shalom* is entirely out of place. Of course, it is Luke who lets the jailor speak and Luke was familiar with the Semitic phrase, as his Gospel shows. But he took great pains in Acts to let Romans say what Romans were known to be saying, of which Gallio's curt reply to Jewish accusers of Paul is a good example (18:14–15). If Luke had placed a distinctly Semitic phrase in the mouth of a Roman official he would have lapsed into an error which he otherwise consciously avoids. This gives rise to the question whether the phrase "Go in peace" in 16:36 cannot be understood differently.

Of course, the phrase remains a parting wish. But its context directs the word "peace" into a different field of meaning. The jailor announces the magistrates' decision, he opens the door to freedom, and his farewell is followed by the magistrates' acknowledgment of wrongdoing on their part against Roman law when they had Paul and Silas beaten, even without due process of investigation (16:37–39). The issue at stake in the closing scene of Paul and Silas's imprisonment in Philippi is the security from unjust acts and the liberty of innocent citizens provided and protected by the law. *Eirene* is an ideal word to combine the notions of security, protection, and freedom in a single noun. Understood thus, the jailor's wish "Go in peace" has nothing to do with a misplaced Semitic phrase. Heavily paraphrased, it would be meant to say: "Depart in the security of an official act of the city authorities, and in the liberty provided you by recourse to a good and well-functioning law that has the strength to right previous wrongs."

If the suggestion is sound to read "Go in peace" in Acts 16:36 contextually, the verse is at once also drawn into the sphere of the idea of the Pax Romana. Universal validity and sound application of Roman law was one of its necessary pillars of support. The other was the Roman military, and to this point we will have to return below.

Assuming now that Acts 16:36 and 24:2 employ the word *eirene* in direct (24:2) and indirect (16:36) reference to the Roman peace, we will have to determine whether the picture of Roman law and administration drawn otherwise in Acts agrees with it.

Some potentially negative observations must first be mentioned. On occasion, Roman officials and Roman justice do not receive high marks in Acts. Luke has not hesitated to incorporate accounts into his work that cast doubt on the personal integrity of Roman officials and on the reliability of the governmental procedures, or on both. Two of the more glaring instances of this are the beginning of the story of Paul and Silas's flogging and incarceration in Philippi, and the description of Felix in his contacts with Paul. The praetors in Philippi, who are in charge of law enforcement in the colony and are susceptible to pressure from wealthy slave owners, inflict a beating on the Christian missionaries and have them jailed, without proper investigation and conviction (16:19–24; cf. 16:37). The question is difficult to answer why Paul and Silas (who is presumed in vs. 37–38 to have Roman citizenship like Paul) do not protest the action by appealing to their rights as *cives Romani,* but it does not need to detain us because the image of a capricious handling of the law by city officials is clear. Their susceptibility to pressure from the rich casts a shadow on the proper functioning of the law and endangers the freedom and the mission of Paul and Silas.

The account of Felix in Acts 24:24–27 is plainly critical. He is presented, together with his Jewish wife Drusilla, as a serious inquirer into Paul's message. But his double dealings stand in the way of his acceptance of the Christian message. It is probably not meant negatively when 24:25 reports his fear when he hears Paul's presentation of the essentials of Christian faith (in Lukan form!) but certainly negative are his vulnerability to receiving bribes, his desire to please the Jewish leadership, and his delay in pronouncing a judgment in the case of Paul.

Other features of the account in Acts could be added, such as the interminable delay of Paul's case in Acts 21–26 by the Roman authorities, which leaves the reader with the impression that the mills of Roman justice grind very slowly indeed. But it is not necessary to go into further detail to justify the observation that Acts has not whitewashed Roman authorities. This makes the other side of the matter appear in even brighter light, and it is this side which Luke intentionally and frequently brings to the attention of his readers. Roman personnel, Roman administration, and especially the force and fairness of Roman law itself protect the advance of the Christian message and its preachers. They are, to put it cautiously, not antithetical to the Christian mission; the Pax Romana is an ally for the Pax Christi—in what sense, and to what degree, is a question to which we will return.

The positive attitude to matters Roman and to Romans in Acts is so broad that a quick sketch of the evidence must here suffice (for a much fuller recent discussion, see Paul W. Walaskay, "*And so we came to Rome,*" in the Select Bibliography). Romans of high standing and office are singled out as examples of receptivity to the word of God. The first pagan admitted to baptism in Acts is Cornelius, a career officer (centurion) in the Roman army, whose story (Acts 10) is the opening door through which the leaders of the Jerusalem church move to their commitment to accept non-Jews into church membership without circumcision and without obligation to obey the law of Moses, although under conditions and for reasons quite different from those advocated by Paul as we know him through his letters. A shining example of unprejudiced openness toward the gospel, and of an eventual full commitment to it, is the proconsul Sergius Paulus on Cyprus (13:7, 12). Time and again, Romans of all ranks act to protect the Christian missionaries, sometimes from mortal danger. Lucius Junius Gallio Annaeanus, proconsul of Achaia, member of a distinguished Roman family and brother of the Stoic philosopher and poet Seneca, Nero's tutor, resists accusations against Christians with aristocratic decisiveness and brevity (18:12–17). Roman soldiers, officers and men alike, repeatedly rescue Paul from mob violence and from the conspiracy to assassinate him (21:31–36; 22:23–24; 23:10, 16–32; 27:42–44). Their attitudes and actions are illustrations of the salutary effects of the Pax Romana on the Christian mission.

More important than that, however, is Luke's repeated weaving of incidents into the narrative which suggest that the principles of Roman law work for the protection of the church. Twice Paul defends himself by the charge that he was punished, or is about to be punished, "uncondemned" (16:37; 22:25). The precise legal meaning of the word is not certain; it can refer to punishment without prior investigation or to the carrying out of a penalty without due sentencing. In either case, it is clear that Paul appeals to a principle of due process in Roman law, and he is successful in both cases. The charge brought against Paul by Jewish opponents in Corinth is summarily dismissed by Gallio in a short verdict which states that Roman justice protects against criminal wrongdoing or a serious piece of villainy, but it does not adjudicate dissensions of people in the provinces that arise from interpretations of their own laws (18:12–15). In the long section, Acts 21:17–26:32, Paul is subjected to a long series of hearings before Roman, Jewish, and mixed tribunals. The outcome is always the same; three times Paul is declared innocent by the Roman officials who are in charge of his case (23:29 in a letter by the tribune of the garrison in Jerusalem; 25:25 by Festus addressing Agrippa II; 26:31 in a joint opinion by Agrippa and Festus). The principle of fair administration of the law is emphasized in a speech of Festus, who, addressing Agrippa and his queen Bernice, declares strict equality before the law to be the touchstone of Roman justice: It was "not the custom of the Romans to hand over anyone before the accused had met the accusers face to face and had been given the opportunity to make a defense against the charge" (25:16). Dom Jacques Dupont, in his article "Aequitas Romana" listed in the Select Bibliography, has made a thorough investigation of this sentence. His article demonstrates that the word translated "custom" (*ethos*) carries the force of a norm-setting obligation incorporated in the law, and that this principle is expressly stated in an impressive number of Roman sources from the first century B.C. (especially Cicero) to the second century A.D. Luke knew the technical language of Roman law and agreed with the claim of its fairness. From the sources quoted in the article, one relatively late example from a popular tale may here be quoted because it shows the longevity of the idea and its adoption by general public opinion in the empire. Apuleius writes (about A.D. 150) about a father who, deceived by the wicked schemes of his wife, seeks the death of his own son, whom he was made to suspect as his brother's murderer. This father "besought the magistrates with tears and prayers, yea, even embracing their knees, for his son's death." The elders of the city and its people were so swayed by the father's appeal that "without any delay of trial or further inquisition or the careful pleading of defenders they cried all that he should be stoned to death." But the justices were fortunately mindful of sound principles of Roman justice and instructed

> the decurions and the people of the city to proceed by examination of witnesses on both sides, like good citizens, and with order of justice *according to the ancient custom*; for the giving of any hasty sentence or judgment without hearing of the contrary part, such as the barbarous and cruel tyrants accustom to use, would give an ill example in time of peace to their successors. (Apuleius, *Metamorphoses* X, 6)

We may, then, draw the conclusion that Luke has presented in Acts a positive picture of the Pax Romana. Not all Roman officials are at all times seen in the best light; greed, the desire to play one side against the other, inefficiency, and plain error of judgment play their games. But by and large the conduct of the Roman soldiers and officials is above reproach. They are committed to preserve, inviolate, the protection afforded by Roman law, which defends the innocent and subjects to punishment only persons found guilty of serious crimes. The strict attention to the principle of equality before the law, the

conviction of its value for all, and the fairness of its administration make Roman law the firm support of the Roman
peace throughout the empire. The Christian mission has
nothing to fear from it; on the contrary, it serves as a means
of protection for the messengers of the gospel and, indirectly,
serves to spread this gospel "to the ends of the earth" (Acts
1:8).

3. Other Meanings of Peace in Acts

Five times in the book of Acts, the word *eirene* is used
without connection to the Pax Romana. Of these instances,
10:36 was discussed in chapter 3. The remaining four verses
will now be considered in the order in which they are found in
Acts.

a. Stephen's speech before the high court in Jerusalem
(Acts 7), in its long section on Moses (vs. 17–44), refers to an
attempt of Moses to promote peace between contending
Israelites (v. 26). Some of the best modern translations do not
make use of the word "peace" at this point. The NRSV
translates 7:26: "The next day he [Moses] came to some of
them as they were quarelling and tried to reconcile them,
saying, 'Men, you are brothers; why do you wrong each
other?'" and the Revised English Bible (REB) renders: "The
next day he came upon two of them fighting, and tried to
persuade them to make up their quarrel. 'Men, You are
brothers!' he said. 'Why are you ill-treating one another?'" A
literal translation of the verse would run like this: "On the
following day he appeared to them as they were fighting and
sought to reconcile them to peace, saying, 'Men, you are
brothers; why do you wrong each other?'"

In Acts 7:23–29 an incident from the life of Moses is
adapted from the report in Exodus 2:11–15: Moses kills an
Egyptian whom he found beating an Israelite, and the next
day he intercedes with two fighting fellow countrymen. The
first part of this incident is recounted in Acts 7:24 in
substantial agreement with Exodus 2:11–12. The scene on
the following day is, however, so substantially altered that the
question of the purpose of the change must be raised. Since
Acts 7 very largely follows the Septuagint, the verses in
question from Exodus 2:13 (LXX) and Acts 7:26 are placed
side by side for contrast.

Exodus 2:13 (LXX)	**Acts 7:26 (lit.)**
Going out, then, on the second day he saw two Hebrew men fighting and he said to the one who did wrong, "Why do you beat your neighbor?"	On the following day he appeared to them as they were fighting and sought to reconcile them to peace, saying, "Men, you are brothers; why do you wrong each other?"

Leaving small details aside, we can observe two alterations from the LXX in Stephen's speech. (1) In Exodus 2:13 Moses addresses one man whom he judges to be doing wrong with the question of why he is beating his fellow. In Acts 7:26 both parties are addressed together by Moses and they are asked why they wrong each other. Moreover, it is not clear in Acts that the two parties involved in the fight are two individuals; they could be groups opposed to each other. The Moses in Stephen's speech does not decide who is wrong, but considers the arising of a fight among Israelites as an evil in which each side wrongs the other. (2) To underline Moses' position above the contending parties, a whole phrase is introduced in Acts which is completely absent from Exodus. Moses is characterized as the man who "sought to reconcile them to peace." This paraphrase of Exodus 2:13 carries the decisive statement of the whole scene: Moses is the peacemaker who seeks reconciliation of a conflict that tears apart the unity of God's people, and the fight of opposing sides against each other is the wrong in which they are mutually involved.

The theological potential of this paraphrase is enhanced if one adds the likelihood that the Moses of Stephen's speech is painted in colors that belong to Luke's palette in his portrait of Christ. Stephen's Moses is said to be a man "powerful in his words and deeds" (7:22), as the two disciples at Emmaus put their memory of Jesus of Nazareth in the phrase, "a prophet mighty in deed and word" (Luke 24:19). Moses in Acts 7 has "performed wonders and signs" (*terata kai sēmeia*, 7:36) as Jesus, in one of Peter's speeches, is said to be "a man attested to you by God with mighty works and wonders and signs (*terasi kai sēmeiois*, 2:22). Perhaps there is also an intentional congruence between Moses the "ruler (*archōn*) and liberator," in Acts 7:35, and the Jesus described in the apostolic confession of Acts 5:31 as "Leader (*archēgos*) and Savior."

It would appear that hints are supplied in Stephen's speech to understand Moses in analogy to Jesus. On the other hand, Stephen's speech is not analogous to the theology of Luke. Rather, Acts 7 seems to be a piece of tradition that Luke incorporated into his second volume without many changes. If, however, the hypothesis is sound that Stephen's speech represents a type of tradition current in the circle of Christian diaspora Jews to whom Stephen belonged (J. Roloff, 118–119; see Select Bibliography), the typology Moses-Christ would become completely understandable.

This encourages the question whether the paraphrase of Exodus 2:13 in Acts 7:26, which makes Moses the reconciler and man of peace, is not a part of a larger typology in which Jesus is also understood as reconciler and peacemaker. We are, however, on shaky ground. Other passages need to be consulted first before even a hypothetical solution can be advanced.

b. In a Lukan summary, Acts 9:31 also employs the word "peace": "Meanwhile the church throughout Judea, Galilee, and Samaria had peace and was built up. Living in the fear of the Lord and in the comfort of the Holy Spirit, it increased in numbers."

The summary looks back on the growth of the church to this point, but also to the difficulties that lay on its way. Judea, Galilee, and Samaria were reached by the Christian mission, realizing part of the objective stated in Acts 1:8. Yet this expansion occurred in the face of serious opposition. The apostles were imprisoned, even their lives were threatened (5:33). The first martyr of the church died (7:60). A more serious persecution broke out, scattering the Jerusalem church but also spreading its influence (8:1). The entry of Saul aggravated the situation (8:3). But now, after the first dispersion (which in historical reality was only the emigration of the Stephen group from Jerusalem) and the conversion of Paul (9:1–30), a temporary period of calm has been reached. "The church had peace" certainly as this development in mind. "Peace" stands for a condition of quiet and safety that has, for the moment, been reached.

But that does not exhaust the meaning of *eirene* in Acts 9:31. The phrase "the church had peace" is followed by two participles ("building up" and "living") that add to the description of the peace of the church. "Peace" is not only, negatively, the absence of persecution; it is also, positively, the church's continued growth and its obedience to Christ's instruction. Two facts of 9:31 would support this interpretation. First, the verse is formulated in a highly unusual way, in that the church throughout Judea, Galilee, and Samaria is given the grammatical form of the singular. This is the only time in all of Acts that a whole network of Christian communities is integrated into the singular "the church"; otherwise in Acts "the church" in the singular is either the church in Jerusalem, or the local Christian community in some city. Only in 9:31 is a "catholic" sense of "the church" expressed which views all existing Christian congregations as one. This one church, located in separate areas, has peace. It enjoys an essential unity which continued in and through its expansion, and as that unity the church has peace. Second, 9:31 is without a doubt a statement of a first stage of fulfillment of the charge in the words of the risen Christ that his apostles should be witnesses "in Jerusalem, in all Judea and Samaria, and to the ends of the earth" (1:8). The peace of the church is linked to this first retrospect on the expansion of the church. Its building up and its obedient "living in the fear of the Lord" is an element of the peace of the church.

c. Not much needs to be said about Acts 12:20. Relations between Agrippa I and the cities of Tyre and Sidon had so deteriorated that the cities considered it necessary to send a delegation to the Jewish king to "ask for peace." The cause for the tension between the king and the cities is not mentioned because the narrative, Acts 12:20–23, is solely interested in the judgment by God on a sovereign who allowed himself to be worshiped like a god. The actual conflict cannot be reconstructed with confidence because the parallel account of Josephus on the death of Agrippa (*Ant.* XIX, 343–350) knows nothing about trouble with Syrian cities. However, the tension between king and cities can hardly be meant to imply the use of military means by Agrippa to coerce the cities, because Roman rule over the region would not have permitted the waging of war on the part of two dependent partners in the empire. Commentators therefore frequently assume that Herod conducted a boycott of grain imports against the two cities, which could not live for long without imports of Palestinian grain. The "asking for peace" by the delegation from Tyre and Sidon would then mean the lifting of the boycott.

Whether or not this hypothesis is correct, it appears that Acts 12:20 contains no more than a snapshot of political complications at the time of Agrippa's death, and that the word "peace" here has no content that would add a theologically important element to Luke's understanding of the word, except that it reinforces what we have already noticed: Luke readily applied the word *eirene* to concrete political circumstances and to practical steps of diplomacy aimed at the safety and order of groups participating in the protected life of the Roman empire.

d. Finally, a look at Acts 15:33 is necessary. The verse has its place at the conclusion of the "apostolic council" in Jerusalem. Therefore it is part of the account of one of the most pivotal events in the outline of Acts. The historical problems caused by the relationship of Acts 15 to Paul's description of the Jerusalem agreement in Galatians 2 are of no consequence for the comprehension of Acts 15:33 within its own context. We are interested here only in the question of what the word "peace" connotes, given the extreme significance in Acts of its immediate context.

The Jerusalem council had to address itself to a threat that, unless removed, would effectively split the church into factions separated from each other by decisions so fundamental that a reconciliation between the parties could never be achieved. The problem is the manner of acceptance of Gentile Christians into a parent body of Jewish Christians who are bound to the Mosaic law. The content of the "apostolic decree," with its theological and historical problematic, we leave aside here, because it is certain that in the view of Luke's chronicle of the event in Acts 15 the decision was agreed upon by the leadership of the church in Jerusalem as well as by the delegation from Antioch, headed by Paul and Barnabas, and thus the unity of the church was secured. Luke reports in Acts 15 about a triumph of conciliation in a situation of extreme stress. It is of the greatest importance that the decision be communicated back to Antioch not only with the backing of the report of the Antiochene delegation, but with a written document authenticated by the presence of a delegation from Jerusalem to Antioch. This delegation is to be made up of Judas and Silas, who in addition to the written agreement are to give it an oral interpretation consonant with the oral reports of Paul and Barnabas.

The events proceed fully as planned, Judas and Silas put their authority as prophets behind the letter from Jerusalem and the report by Paul and Barnabas. There is rejoicing in Antioch about the agreement and the prevention of a disastrous split; and Judas and Silas are fully accepted there as legitimate teachers (15:31–32). At the end of this time of solidifying a concord of unity, Judas and Silas are sent back to Jerusalem "with peace" (15:33, lit.).

A large majority of commentators are content with saying that the send-off "with peace" is no more than the usual dismissal of friends to the journey with the formula of the traditional farewell wish. In contrast to Acts 16:36 there is nothing wrong with this comment. Jews are sending off other Jews in Acts 15:33 and it is quite certain that they would do so in words such as "Go in peace" (Luke 7:50; 8:48). But it is entirely unbelievable that the whole mood, the gladdening message of Acts 15, should not reverberate in this wish of departure. A whole chapter bristled with tension about a mortal danger to unity and about the triumph of its preservation through the presence of God's Spirit; and should not the wish of peace at its conclusion echo this story of a sickness unto death and its cure?

Judas and Silas could very well have been dismissed from Antioch with the simple verb "they were sent off," as they were, only three verses earlier, "sent off" (without *met' eirēnēs*, but with the same verb) from Jerusalem to Antioch (15:30). The farewell "in peace," in 15:33, is loaded with the freight of an achievement that has rescued the unity of the church, and it carries the announcement of its full and joyous acceptance in Antioch back to Jerusalem.

We look back on the four verses considered in this section. With the exception of Acts 12:20, the remaining three passages mentioning peace are located at important junctures of the developing story in the book. The Moses of 7:26 is the reconciler of conflicting parties, perhaps typologically related to Christ in that capacity; and 9:31 stresses with a very unusual expression the oneness of the church in its expansion into new—and formerly hostile—territories, by way of a Lukan summary that surveys the whole narrative from chapter 1 to the present. Chapter 15:33 caps the success of an agreement preventing different groups within the church from sliding into alienation from one another. The use of the word *eirene* in Acts 7:26; 9:31; and 15:33 displays, then, if the context is allowed to help in providing meaning, a remarkable consistency and a common trend. Peace, in the first half of the book of Acts, signifies the power of mediation through which a goal of unity can be reached, and which protects its (as yet partial) realization.

This is consequently also the specifically Lukan meaning of the designation of the word of God as the good news of peace through Jesus Christ (10:36). More than in the other Gospels, Christ is presented by Luke as the mediator between God and humanity. The spreading of the gospel to the ends of the earth aims at the formation of one people of God in which the division between Israel and the pagan world is overcome. Luke cannot but acknowledge that a large sector of the Jewish people of his time could not be persuaded to accept the offer of the Christian gospel to join with former Gentiles in a new worldwide community, but he has never relinquished the hope that the invitation to Jews to join this community might remain open. Nor was Luke willing to close his eyes to the fact that the progress of the gospel among the pagan population in the Greco-Roman culture of his day was difficult, and it encountered resistance and rejection from this side as well. But that did not hinder him from viewing the Pax Romana as a cultural reality that worked frequently for the protection of the Christian mission and its pioneers. François Bovon has shown that Luke values highly the human, cultural, and social tools of mediation that serve as a means in the all-important task of offering the good news of peace to the entire world (*Theologische Literaturzeitung*, see Select Bibliography). Luke's positive view of the usefulness of the Pax Romana for the achievement of this goal is a part of his appreciation of those factors in history which can serve as cultural mediators with which the power of God can work.

Select Bibliography

Bovon, François. "L'Importance des médiations dans le projet théologique de Luc," *New Testament Studies* 21 (1974): 23–29.
———."Israel, die Kirche und die Völker im lukanischen Doppelwerk." *Theologische Literaturzeitung* 108 (1983): 403–414. (Excellent sketch by one of the world's foremost specialists in Lukan studies today.)

Comblin, J. "La paix dans la théologie de Saint Luc." *Ephemerides Theologicae Lovanienses* 32 (1956): 439–460. (Emphasizes the political and pragmatic elements in the use of *eirene* in the Lukan work.)

Conzelmann, Hans. *The Theology of St. Luke.* New York: Harper & Brothers, 1961. (On our subject see especially pp. 138–144.)

Dupont, Jacques. "Aequitas Romana. Notes sur Actes 25, 16." In *Études sur les Actes des Apôtres,* 527–552. Paris: Cerf, 1967. (Outstanding collection of evidence for Roman conviction about the fairness of their laws.)

———. "The Salvation of the Gentiles and the Theological Significance of Acts." In *The Salvation of the Gentiles: Studies in the Acts of the Apostles,* 11–33. New York: Paulist Press, 1979.

Fuchs, Harald. *Augustin und der antike Friedensgedanke.* 2nd ed. Berlin and Zurich: Weidmann, 1965. Repr. New York: Garland Publishing. (Of particular importance for this chapter is Appendix 3 on the Greek and Roman concepts of peace, pp. 167–223.)

Roloff, Jürgen. *Die Apostelgeschichte.* 17th ed. Das Neue Testament Deutsch 5. Göttingen: Vandenhoeck & Ruprecht, 1981.

Walaskay, Paul W. *"And so we came to Rome": The Political Perspective of St. Luke.* Cambridge: Cambridge University Press, 1983. (Advocates the interesting thesis that Luke is not an apologist for the church addressing himself to Roman readers, but an apologist for the Roman empire to his Christian readers.)

Wengst, Klaus. *Pax Romana and the Peace of Jesus Christ.* Philadelphia: Fortress Press, 1987. (A very comprehensive description of the Pax Romana and attitudes toward it displayed in the New Testament.)

6

Peace
in the Letters
of Paul

An understanding of the letters of the apostle Paul hinges to
a large degree on the comprehension of some key concepts.
Words and phrases like "the righteousness of God," "faith,"
and "life in the Spirit," among others, contain results of the
most sustained energy of theological reflection collected into
a single expression. All of Paul's leading concepts have a rich
tradition behind them, but none is a simple restatement of
terms provided by his heritage. An incredibly intense mind,
and a life possessing the courage of radical existential hon-
esty, has molded each of these concepts and given it a distinctive character that cannot be confused with the language
of anyone else in the first century A.D.

The word *eirene* does not belong to this group of key
concepts in Paul's thought. It is, however, correlated with
several of the most important, and characteristically Pauline,
ideas. A severing of this correlation would immediately obscure the meaning of peace in Paul's letters. It will be
necessary, therefore, to observe and preserve the links with
dominant Pauline words and phrases that the use of the word
eirene displays.

In this chapter we will be concerned only with letters whose
authorship by Paul is today virtually undisputed. The letter to
the Colossians and the letter that has come down to us with
the dedication "to the Ephesians" will be reserved for chapter
7. There are two reasons for this. First, I share the opinion of
those who consider both Colossians and Ephesians to be

writings originating with someone other than Paul himself, but composed by heirs of Paul's legacy. Second, in Ephesians the subject of peace has become so primary an issue that a separate treatment of it is demanded by the weight of the subject alone.

1. The God of Peace

Already in the Old Testament, and continuing in the literature of early Judaism, the action and nature of God are sometimes described by the combination of the name of God with a noun in the genitive. We find expressions like "the God of faithfulness" (Deut. 32:4, lit.), "the God of truth" (Isa. 65:16, lit.), "the God of glory" (Ps. 29:3), and many others. The New Testament continued this way of capturing an aspect of God's reality with a predicate noun.

In comparison to the frequency of those forms of language in Old Testament and early Jewish traditions, the New Testament tends to reduce the number of nouns employed as predicates of God. It displays a decided preference for nouns expressive of particularly basic matters that have great theological weight. We hear of "the God of glory" (Acts 7:2), or the "Father of glory" (Eph. 1:17), noting that this way of characterizing God can also be christologically used, since the designation "Lord of glory" is applied to Christ also (1 Cor. 2:8; James 2:1, lit.). The New Testament can talk of "the God of all grace" (1 Peter 5:10), of "the King of the ages" (1 Tim. 1:17), of "the Father of mercies and God of all consolation" (2 Cor. 1:3). There is a "God of steadfastness and encouragement" (Rom. 15:5), a "God of hope" (Rom. 15:13), and a "God of love" (2 Cor. 13:11; together with "peace").

In light of this it is not surprising that we also find the phrase "the God of peace" in the New Testament. In this form the phrase occurs in Romans 15:33; 16:20; 2 Corinthians 13:11 in combination with "love"; Philippians 4:9; 1 Thessalonians 5:23; and 2 Thessalonians 3:16 in the form "the Lord of peace" with christological meaning; outside the letters of Paul the phrase "God of peace" is used only once, in Hebrews 13:20.

This evidence calls for some comments. First, the expression "the God of peace" is very much more frequent in Paul than anywhere else in the New Testament. Paul is not its inventor; Hebrews 13:20 shows that groups in early Christianity outside the sphere of Paul's influence could use it equally well. But with Paul the phrase "the God of peace" has become a favorite. Second, Jewish literature prior to or roughly contemporaneous with the New Testament uses the phrase only once. It occurs in the Testament of Dan 5:2 in the context of a passage to which we shall have to return in the next section; no other evidence of it has so far come to light.

It is likely that Paul's preference for the phrase "the God of peace" is, at least in part, due to conventions of Jewish piety. Paul uses the phrase with some frequency at the end, or near the end, of letters (Rom. 15:33; 16:20; 2 Cor. 10:11; 1 Thess. 5:23) within blessings or wishes for his congregations. Since the word "peace" is traditionally associated with blessings and farewell wishes, the formation of the expression "the God of peace" in such contexts is natural. But that does not eliminate the fact that "the God of peace" is a favorite term for Paul.

In Paul's thought, then, "peace" is a reality and a power that deserves to be associated with God so closely that it can describe a fundamental aspect of the act and being of God. Paul knows of a wrath of God, and of judgments of God. But he never spoke of a "God of wrath" or of a "God of judgment." Peace is more deeply associated with God, more comprehensively descriptive, and more ultimately revelatory of God, than other words of human language that can and must be used as opposites to peace. Therefore, the phrase "the God of peace" is a small, but still significant, pointer toward a proper understanding of Paul's letters in their entirety. Paul is the servant of a God who loves, accomplishes, and preserves peace.

2. Peace in the Addresses and Endings of the Letters

One typical address of Paul's letters reads:

> Paul, an apostle of Christ Jesus by the will of God, and Timothy our brother, To the church of God that is in Corinth, including all the saints throughout Achaia: Grace to you and peace from God our Father and the Lord Jesus Christ. (2 Cor. 1:1–2)

Reduced to its basic components, the address has three parts; the sender, the addressee, and the wish of grace and peace. In this structure, the part of the sender and the part of the addressee are often enlarged by explanatory statements that can occasionally move into highly theological wording (for the sender: Rom. 1:1b–6; Gal. 1:1; for the addressee: 1 Cor. 1:2). On the other hand, the third part of the structure is far more consistently preserved, although Galatians 1:3 shows that this usual consistency could also be broken if the situation required it. By and large, however, the sentence "Grace to you and peace from God our Father and the Lord Jesus Christ" constitutes the third part of the address of almost all letters of the apostle (Rom. 1:7; 1 Cor. 1:3; 2 Cor. 1:2; Gal. 1:3; Phil. 1:2; slightly changed in 1 Thess. 1:1; 2 Thess. 1:2; Philemon 1:3). The general structure, and especially its third part, is also found in letters whose authorship by Paul is uncertain or unlikely (Eph. 1:2; Col. 1:2; 1 Tim. 1:2 and 2 Tim. 1:2 augment "grace" and "peace" with "mercy"; Titus 1:4). Beyond Paul, the third part of the address is essentially maintained in 1 Peter 1:2; 2 Peter 1:2; 2 John 1:3 (with "mercy") and is more varied in Jude 1:2, where "mercy," "peace," and "love" are combined. It is certain that Paul shared in a very common tradition with regard to the address of letters in the early church, in which peace was a constant part of the wish extended to the addressees.

The most common Pauline form of the address can be abbreviated to the formula "Paul, to addressees, grace and peace from God and Christ." It has long been assumed that this formula adopts and changes the standard form of Hellenistic and Semitic addresses in letters. The Hellenistic form is generally very brief, saying only "Sender, to addressee, greetings (*chairein* [*legei*])," found in the New Testament in James 1:1. The Semitic form runs "Sender, to addressee, peace," as in Daniel 4:1. It has seemed that the structure of address in Paul's letters was a deliberate combination of the third part of the address by adopting grace (*charis*, related to *chairein*) from the Hellenistic, and peace from the Semitic form.

However, this view has been found too superficial (see K. Berger in the Select Bibliography). In Jewish writings an address very similar to the form found in Paul is preserved in *2 Baruch* 78:2: "Thus speaks Baruch, the son of Neriah, to the

brothers who were carried away into captivity: grace and
peace be with you." The combination of "peace" with the
words "grace" or "mercy" is quite frequent in Jewish literature apart from its use in letters. It is found particularly in
phrases that speak of a blessing imparted by God to his
people. "Grace" is associated on many occasions with the
idea of characterizing the special status of a person who was
granted a revelation by God. Since in the Hellenistic letter the
words "*from* A to B" always signify "A" as the author of the
letter, it can well be argued that Paul's phrase "grace and
peace *from* God our Father and the Lord Jesus Christ" means
to convey not only that God, in his Christ, is the origin and
source of grace and peace, but also that the letter itself is the
actual and concrete form of God's grace which grants the
disclosure of God to the recipients.

The address of Paul's letters is, then, not an almost
mechanical combination of two distinct forms of letter
writing at this time, one Hellenistic and one Semitic. Rather,
it has the power of a blessing in which the apostle communicates a message whose origin is from God. The address
clarifies the ground on which the entire letter is built, and it
sets the tone in which the letter as a whole is to be understood. This ground and tone are the grace and peace that
come from God. The letter, whatever it may contain, is
ultimately brought about by a divine act of re-creation in
which the enmity between God and human beings is overcome, and it imparts a blessing in which the restoration to a
life of filial trust and obedience is initiated and nourished.

It can come as no surprise, then, that the wish of peace can
also close a letter. Paul's letters frequently end with a blessing
of peace, as they began. Romans 15:33 was, at some time, an
ending to the letter before chapter 16 was added to it. It closes
Paul's writing to the Roman Christians with the words, "The
God of peace be with all of you. Amen." Similar blessings
with peace occur, if not in the last sentence, in the concluding
section of other letters (2 Cor. 13:11; Gal. 6:16; 1 Thess. 5:23;
2 Thess. 3:16; in dependency on Paul in Eph. 6:23; and once
also outside the Pauline collection of letters, in 1 Peter 5:14).

Peace, then, is regularly a part of the opening, and frequently a part of the ending, of Paul's letters. The word has
the dignity and value to summarize the essential content of
each of the apostle's writings. Whatever else these letters may

have to say, they say it in the name of the God whose peace is start and finish.

3. Peace in the Apocalyptic Mode

What kind of peace does Paul have in mind? We can begin an answer to this question with the observation that the word "peace" occurs in an unambiguously apocalyptic context in two letters dating from the very beginning of the apostle's preserved correspondence (1 Thessalonians), and from the period of its completion (Romans). That allows the conclusion that an apocalyptic setting for the concept of peace could be maintained by Paul from the inception to the conclusion of his activity, insofar as we can still trace it with the help of existing literary documents.

In 1 Thessalonians 5:3, the Christian community of Thessalonica is warned: "When they say, 'There is peace and security,' then sudden destruction will come upon them." The sentence belongs to a series of comments about the "coming of the Lord" (4:15) in answer to anxieties about the future of Christians who had died (4:13–18), and to a sequence of exhortations on living in the expectation of the day of the Lord (5:1–11). The vocabulary immediately surrounding 1 Thessalonians 5:3 is filled with terms belonging to the Christian hope of the impending coming of Christ in power. The question about "the times and the seasons" (5:1) is related to the inquiry "When will this be?" and the saying concerning "that day and hour" in the "little Synoptic apocalypse" (Matt. 24:3 and 36: Mark 13:4 and 32: Luke 21:7); the picture of the thief breaking into the house by night (1 Thess. 3:4) is also common in apocalyptic discourse (Matt. 24:43; Luke 12:39f.; Rev. 3:3); and so is the watchword "keep awake" (1 Thess. 5:6; Matt. 24:42; Mark 13:35, 37; the Greek verb used in each of these verses is identical).

In the apocalyptic context of 1 Thessalonians 5:1–11, "peace" is used in a negative sense. The Christians in Thessalonica are warned against "peace and security" because the approaching day of the Lord demands wakefulness, the active marshaling of energy that is expected of a person in the hours of daylight. The warning against being lulled into a false sense of peace recalls similar prophetic criticisms (Jer. 6:14; 8:11; more generally Jer. 12:12; Ezra 7:25). Although the circumstances of these warnings vary greatly, there is also an important point of contact between them. The leadership and population of Judah, in the time of Jeremiah, relied on the presence of Yahweh in the temple as a guarantee that Yahweh was bound to be on Jerusalem's side, regardless of the condition of the people before their God. Analogously, the Thessalonians have heard and believed the message that "God has destined us not for wrath but for obtaining salvation through our Lord Jesus Christ, who died for us" (1 Thess. 5:9), and there are apparently some in the community who derive from this the assurance of peace and security in a way that rocks conscience and energy to sleep. But the time between the salvation by Christ and his coming in power is totally and fatefully misconstrued if it is taken to initiate a peace of slumber. Rightly perceived, Christ's death is the reveille in the morning that calls to the work of the day.

Situated on the other side of the spectrum is Romans 16:20: "The God of peace will shortly crush Satan under your feet." Peace is, in this verse, the sum total of an all-decisive victory of God over his opponent. The benefits of this victory can be focused in the single word "peace."

Romans 16 is a chapter embattled by critics, and it is necessary to indicate how its 20th verse is affected. It is noticeable, in Romans 16:17–20, that a sharp polemic prevails which is difficult to reconcile to the predominating mood of evenhandedness and flexibility characteristic of the discussion about the issues concerning "the strong" and "the weak" in Romans 14:1–15:6. A spirit of mutual respect is absent from 16:17–20; a line is sharply drawn and compromise is out of order. The "dissensions and offenses" brought into the congregation are not alternatives dictated by a strong or a weak Christian conscience; rather, they are flatly contrary "to the teaching that you have learned" and they must be avoided (16:17). Persons made responsible for these upheavals are said, quite unequivocally, not to "serve our Lord Christ" (16:18), a polemic far more reminiscent of Paul's bitter controversy with opponents who were out to destroy his credibility as an apostle (2 Corinthians 10–13) than with the careful argument in Romans 14–15 which attempts to let each of the sides involved in the dispute have their relative right. The attack on the sowers of dissensions is motivated by the charge that, rather than serving Christ, they serve their own bellies (*koilia,* 16:18). The same charge is brought forward in Philippians 3:19 against people who make their belly a god and glory in their shame, thus making them enemies of the cross of Christ. It seems quite consistent to assume that behind those responsible for dissensions in Romans 16:17–20 is a group essentially similar to Paul's opponents in Philippians 3:17–21. The latter are, in turn, of one mind with a group discernible in Corinth that appears to have argued that a Christian male is free to consort with a prostitute because sexuality is a matter of the belly (*koilia*) and of nothing more (1 Cor. 6:12–20). In 1 Corinthians, Paul presumes acquaintance with an argument of which he only introduces a few distinctive fragments and which, if reconstructed, might have run about like this: "The belly is made for food, and it desires regular satisfaction to avoid hunger; human sexuality is located in the belly and follows the same rule; since the Christian is a spirit-person, all matters concerning the belly—sexuality included—are of no consequence and can be dealt with in complete freedom." The point of Paul's argument against this position is the denial that sexuality is purely a biological function subject to the rhythms and rules of the belly. For Paul, human sexuality is part and parcel of the human self, which, as body, is related to other selves, receiving itself from others and giving itself to others, and so living in mutual relationship and dependency. As this kind of "body" (*sōma*), the Christian is claimed and owned by Christ, and therefore this self, which lives in concrete, material form ("bodily" in our sense of the word), is designated for eternal life together with its Lord.

This line of argument connects Romans 16:17–20 with Phillippians 3:17–21 and 1 Corinthians 6:12–20, assuming in the case of these passages an opposition to Paul roughly united by comparable and similar intentions and thoughts. This all but demands that we consider Romans 16:17–20, or all of Romans 16, as a fragment independent of, but later somehow attached, to Paul's letter to the Christians in Rome. The critical issue is, as such, of no primary importance for our search. But it could not be passed by because it provides the setting for the statement that the God of peace will soon crush Satan under the believers' feet.

The exclamation, "The God of peace will shortly crush Satan under your feet," must be understood as a final word of hope giving direction for the resistance to a group of people who spread poison in the Christian community by their teaching. That implies that Satan is the operative who is at work in the activity of those who "do not serve our Lord Christ, but their own appetites" (Rom. 16:18). The peace of God is threatened and damaged if advocates of pestilent teaching are permitted to do their work.

On the other hand, the statement "God will crush Satan" is apocalyptic through and through, looking forward to an ultimate victory in the future. The sentence is similar to a Jewish tradition about the emergence of a priest-messiah in the time of the end of whom it is said, "Beliar shall be bound by him: And he shall grant to his children the authority to trample on wicked spirits" (*Test. Levi* 18:12). As in the Synoptic material, discussed earlier, the decisive victory of God cannot be won unless and until an opposition is defeated which contests the total rule of the one God. Then, and then only, will the God of peace be the uncontested sovereign of his creation. Then only will peace prevail over all.

The Synoptic sayings of the defeat of Satan speak of the accomplishment of a victory in the life of Jesus that has the power and the character of God's final triumph: In them a campaign is successfully completed and further resistance is no longer possible. In contrast to that, Paul expects the crushing of Satan, and with it the dawn of peace, to happen in the future. In the communities given to his care the apostle notes the signs of a presence of Satan whose influence has by no means been eliminated once and for all. This raises questions endemic to Paul's theology, and the concept of peace within it cannot be understood unless they are answered. We will return to this question at the conclusion of the chapter.

4. Peace as Reconciliation (Romans 5:1–11)

Only once in the undisputed letters of Paul does the word "peace," together with other related terms, give a thematic unity to an entire section. The opening statement of that section (Rom. 5:1–11) and its last few sentences provide a cohesive argument to which peace is central.

> Therefore, since we are justified by faith, we have peace with God through our Lord Jesus Christ. (v. 1)

> Much more surely then, now that we have been justified by his blood, will we be saved through him from the wrath of God. For if while we were enemies, we were reconciled to God through the death of his Son, much more surely, having been reconciled, will we be saved by his life. But more than that, we even boast in God through our Lord Jesus Christ, through whom we have now received reconciliation. (vs. 9–11)

Compared to the Synoptic Gospels, the theme of peace in these verses is transposed into a different key. The evangelists told of Jesus the peacemaker through the media of narratives and sayings that involved individuals and groups at given times and in known places. Disciples and opponents, crowds now admiring, now hostile, meet the messiah of peace. They experience his presence in villages and towns, in the countryside and in the temple, at certain moments of their lives which, at least in principle, are datable by month, day, and year, even if the nature of our sources precludes any attempt to arrive at historically precise information. The same peacemaker is seen by Paul from a different perspective. All individuals and groups with their special histories and problems have disappeared. They are concentrated into a "we" that represents, from the standpoint of faith, human life as a single unit, and this one body of humanity is confronted with a Lord who lives beyond the limits of our time and space in the manner of God. While this Lord is identical with the human individual Jesus, he stands over against the whole history of humanity as the new Adam who brings to life a new form of humanness that is radically discontinuous with the old. Faced with Christ, all human history melts into a single unit because it is the outcome, consequence, and ever-renewed actualization of the first Adam whose disobedience to God subjects human existence to alienation from God (Rom. 5:12–21).

The reality and truth of peace are placed, for Paul, within these all-encompassing blocks of human history, the history of the old Adam with his offspring who have no peace with God, and the history of the new Adam with his children who live in peace with God. With regard to that peace, every human individuality is incorporated into one of these blocks. Great achievements for the well-being of nations, the savagery of ruthless murderers, and the drab sameness of floating along in a stream of accommodation and compromise—all have been made uninteresting and ultimately inconsequential when placed against an act of making peace that decides the destiny of the world history before God. The coming of Christ as the new Adam was to Paul an event of that unparalleled magnitude, an event that reduces the wealth and importance of historical differences to a single point determined solely by its relation either to the old Adam or to Christ. The making of peace, in Romans 5:1, introduces a concept of peace that draws meaning from the act of God in Christ, an act that reverses the direction of all human history prior to it.

The peace with God is contrasted, in Romans 5:1–11, with a number of nouns describing a condition of hostility between humans and God. Our reconciliation to peace with God was brought about when the recipients of this gift were still in a condition of weakness caused by perceptions, attitudes, and acts that are signs of people who are living without God (5:6). In sharper terms, reconciliation was effected for us "while we still were sinners" (5:8). Living without God as sinners, we were enemies of God (5:10).

On the other side of the issue, peace is also accompanied by a sequence of related terms, each interpreting the other. To live in peace with God is the same as being justified by God (5:1, 9). This means having free access to God, even as the high priest has permission to enter the holiest precinct in the temple to step into God's presence (5:2). Having peace with God is identical to being reconciled to God (5:10, 11), and it entails also the hope of sharing in God's glory (5:3), which will not come to rest until it has achieved a final salvation in which we will share in the life of the risen Christ (5:9, 10).

What can give substance to these stupendous claims? Paul has stated that the justification which brings peace with God is realized by faith (5:1). He has taken care to underscore the importance of faith in the earlier parts of Romans, and faith is made a key word by which the reader of the letter is introduced to an understanding of the ground for the separation of humanity into two groups: God's enemies and the reconciled who have peace with God.

The gospel is God's power of salvation for everyone who lives by faith (Rom. 1:16). Faith receives the gospel in the way of Abraham, the father of faith (4:11). That entails, first and foremost, that faith receives God's unearned forgiveness as both Abraham and David received the grace of God in a condition in which they lived godlessly (4:5–6). Yet this is not enough for Paul. To say that faith is based on God's grace and not on works could still be construed to mean that faith provides an escape ladder for emergencies: when normal goodness and justice break down, an emergency provision can be utilized that permits reliance on the forgiveness of God where and when my own best efforts happen to falter. But that is not what Paul had in mind when he called faith the realization of our salvation. He recalled the life of Abraham to illustrate the nature of faith. The old Abraham and the old Sarah are unable to generate new life. Abraham is about a hundred years old when the promise for a child is given him. In matters of fathering new life he is as good as dead, and Sarah is a barren woman. In spite of that, in the face of its complete contradiction by the state of his and Sarah's bodies, Abraham believed the promise of God. Faith is disclosed as what it is when it is expressing its trust in the God who gives life to the dead and calls into existence the things that do not exist (4:17–22). The righteous person lives by faith because faith relies on God's creative power, which is the basis upon which everything else is built. The unearned, and unearnable, grace of God can neither be prepared, nor reached, nor supplemented by human works because it is the manifestation of God's lordship over all of human history, every individual life included.

Paul has added to the positive explanation of faith through Abraham's life a stinging negative counterpart, and it is probably not by chance that he has given it the form of a personal confession (Romans 7:7–12). In explanation of his thesis that faith excludes all reliance on the fulfillment of Moses' law, and in defense of the concomitant assertion that Moses' law as God's gift to Israel is holy, just, and good, Paul has introduced an argument in the first person singular that is meant as a confession. But the confession is cast in words so definitely reminiscent of the story of Adam in Genesis 2 and 3 that it has been said, with good reason, that the Adam of Romans 5:12–21 has been given speech—the speech of Paul—in Romans 7:7–12, and vice versa, that the confessor Paul speaks of his own deepest failure through the person of Adam.

Paul states in his confession that the law says "You shall not covet" (*epithymeō,* 7:7). This laconic sentence is meant to have the force of a definition. The object of the covetousness is not stated and the general form of this statement reminds one of the desire of Adam and Eve to eat of the forbidden fruit (Gen. 3:6). Thus the sentence "You shall not covet" expresses the basic rule of the law of God. In the context of Genesis 3:5 the prohibition of desire states the law's fundamental intent: It wants to guard against the attempt by the first pair of humans—and with them all succeeding human generations—to decide about their own destiny and to ape God in projecting themselves into the deadly illusion of being in control of their own good.

The law reduced to its single purpose, stated negatively, says, "Do not desire divine status for yourself"; positively put, this may be translated into the sentence "God alone is your lord, therefore, you may trust him totally." But sin, which is not produced by the law in Romans 7:7–12, usurps the good law of God and, forcing it into its services, uses it as a beachhead for an assault aiming at the total occupation (by sin) of a territory that does not belong to it (the law). The word "opportunity" in Romans 7:8 and 11 (*aphormē*) can be used in military language for a base of operations from which an invasion can be launched. While it is not suggested that Paul wished to evoke the special military significance of the word, it does provide a useful point of comparison. The law states that those who fulfill it will live (Rom. 3:12; Rom. 10:5 in quotation of Lev. 18:5; cf. also Deut. 30:15–16). Wishing to live, the person dominated by sin presses God's commandments into service and distorts the law, which is intended to protect the freedom of God's grace, into an instrument of self-exaltation. Now the law begins to insinuate: Do this and you will be pleasing to God, or avoid that and you will earn yourself distinction, special privileges, and the glory of moral superiority. If that happens, sin has succeeded in occupying a beachhead through the law itself and will from there drive on until the entire land is occupied. Through its very commandment, therefore, sin can draw God's good law over to its side, corrupt it totally, and lead—against the law's will—into a condition of enmity with God, whose honor and goodness is despised if the unconditional freedom of his pure grace is questioned.

But there is yet another aspect to faith, of equal importance to Paul as the first, and this second aspect is also illustrated by the Old Testament's Abraham narrative. Abraham was promised descendants as numerous as the stars in the sky; he trusted the divine promise, and in placing his trust on God's truthfulness and reliability he was righteous. Now, God's promise was made and Abraham's faith happened before Abraham was circumcised. It follows, so Paul argues, that as faith in the promise precedes circumcision, righteousness by faith precedes the law (Rom. 4:9–15). It is helpful to notice that earlier, in the letter to the Galatians, Paul has argued somewhat differently. In Galatians 3:15–18 he had used the 430 years that elapsed between the promulgation of God's promise, in which Abraham believed, and the promulgation of the law on Sinai to make the point that the divine promise precedes the law. In Galatians 3:15–18 the contrast is between promise and law; in Romans 4:9–12 the contrast is drawn between the blessing of forgiveness and circumcision. The reasons for this change need not detain us now, but it is evident that law and circumcision become alternate terms. Circumcision stands for the covenantal sign of Jewish life dedicated to the Mosaic law. Consequently, Abraham was justified in faith before the covenantal sign existed which sets Judaism apart from the other nations. Faith is a clinging to God's promise and blessing in trust, and this faith is not bound to membership in the Jewish community. Therefore, as recipient in faith of God's blessing and promise, Abraham is the father of all who have faith, whether they be Jews or non-Jews. Faith is the only requirement to inherit the blessing of the God of Abraham. It breaks down the barrier between Jews and non-Jews, opens every human life to the possibility of receiving God's grace, and is, consequently, the basis for Paul's mission to offer the gospel to all nations. In Paul's own words: "The scripture says, 'No one who believes in him will be put to shame.' For there is no distinction between Jew and Greek; the same Lord is Lord of all and is generous to all who call on him. For 'Everyone who calls on the name of the Lord shall be saved'" (Rom. 10:11–13). It is interesting to note that in the context of the long argument in Romans 2:1–3:20 against the pride of Jews, and Jewish Christians, in the law, Paul has used the word "peace" to mark God's impartiality, which consigns every member of the family of Adam to one and the same place. In 2:1 an argument begins against the proclivity to judge others as morally inferior. The last judgment of God will pass sentence on each individual in complete disregard of religious or ethnic membership. It will bring to light exclusively the actual truth about each life: The final verdict of God will impart the full blessing, "glory and honor and peace," to those who do good, "the Jew first and also the Greek. For God shows no partiality" (2:10–11). Toward the end of this argument, Jews and Greeks are together placed under the condemnation of scripture. A sequence of Old Testament sayings addresses them both, leading to the sentence, "'No human being will be justified in [God's] sight' by deeds prescribed by the law" (3:20). Into this chain of quotations is put a part of Isaiah 59:7–8: "Their feet are swift to shed blood, ruin and misery are in their paths, and the way of peace they have not known" (Rom. 3:15–17). In Romans 2:10, "peace" stands for the eternal benefit of salvation, while in 3:17 it describes the nature of human behavior. But in both verses, "peace" is a reality that is at stake in the human presumption to be set apart from others in the illusion of an excellence before God which stems from the disregard of God's all-inclusive grace.

We had set out to consider the sentence, "Since we are justified by faith, we have peace with God through our Lord Jesus Christ" (Rom. 5:1), and this had led us far afield in search of what justification by faith might mean. But this excursion was necessary because it provides much of the content which is, in Paul's thought, enveloped in the word "peace." God has made peace with us through Christ's work of reconciliation, and that says that we who are "weak," "godless," "sinners," and "enemies" have been released from this awful condition and placed in a position in which peace with God prevails. This place at peace with God is occupied by faith, and faith explains what it actually implies to be weak, godless, a sinner, or an enemy of God. Human life is at war with God when it usurps God's lordship by making the human ego into a god, and by the desire to use life as a means to produce excellence and distinction before God in violation of the free and abundant grace of God, which is the only and all-sufficient ground for human response to the God of Abraham and of Jesus Christ. Peace with God is enjoyed when, through faith, the illusions of grandeur and the pretenses of separate excellencies are abandoned, and when all human beings without exception are allowed to be firmly united at the one crucial point, their common and total dependency on God's unearned goodness.

The faith which lives in peace with God is accessible to Jews and non-Jews. But it is not spontaneously produced by either Jew or non-Jew. It is called forth, in Paul's thought, by the death and the resurrection of Jesus, who is the act of reconciliation by which God makes peace with his enemies. The opening and closing sentences of Romans 5:1–11 are obviously correlated: to be "justified by faith" is conjoined to being "justified by [Christ's] blood" (5:1 and 9), and to have "peace with God through our Lord Jesus Christ" is inseparable from the statement "While we were enemies we were reconciled to God by the death of his Son" (5:1 and 10).

The work of reconciliation, the making of peace with God, is completely misconstrued if it even faintly smacks of the idea that Christ's death changed a God of wrath into a God of love. The death of Christ is the outcome of the love of God toward his enemies, its very showpiece (Rom. 5:8). The love of God comes into its own in the act of reconciliation: "All this is from God, who reconciled us to himself through Christ and has given us the ministry of reconciliation; that is, in Christ God was reconciling the world to himself, not counting their trespasses against them" (2 Cor. 5:18–19).

Paul gave serious consideration to the wrath of God. The passage that is before us in this section speaks of it: "Much more surely then, now that we have been justified by his blood, will we be saved through him from the wrath of God" (Rom. 5:9). The wrath of God has, for Paul, an eschatological and a historical aspect. It signifies the final rejection by God of the chaos in human history that is caused by the ever virulent and idolatrous human urge to elevate elements of nature to the position of divine honor (Rom. 1:18–32), and by the self-deception on the part of the religious ethicists who claim a moral distinction and excellence that sets them apart from others (Rom. 2:1–3:20). The wrath of God is, on the historical side of the issue, in full operation through God's giving up of idolaters to their own designs (Rom. 1:24, 26, 28) in which they reap the foul fruit of their own planting. It is, on the eschatological side, ultimately and irrevocably endorsed in God's final judgment (1 Thess. 1:10; 5:9; Rom. 2:5, 8). The idolator and the moralistic pretender are under the wrath of God, and they are, in that condition, enemies of God. The gospel of God's saving power (Rom. 1:16) reveals also God's wrath (Rom. 1:18ff.), and there can be no doubt that the reconciliation of God and humans is not intended, by Paul, to cancel out the reality and the weight of God's wrath. Before and after Christ, God's resistance against, and rejection of, idolatry is final, be it in the form of the adoration of natural forces or in the form of moralistic, ethical self-exaltation. Rather, it is in the death and resurrection of Christ that God's wrath is forever established as a necessary consequence of the love of God.

Perhaps the last sentence will seem to many readers to be an irresponsible and confusing game with words. It certainly calls for explanation, and an explanation encounters the difficulty that Paul was not very specific and expansive when he made use of christological and soteriological language. I will therefore take the risk of stating in very brief and thetic form what, in my reading of Paul, appear to be assumptions about Christ's work of reconciliation more hinted at than developed in the apostle's letters.

Paul underscored greatly that Christ's obedience and right-eousness were lived in contrast to Adam's disobedience and trespass (Rom. 5:12–21). At the same time, Adam's sin is repeated over and over again by all succeeding generations until the coming of Christ (Rom. 5:12). Paul's confession through the voice of Adam (Rom. 7:7–12) and his analysis of idolatry and moralistic deception (Rom. 1:18–3:20) give us the concrete image of what Paul considered to be Adam's disobedience. Be it said again, this disobedience, whether in the form of Adam's fall, or in the form of Paul's own former life as a zealot for the law, was always, is now, and ever will be subject to the wrath of God. The very confirmation of this statement is the cross of Jesus the reconciler. Paul has said not only that Christ died for us, but that he died in becoming a curse for us (Gal. 3:13), or that he died becoming sin for us (2 Cor. 5:21). As Adam's counterpart, Christ's life was from its ground up free from idolatry. It was the first-time appear-ance of a human who trusted solely, for himself and for all others, in the sufficiency and glory of God's free and all-inclusive grace. Precisely as that unique person he lived together with all the thousands of reincarnated Adams whose contemporary he happened to be. He lived among them— with respect to the basic orientation of his life as the one obedient to God's free and universal grace—like a total stranger. In that companionship with the strangers he perse-vered; had he not done so he would himself have denied both the freedom and the universality of God's gracious love. The presence of this stranger, and his perseverance in their midst for their benefit, the Adams of the time of Christ could not tolerate. They decided to do away with him as a disturbance of their order and a troubler of their peace. Therefore they executed him and let their order and peace prove to be in command in the world. The Adamites had unleashed their chaos on him, Christ was swallowed by the curse of their law, and the arrogance and pride of Adam's sin had made Christ its victim.

If, then, the wrath of God is opposed to Adam's sin, it can be said that Christ's death is its ultimate disclosure. But this wrath of God is not opposed to God's love. The message of the love of God, the declaration of our peace with God, does not by any means lead to the conclusion that God changed in the act of reconciliation, or that the wrath of God was found out to be an unenlightened superstition unworthy of Christian faith. But the love of God—and the declaration of our peace with God—does mean that the Christian is saved from the wrath of God, and that is seen, again, in both its historical and its eschatological dimensions. In saying this, we are entering into another aspect of the peace of God in Paul's writings which is to be the subject of the next section.

5. Peace as Life in the Spirit

Our peace with God, in Romans 5:1–11, is described as an act of God in which God establishes our reconciliation through the death of his Son. But this is only one side of the matter. Peace with God has also a future aspect; in fact, the future of God's peacemaking with us will surpass the present benefits. We are now already justified by Christ's blood. "Much more surely then, now that we have been justified by his blood, will we be saved through him from the wrath of God. For if while we were enemies, we were reconciled to God through the death of his Son, much more surely, having been reconciled, will we be saved by his life" (5:9–10).

To our way of thinking, peace is a condition that prevails between equal partners who have agreed to live together without resort to violence, and who respect the order that regulates their relationship by mutually recognizing an integrity and freedom within which each partner can exist without hurtful interference from outside. Of course, this condition of peace can be relatively secure, or it can be fragile and threatened; and it can exist between parties whose powers are uneven. But it remains a condition reached by the mutual agreement of partners who have the will to peace. The peace with God of which Paul speaks in Romans 5:1–11 is of a different kind. It is a peace between utterly unequal partners. The superior partner in this conflict makes and proclaims the peace while the other party is still fully engaged in the conflict ("while we still were sinners," "while we were enemies," 5:8 and 9). In fact even now, after the superior party has offered the peace, a majority of the members of the inferior party have hardly heard of it, let alone accepted it, and among those who have positively responded to the offer there is still some considerable doubt whether the terms of the peace can be unconditionally accepted. In other words, a condition of peace, fully accepted by both parties, has not yet been reached. This peace is, from the side of the inferior party, still in jeopardy. If it is to succeed it will have to win universal compliance with its terms in the future.

The word "salvation" in Romans 5:9 and 10 marks that time in the future at which the peace that God has made, offered, and proclaimed to his human enemies will be unconditionally accepted. Only then will the peace with God be so established that no resistance to it can put its validity in doubt. Then and only then will peace between God and his human creation have become a condition that truly and fully describes their relationship from the side of both partners. Paul has associated the expected arrival at this point in the future with the life of the risen Christ (5:10). It is by the power of Christ's resurrection that God's peace, already made, offered, and published for us, will ultimately prevail.

The apostle Paul has never talked of Christ's resurrection in isolation from its power through which those who belong to Christ are made participants in resurrection. "If the dead are not raised, then Christ has not been raised" (1 Cor. 15:16) but since he has been raised, his resurrection is only "the first fruits of those who have died" (1 Cor. 15:20). The power of Christ's resurrection will not have spent itself until death is defeated and God is all in all (1 Cor. 15:26, 28). It is not only active in the raising from the dead of the Son of God, and then again in its ultimate victory over death; it is also at work with and in those who live between this resurrection and the final disclosure of its power. Paul has identified the power of Christ's resurrection in the midst of historical human life and the operation of God's Spirit in the believer, and the word "peace" is associated with this identity of the power of life and the Spirit of God. Two verses are, in this respect, of particular importance:

> The fruit of the Spirit is love, joy, peace, patience, kindness, generosity, faithfulness, gentleness, and self-control. There is no law against such things. (Gal. 5:22–23)

> To set the mind on the flesh is death, but to set the mind on the Spirit is life and peace. (Rom. 8:6).

In Galatians 5:22, the word "peace" is linked to eight other nouns describing the nature of a life lived in the Spirit of God. "Peace" is not particularly emphasized in this chain, and neither the order nor the number of the words in the chain appear to be meant as more than illustrations without an attempt being made to produce a system of "virtues." In the neighborhood of so many general terms, "peace" is hardly intended to carry a precise meaning. In this list much more emphasis is placed on the origin of peace and its opposition to other characteristics of life.

We said above that the peace with God envisioned in Romans 5:1 is not an achieved condition of human life. Galatians 5:19–21 brings together a list of "works of the flesh" which are contrasted to the fruit of the Spirit, 5:22–23. Peace belongs on one side, and not on the other. It is a product of the Spirit, and therefore completely opposed to the products of "flesh." Spirit and flesh are mutually exclusive; there is a rivalry between them that cannot be reconciled, "for what the flesh desires is opposed to the Spirit; and what the Spirit desires is opposed to the flesh; for these are opposed to each other" (Gal. 5:17). The origin of peace is in the Spirit; the flesh does not want peace, cannot strive for peace, and if it should produce anything resembling peace it will be only a cover over the surface of a reality of "enmities, strife, jealousy, anger, quarrels, dissensions, factions" (Gal. 5:20). If peace is an effect of life in the Spirit, it follows that peace can be had, preserved, and promoted only by opposition to flesh and its works. Peace of the Spirit does not remove into a land of paradise untouchable by conflict and effort. Rather it is of a kind that guarantees struggle and exertion. As the fruit of the Spirit of God, peace is quite distinct from an equilibrium of mind, or a harmonious balance of forces advantageous to a condition of minimal disturbances. In its opposition to the works of the flesh, the peace of the Spirit of God is a force readying the Christian for vigilance and confident resistance to whatever flesh proposes.

The same tension as in Galatians 5:16–18 finds even stronger words in Romans 8:6–8. To have one's mind set on the flesh is death and enmity to God; to have the mind oriented toward the Spirit is life and peace. Flesh and Spirit are perceived as powers that shape and direct human life toward opposite destinies. To be human is to be "empowered" in the sense that human life is necessarily dominated by the field of force which is either "flesh" or "Spirit." The human being is no independent, self-directing subject, free to make its own choices; rather, it is "in the power" of flesh or Spirit. When flesh rules the human subject it is dominated by motivations and convictions, impulses and aims that arise from within itself without regard to a direction from God. Paul has perceived the domination of flesh over human life by no means exclusively in low appetites and moral corruption. They are certainly included in the "works of flesh," as the list in Galatians 5:19–21 demonstrates. But domination of the flesh comes also in the guise of religious and moral achievements. In retrospect of his own life, the apostle gives us an astonishing account of what he considers "works of flesh" in his own case. "If anyone else has reason to be confident in the flesh, I have more: circumcised on the eighth day, a member of the people of Israel, of the tribe of Benjamin, a Hebrew born of Hebrews; as to the law, a Pharisee; as to zeal, a persecutor of the church; as to righteousness under the law, blameless" (Phil. 3:4b–6). Flesh is most virulent when it exercises its spell in the form of exceptional distinction and achievement, which presents the ground for pride in one's own accomplishments and excellencies. The moral flesh, and especially the religious flesh, is worse than any other because it produces an enmity against God in his pure grace and casts a mantle of great honor over life which, due to its pride, is on its way to self-destruction.

Life and peace, on the other side, are the fruit of empowerment by the Spirit. In Romans 8:9–11, Paul uses a sequence of correlated phrases through which the action of the Spirit is described.

> But you are not in the flesh; you are in the Spirit, since the Spirit of God dwells in you. Anyone who does not have the Spirit of Christ does not belong to him. But if Christ is in you,

> though the body is dead because of sin, the Spirit is life because of righteousness. If the Spirit of him who raised Jesus from the dead dwells in you, he who raised Christ from the dead will give life to your mortal bodies also through his Spirit that dwells in you. (Rom. 8:9–11)

The passage shows a number of identifications. To live in the Spirit means the indwelling of the Spirit of God. In the same way, to have the Spirit of Christ is identical with having Christ within oneself. Finally, the Spirit of God is the power that raised Jesus Christ from the dead, and this same power is at work in believers through the Spirit which dwells in them. The intention of this sequence is the closest possible linkage between the Spirit of God and the Spirit of Christ. Being in the Spirit of God could be confused with a state of enthusiasm, with mystical contemplation, or with a possession of miraculous powers. But the true Spirit of God has the concrete marks of Christ's Spirit, and that means for Paul the Spirit of one who serves others to the point of death, expecting vindication completely though the power of God which brings life out of death. In this Spirit, the believer has life and peace.

Peace with God (Rom. 5:1) is at the same time peace through God's Spirit (Rom. 8:6). In both verses the peace is explained by the context as being brought about by God's justification of his enemies and completed in the eternal peace assured through the God who "calls into existence the things that do not exist" (Rom. 4:17). But this same Spirit of peace is also at work in and during the believer's life on earth through the service in which one member builds up the other in a community of peace.

6. Peace in the Service of God

The sentence "It is to peace that God has called you" (1 Cor. 7:15) is placed, in Paul's advice to a specific group of Christians in Corinth, within the framework of his discussion of questions concerning marriage. First Corinthians 7 is the beginning of Paul's answer in the letter to specific concerns that had been submitted to him ("Now concerning the matters about which you wrote," 7:1; repeated in similar form in 7:25; 8:1; 12:1; 16:1, 12). The interpretation of Paul's instruction and advice about matters of marriage hinges in

large measure on the assessment of the spirit prevalent in
Corinth, which is reflected in the whole letter and in the
apostle's concrete answers to the individual concerns with
which he was approached. I assume, here, without further
justification, that the tendencies and ideals behind the questions that prompted Paul's answer in 1 Corinthians 7 are best
understood as coming from a desire for a perfection of
Christian life that tended to disregard, and even despise, the
natural and material facts of human life. The slogan "All
things are lawful" is in vogue in Corinth (1 Cor. 6:12; 10:23).
It projects an ideal in which normal societal and individual
limits of freedom are cast aside to make room for the reign of
a spiritual existence that incorporates a liberty from all bonds
of earthly human behavior. In regard to the question of
marriage, this has produced in Corinth the desire to be free
from the limitations imposed by married life. There are some
who wish to maintain a married life without having sexual
relations any longer; they are warned against fooling themselves into the illusion that the natural sexual drive has ceased
to be a powerful reality (7:3, 5). There are others who want to
dissolve their marriages to live a more spiritual life; they are
answered by Jesus' instruction against divorce (7:10–11).
Unmarried and widowed persons are given the advice to stay
as they are, in accordance with their wishes, but without
forcing a decision upon themselves which they might not be
able to cope with in the long run (7:8–9).

A special group addressed are members of the community
in Corinth who live together with a non-Christian partner
(7:12–16). It is understandable that the drive for spiritual
perfection caused those Christians to wish to end their
marriages. Paul's advice ("I say—I and not the Lord," 7:12)
in this issue shows an amazing composition of confidence in
the sanctity of Christian life, sobriety with regard to its
limitations, and concern for the unforced spontaneity of
decisions. Paul counsels that the Christian partner in a mixed
marriage should not strive for divorce as long as the non-
Christian partner wishes to remain in the marriage (7:12–
13). Any fear of contagion by pagan practices and attitudes
does not need to force separation because the life of the
Christian part in the marriage is made holy to the degree that
even the children of this union are sanctified (7:14). Paul
dares to expect that life as spiritual service (Rom. 12:1) by
one partner in the marriage is stronger than the dangers that

might well arise from consorting with the unbeliever; the whole marriage is made holy, including the partner who does not believe. On the other hand, the Christian in a mixed marriage should not be troubled by being impelled to the obligation or responsibility to convert the nonbelieving partner (7:16). Such obligation is invalid because it is not within the power of any human to create faith. The possibility in a mixed marriage exists also that the unbelieving partner wishes a divorce (7:15). In that case the believer in a mixed marriage is free to divorce. The teaching of Jesus against divorce (7:10) is not to be turned into a prison in perpetuity when the will of the unbeliever to separate would cause the Christian partner to live in a situation of unmanageable and constant discord and strife if the union was not dissolved. The Christian partner, in this case, is not to be tortured by feelings of being chained to a married life which has turned into a breeding ground of resentment and dissatisfaction.

This advice to Christians living in a mixed marriage is summarized by the general statement, "It is to peace that God has called you" (7:15). It is manifest that this peace has to do with life on earth in the aspect of the right forms of marriage. Peace embraces all the elements in Paul's argument. It grants room to live with a good conscience in a marriage whose composition contains the seeds for potential trouble because the Christian faith does not bind both partners in a common bond. It gives the freedom to terminate a condition of marriage in which the nonbelieving partner desires divorce. And it liberates from a compulsion to expect of oneself the impossible by experiencing the obligation to convert the partner. It is hardly possible to unite all these aspects of peace in a single term. What is important is not its definitional accuracy but the sense of its overarching benevolence.

As the sentence 1 Corinthians 7:15 draws a differentiated discussion into one maxim, so does the statement in 1 Corinthians 14:33, only in a different context: "God is a God not of disorder but of peace." The theme in 1 Corinthians 14 is a form of worship that helps in building up the congregation. The contributions of prophets in worship are especially desired because they lead to "upbuilding and encouragement and consolation" (14:3). Three times the task of edifying the community is mentioned in sounding a caution against a speaking in tongues that is not understood by all, visiting outsiders included (14:24), unless this enthusiastic praying is also interpreted (14:4–5). The concern for building up each other in worship is repeated in 14:17 and put in the general principle, "Let all things be done for building up" (14:26).

We may be inclined to understand Paul's emphasis in 1 Corinthians 14 as a concern for "decency and order" (14:40). But that is hardly the case. The freedom he allows goes far beyond the limits to which we are accustomed through our orders of worship, even if they represent a nonliturgical tradition. One comes together with the congregation in Corinth and feels invited, under the Spirit's prompting, to offer "a hymn, a lesson, a revelation, a tongue, or an interpretation" (14:26). It has happened that those speaking in tongues have talked simultaneously, two or three on top of each other (14:27). Paul was not about to do battle against freedom of expression. But he insisted on a number of requirements that must govern an assembly of Christians in worship even if the spontaneity of the Spirit is not curbed. Understanding of ecstatic exuberance is to be ensured (e.g., 14:11); imbalance in contributions is to be avoided (14:27, 29); a speaking of several at one time must be stopped (14:27); and prophets must respect each other's words (14:29–32).

All of these instructions aim at steps undertaken to foster a productive freedom during worship whose decisive aim is the mutual upbuilding of one another and the avoidance of an egocentrism in worship that revels in self-expression at the expense of others (14:4). If that aim is borne in mind, worship will honor the God who is not a God of disorder but of peace. The peace envisioned is the free exercise of many different forms of contributions in worship under the discipline of the concern that all be made serviceable to the common good.

In yet another set of circumstances, the concept of peace plays a part in Romans 14–15. In these chapters, Paul is clarifying his position about proper Christian behavior in the face of divisions within the Roman congregation. The issue at hand is one of dietary restrictions and conformity to a specific calendar of holy days and seasons (Rom. 14:2, 5–6). Those who consider themselves above diet laws and feast days call themselves "the strong"—and Paul leaves no doubt that for his own part he joins their conviction (14:4)—but others, "the weak," cannot in good conscience transcend boundaries to which their upbringing and background have led them. Paul's reasoning drives home the point that each individual form of faith must be protected and respected if the Spirit of Christ, who came to serve all in their weakness, is to be honored (15:1–3). In this connection the word "peace" is repeatedly employed. The rule of God is not decided by conformity or nonconformity to food laws, but it is manifest in "righteousness and peace and joy in the Holy Spirit" (14:17). Therefore, in a combination of words reminiscent of 1 Corinthians 14, Paul admonishes that everyone, strong and weak together, "pursue what makes for peace and for mutual upbuilding" (14:19). Finally, in concluding his discussion, but also in summarizing it, the apostle closes with the wish, "May the God of hope fill you with all joy and peace in believing, so that you may abound in hope by the power of the Holy Spirit" (15:13).

The rule of peace, then, is the genuine order of congregational life. Recriminations and accusations have the capacity to undermine the unity of the community, which is achieved not by the enforcement of a single standard of conduct but by an unfeigned respect for everyone's faith, for only that which does not proceed from faith is sin (14:23).

For Paul, the concern for peace was, first and foremost, a concern for establishing a helpful, upbuilding, and unselfish conduct within the Christian community itself, which cannot take a condition of peace for granted. But for him the reach of the task of peacemaking extends beyond that. "If it is possible, so far as it depends on you, live peaceably with all" (Rom. 12:18). In their attitude to each other in the Christian community, but also in their will and work for peace with everyone, Christians are placed under the blessing, "The peace of God, which surpasses all understanding, will guard your hearts and your minds in Christ Jesus" (Phil. 4:7).

7. Jesus and Paul

Jesus the peacemaker is described in the Synoptic Gospels through the medium of sayings and narratives. In Luke, the gospel is the good news of peace. The account of Jesus' words and works is bracketed by the praise of God who, through Jesus' life, establishes peace on earth in accordance with the peace that reigns in heaven. What peacemaking is can consequently be understood if the entire flow of Luke's Gospel is seen as the explication of God's peace, which makes a home on earth in the teaching and activity of Jesus. For Matthew, the messianic peacemaker is more specifically identified with characteristic facets of Jesus' life. The messianic peace is, in Matthew, first and foremost the healing of every manner of mental and physical disease and infirmity. But it is also manifest in Jesus' compassion and help for a confused and leaderless crowd whose hunger he satisfies, whose sins he forgives, and whose low status he protects against neglect and derision.

In the Gospels of Matthew and Luke, the accomplishment of Jesus the peacemaker is bound up with concrete people and their real needs. Both evangelists have made it clear that this peacemaking transcends the narrow horizon of a specific time and place in the life of Palestinian people, because God's ultimate right over his creation, his kingship over all, takes hold of the earth here and there whenever, in Jesus' teaching and action, this kingship of God manifests itself. But in the Gospels, the people to whom God's peace comes remain individuals with their specific and time-bound needs.

Jesus is the peacemaker for Paul no less than he is for the Synoptics. But in Paul's letters peace is associated with wide-reaching concepts that appear to have lost touch with concrete and individual problems and needs. Now, in place of concrete sufferers stands all of humanity marred by the sin of Adam. The time in whose perimeter peace is made is no longer datable, at least roughly, in the years around A.D. 30; rather, it is immeasurably expanded to cover the whole aeon from the inception of human history to the Christ event. The problems and needs to which peace brings resolution are no longer the identifiable realities of sickness, depravity, and destitution; peace is now determined by the internal struggle between Spirit and flesh which overshadows every individual concretion. In the Synoptics, the messianic words and works of peace are like flares in the night which announce the coming of the day in the midst of history, but in Paul's apocalyptic modes of thought the peace of God is still relegated to its disclosure in the future. And the immediacy of Gospel narratives that tell of acts of messianic peacemaking gives way, in Paul, to admonitions for peace that, in comparison to the Gospels, appear pale and abstract.

Is the peacemaker seen so differently, in the Synoptics and in Paul, that the attempt to discover essential common ground which unites them is doomed to failure? An answer to this question can perhaps be found if we take into account cases of concrete and specific problems, which quite frequently are discussed in Paul's letters. We will proceed very selectively, isolating as test cases Paul's statements about two issues that are centered in social needs and problems: the collection for the Christian community in Jerusalem, and the disorder in the celebration of the Lord's Supper in Corinth. (For this entire section, see the essay by Ulrich Luz, "Friedenshandeln," in the Select Bibliography.)

In the strategic agreement between Paul and the apostolic leadership in Jerusalem, it was stipulated that Paul should "remember the poor" (Gal. 2:10) in his work among Gentiles. Related passages in Paul's letters leave no doubt that this "remembrance" means the collection of funds on the Pauline mission field for impoverished members of the Christian community in Jerusalem. There is a segment of the community in Jerusalem who are "the poor among the saints" (Rom. 15:26). This group in Jerusalem suffers want (2 Cor. 8:14; 9:12). Although the expression "the poor" may be connected to an honorific title equating "the poor" with the truly elect, Paul speaks of the poor in Jerusalem consistently in the sense of people who are economically disadvantaged. In view of this, it is remarkable that in all longer passages in Paul's letters in which the apostle talks about the collection (Rom. 15:25–33; 2 Corinthians 8 and 9) there is nothing to suggest a planned relief action for the removal of poverty among the Christians in Jerusalem. The emphasis, rather, is on the demonstration of solidarity in faith which unites the Gentile Christians with their fellow believers in Jerusalem. The word "common bond" (*koinōnia*), ordinarily used by Paul for communion with God and other Christians, is applied to gifts toward the collection (Rom. 15:26; 2 Cor. 8:4; 9:13, translated in NRSV "shar[ing] their resources," "sharing in this ministry" [*koinōnia tēs diakonias*], and again "sharing"). The collection is important as a sign of acknowledgment that Gentile Christians owe their "spiritual blessings" to the Jewish heritage for which the church in Jerusalem stands as the historical link (Rom. 15:27). The collection, therefore, answers to a concrete social need. But the service of this need is not an end in itself. Rather, it is the occasion calling for the realization of the common bond between Jewish and Gentile Christians who, through the collection, demonstrate their unity and mutual dependence.

Surprisingly, Paul's concern about disorders in the celebration of the Lord's Supper in Corinth points in the same direction. What appears, at first sight, to be dictated by the desire for a proper liturgical form turns out, at closer inspection, to be permeated by social problems. Assemblies of the whole Christian community at Corinth are experiencing difficulties that are connected with the Lord's Supper (1 Cor. 11:17–33). Apparently, the time of worship is divided at least into two main sections; there is a common meal at the beginning, which is then followed by the remembrance of Christ's death in the communion of bread and wine. The normal meal at the beginning must have been a very loosely structured occasion. Some arrive late; so late, in fact, that they miss the dinner altogether and remain hungry because the participation in the distribution of bread and wine is not meant to satisfy hunger (11:33); others arrive in plenty of time, help themselves to whatever is spread on the table, and enjoy the wine to the point of getting intoxicated (11:21, 33). But the division (11:18) between early arrivals and latecomers is combined with the social stratification of the community's members. Some have houses, implying that they belong to a wealthier group; but others have nothing, probably that section of the community which consists of slaves and poorer members of the free society (11:22). The wealthier members of the community, being in control of their time, could arrive early and enjoy a plenteous dinner. The poorer members, however, could not so easily make time to attend the whole meeting, but managed only to arrive for the "sacramental" part of the service, and consequently remained hungry. Paul's criticism of this practice attacks the separation of a "sacramental" part of the service, from a "secular" portion which has no other purpose but to satisfy hunger and thirst. That separation, in fact, despises the poor, and consequently also the entire community (11:22). Paul condemns the opinion that only the "sacramental" celebration matters, while the feeding of the physical needs of the body may be left to everyone's discretion. The spiritual-physical union of life is disregarded in this practice, the poorer in the community are made to feel second class, and in precisely that procedure is the body and blood of Christ profaned (11:27).

There is no question, then, that concerns for social equality play a part in Paul's criticism of the communion practice in Corinth. But this has not led him to the conclusion that the entire social structure in the Corinthian church needs to be reshaped according to an ideal of social equality. He would not object if the wealthier members met in their own houses to have their own meal (11:34). And conclusions are not drawn from the communion of the body and the blood of Christ that would amount to feeding programs for the hungry in Corinth. The sacramental part of the Lord's Supper remains Paul's predominant concern, and from that point he argues for a form of worship in which mutual love prevents a practice that does injury to the socially disadvantaged by neglecting their physical needs. The sacrament is the point at which the unity of the body of Christ craves an expression that approximates as much as possible the essential equality of all members of the body. But consequences for egalitarian social structures are not drawn from this model.

The list of test cases could be considerably expanded, but we break off at this point in the opinion that further observations would lead to similar results (Luz, "Friedenshandeln," discusses many more issues under the headings of need, lack of freedom, and violence). Rather, we return to the questions posed at the beginning of this section.

Concern for the poor and disadvantaged and care for the hungry are, especially in the Gospels of Matthew and Luke, part of the messianic peacemaking that takes place in Jesus' life. Issues dealing with similar needs are, in Paul's letters, not associated with the idea of peace (the wish of peace, Rom. 15:33, is an old ending to the letter, not a summation to the topic of the collection). Is there an explanation for this difference?

It was noted earlier in this chapter that Paul expects the coming of God's ultimate peace in the future when the power of Satan will be crushed. On the other hand, Christ's death is the effective reconciliation between God and a new humanity that lives, through its faith, in peace with God. Peace has, therefore, both a present and a future dimension. Faith grasps the gift of God that is offered in Christ's reconciling death. In this life of faith, the Spirit of God already rules the believer's present, and in this life the peace of God is already established. But this does not negate the other aspect, that God's peacemaking in Christ also has a future that will be victorious over every reality which still denies the validity of Christ's death for the peace between God and all creation.

This tension between present and future is also deeply

ingrained in the Synoptics' account of Jesus' life. On the one hand, there is the insistence that the peace of God's gracious rule on earth is already won in Jesus' acts of healing, in his compassion and care for the lost. But there remains, on the other hand, the realization that the final victory of God's rule in heaven and on earth is still to be expected in the future. The realized kingship of God implies the total and exclusive rule of the one God over all of creation, and this realization has not yet come.

Paul has maintained with great insistence the validity, even the necessity, of this tension. For him the concept of peace is determined by the full content of the eschatological absoluteness of God's saving act in Christ for the benefit of all creation and all of its history. It is a peace that grows out of the indefatigable love of God, which reverses the curse on Adam, turning it into the blessing of Christ's death, which inaugurates the new creation. And it is a peace that is hoped for and expected to win the final victory when the truth of God's reconciling the world in Christ will be manifest to all and in all. This central affirmation is, for Paul, the heart of the issue of peace.

Our test cases have shown that Paul was not about to assume that the peace of the new creation could be given instant expression by the elimination of all those facts of life which produce conflict and inequality even within the Christian communities. It is necessary to ask why the apostle could remain reluctant to claim too much "peace" in fashioning the reality of everyday life in his congregations.

The answer has often been advanced that Paul expected the coming of the victorious Christ with such immediacy that the reformation of social structures became to him a matter for which no time remained. But it has often been pointed out that Paul's arguments for the good order of Christian life are not based on his convictions about the closeness of Christ's parousia.

It is also argued that Paul was too much of a political realist to set in motion in the Christian communities reform programs that were bound to be wrecked by the resistance of powerful societal realities in the Roman empire. But this argument also second-guesses the apostle by attributing to him unstated motivations. The fact remains that Paul's own reasoning does not proceed on lines of political expediency.

In Paul's own thought, the tension between the fruition of

God's peace in the present and the impossibility of concretizing this peace in all aspects of life, through corresponding social structures, is connected to his understanding that Christ's death has the power to draw the believer's life into participation with this death. It is precisely in dying with Christ that the force of God's reconciliation is active and the peace of God is at work. The peace of God shapes the one desire of Paul's faith: "I want to know Christ and the power of his resurrection and the sharing of his sufferings by becoming like him in his death, if somehow I may attain the resurrection from the dead" (Phil. 3:10–11). As the suffering of Christ is the concrete form of God's love for the world, so participation in this suffering is the core of the Christian's love for others. Love does not jump over reality to build figments of paradise. Love meets reality, sin-drenched and death-ridden reality, without escape into projections of ideals through which we desire to make the world lovable. Therefore it is not a contradiction to the peace of God in Christ's death, but its very proof, that Paul can say of himself: "As servants of God we have commended ourselves in every way: through great endurance, in afflictions, hardships, calamities, beatings, imprisonments, riots, labors, sleepless nights, hunger" (2 Cor. 6:4–5; cf. 2 Cor. 11:23–29).

Paul has not expected every member in the Christian communities to experience the same extremes of trouble. But he has insisted that they are capable and worthy of understanding, and of living, the reality that God's peace involves subjection to the experience of oppression and injustice. The faith that lives in the peace of God in Christ knows that only in bearing evil can evil itself be defeated.

Select Bibliography

Berger, K. "Apostelbrief und apostolische Rede: Zum Formular frühchristlicher Briefe," *Zeitschrift für die neutestamentliche Wissenschaft* 65 (1974): 190–231.

Brandenburger, Egon. *Frieden im Neuen Testament*, 25, 51–65. Gütersloh: Gütersloher Verlagshaus Gerd Mohn, 1973.

Käsemann, Ernst. "On Paul's Anthropology." In idem, *Perspectives on Paul*, 1–31. Philadelphia: Fortress Press, 1971.

———. "The Saving Significance of the Death of Jesus in Paul." In idem, *Perspectives on Paul*, 32–59. (Neither of Käsemann's essays deals with peace. But they are fundamental for an appreciation of the soteriological and anthropological horizon within which Paul's concept of peace is placed.)

Luz, Ulrich. "Eschatologie und Friedenshandeln bei Paulus," in U. Luz, J. Kegler, P. Lampe, and P. Hoffmann, *Eschatologie und Friedenshandeln: Exegetische Beiträge zur Frage christlicher Friedensverantwortung.* Stuttgarter Bibelstudien 101. Stuttgart: Katholisches Bibelwerk, 1981. (All four essays take their starting point from a contemporary analysis of peace.)

Schweizer, Eduard. *"Pneuma," Theological Dictionary of the New Testament,* VI, ed. G. Friedrich, trans. G. W. Bromiley, 415–437. Grand Rapids: Wm. B. Eerdmans Publishing Co., 1968.

———. *"Sarx," Theological Dictionary of the New Testament,* vol. VII (1970), 125–135.

Wolter, Michael. *Rechtfertigung und zukünftiges Heil: Untersuchungen zu Röm 5, 1–11.* Berlin and New York: Walter de Gruyter, 1978. (The only recent monograph on Rom. 5:1–11. Provides a great deal of background material for every important term in the passage.)

7

Universal
and Global Peace:
Colossians
and Ephesians

This chapter deals with the subject of peace in the letters to the Colossians and to the Ephesians. These letters are set apart from the previous chapter, dealing with Paul, for three reasons. First, Pauline authorship of Colossians and Ephesians is so much in doubt that a separate treatment appears to be preferable. In fact, this chapter is written in the opinion that neither Colossians nor Ephesians was Paul's own work, but that both are the products of leaders in the churches belonging to Paul's sphere of activity. Second, the interdependence between Colossians and Ephesians is so certain that a joint treatment of these letters is suggested by their internal relationships. Third, and most important, the subject of peace is given new dimensions in these letters which are unique within the New Testament. Colossians, in one unparalleled statement, extols God's work of reconciliation as an act of making peace through which all of creation, in heaven and on earth, is delivered from the chains of hostility against its creator. And Ephesians envisions the church as the token of a new humanity in which all divisions have become obsolete and through which a global peace is reality and obligation.

1. Colossians: Universal Peace

The letter to the Colossians makes two statements about peace. The second of these statements, in 3:15, is part of an exhortation, similar to passages in Paul's epistles that were discussed in chapter 6. It will therefore not be considered again.

The matter is very different regarding Colossians 1:20, which associates peace with the reconciliation of all things through Christ. The verse makes a singular assertion. It has connections to Paul's hope for the ultimate release of all creation from the bonds of futility (Rom. 8:18–25), but it focuses this hope into a creedal or hymnic affirmation that has no peer in the New Testament.

Colossians 1:20 is the concluding sentence of a larger unit (1:15–20) that, in style and content, is clearly set apart from its context. Grammatical characteristics and a definite structure of thought and expression isolate this unit from what precedes and follows. The assumption is well founded which perceives in it an originally independent piece of Christian poetry that may have had a liturgical, creedal, or hymnic purpose of its own.

> [15]He is the image of the invisible God,
>   the firstborn of all creation;
>   [16]for in him all things were created,
>   in heaven and on earth,
>   visible and invisible,
>   whether thrones or dominions
>   or rules or authorities—
>   all things were created through him and for him.
>   [17]He is before all things,
>   and in him all things hold together.
>   [18]He is the head of the body, (the church).
>   He is the beginning, the firstborn from the dead,
>   so that in everything he might be preeminent.
>   [19]For in him all the fullness of God was pleased to dwell,
>   [20]and through him to reconcile to himself all things,
>   whether on earth or in heaven,
>   making peace (through the blood of his cross).
>   (Col. 1:15–20, NRSV alt.)

This poem is divided into two main sections. The first section (15–18a) praises Christ as the image of God and the firstborn of creation, the second praises Christ as the beginning of a new creation and the firstborn from the dead (vs. 18b–20). There is wide agreement among commentators today that the poem has received some editing comments and that its immediate context also serves commenting purposes. While the extent of the interpretive additions within the poem itself remains controversial, I have placed in parentheses, in the translation above, those additions which can be considered explanatory notes with a high degree of probability: In 1:18a "the church" is misplaced in its context because the first section of the unit speaks of creation; the phrase "through the blood of his cross" in 1:20 produces in Greek an extremely awkward repetition of the preposition *dia* and is out of harmony with the governing idea of the victory over death in the second section. Without these comments, the poem displays two clear thematic units: creation and re-creation through resurrection. The passage immediately following the poem, 1:21–23, picks up on its themes ("estranged and hostile" as counterpoint to "peace" and "reconcile[d]" in 1:20) and provides further comments exactly in the spirit of the additions within the poem itself. It is helpful for the interpretation to recognize the distinct movement of thought in the presumably original form of the poem, but the additions and comments will also be taken seriously.

If the phrase "through the blood of his cross" is set aside, for the time being, as an interpretive addition, Colossians 1:20 states that Christ made peace, as the firstborn from the dead, both on earth and in heaven, by God's reconciling in him all things to himself. This implies that, before and outside of Christ's making peace in his resurrection, there was hostility and conflict on earth as well as in heaven.

It is not difficult to see what Colossians has in mind when hostility on earth is in view. The members of the Christian community in Colossae are reminded of their former life outside the field of power into which they were transplanted when they acknowledged Christ as their head. They were once "estranged and hostile in mind, doing evil deeds" (1:21), captives of a "power of darkness" (1:13) that, if allowed to dictate their lives, produces all kinds of poisoned and poisonous behavior (3:5–7). The enmity against God on earth is concentrated entirely in that form of human life which is lived outside the sovereign rule of God's beloved Son (1:13). The subject that spawns and carries out hostility on earth is the human self insofar as it does not yield its will and action to Christ the reconciler.

Far more complicated is the question of what the author of Colossians was thinking about when he spoke of hostility against God in heaven. Heaven is described in the poem, in decidedly Hellenistic terminology, as the domain of that which is invisible, and then, in a more Jewish turn of phrase, as the home of "thrones, dominions, rules (*archai*), and authorities (*exousiai*)" (1:16, lit.; although the list of four powers may belong to the explanatory additions). In Christ, every rule (*archē*) and authority (*exousia*) has its head (2:10), but the sentence implies that, left to themselves without the governance of the head, they have the drive to run on their own power in ways dictated by their own inherent forcefulness. In Christ, however, their might is not only checked but defeated. The rules (*archai*) and authorities (*exousiai*) are disarmed, as after a military campaign, and publicly paraded about like prisoners of war who are led in chains behind a victorious Roman general who is given permission to celebrate a triumph in the capital of the empire, and to exhibit his exploits (2:15). Relatives of the same family appear to be the "elemental spirits of the universe," at least to the translators of the NRSV, who rendered with this phrase the *stoicheia tou kosmou* of Colossians 2:8 and 20.

We begin with the *stoicheia tou kosmou.* They must have played a leading role in shaping that philosophy which, in the judgment of the writer of Colossians, adversely affected the Christian community (2:8). The Greek phrase, literally translated, means "elements of the world" and refers in Greek, Hellenistic, and Jewish writings, well before New Testament times but down to the second century A.D., to the basic substances out of which the whole universe is made. Eduard Schweizer has placed the interpretation of the Colossian philosophy on this background. In a sequence of articles culminating in his commentary on Colossians he has succeeded in offering an approach so convincing that I have adopted it here. The following sketch of the background for the Colossian philosophy is a much abbreviated summary of his work (see Select Bibliography).

The philosopher Empedocles (born 483 B.C.) is credited with the theory that everything in existence consists of four basic elements: earth, water, air, and fire. These elements carry properties opposed to each other, such as wet and dry, cold and hot. The elements are the four roots of being, imbued with contrary properties that tend to commingle with each other to establish a balance, and this exchange of properties (Empedocles's "love") produces movement and pacifies the strife between clashing properties. Later times developed Empedocles' theory, giving it further theological and anthropological significance. Heaven, the abode of the gods, consists of the purest and lightest element, air or ether, and the human being is made of all four elements, having a soul that possesses the properties of air and seeks, after death, to ascend to the highest and purest regions of the universe. Inappropriate ways of living, however, encumber the human soul with heaviness so that, after death, it cannot freely rise to the heights and is condemned to get caught in the lower regions of the air. Several texts shortly before and during New Testament times attest to the practice of issuing certain instructions governing human conduct designed to preserve the soul pure and ready to reach its happy destination in the ethereal world. These instructions are almost entirely paralleled by the regulations for living insisted upon by the Colossian philosophy: abstinence from certain foods and objects (Col. 2:21); the observation of special seasons (2:16); veneration of angels, which are in Hellenistic garb the souls (demons) of the departed (2:18); ascetic practices (2:18, 23); ablutions comparable to baptism (2:12).

Moreover, it is certain that the theory of the four elements of the world with its theological and anthropological elements had found entry into Hellenistic Judaism. Philo particularly adopts it, although with significant modifications dictated by his commitment to monotheistic faith. It is especially significant that Philo, in his discussion of the "feast of trumpets" (the new year festival), calls God the peacemaker and peacekeeper of the universe. The trumpet call at the feast has a significance which is common to all humanity. For, as a trumpet is sounded in war to signal the end of hostilities after a battle, so the trumpet sound at the cultic festival signifies a "thank offering to God the peacemaker and peacekeeper, who destroys faction . . . in the various parts of the universe and creates plenty and fertility and abundance of other good things" (*On the Special Laws* II, 192). God's peacemaking and peacekeeping is necessary because, based on the theory of the conflicting properties of the four elements of the world, "there is another war not of human agency when nature is at strife in herself, when her parts make onslaught one on another and her law-abiding sense of equality is vanquished by the greed for inequality." Human wars cause widespread destruction, but there is also a war in nature which results in "drought, rainstorms, violent moisture-laden winds, scorching sun-rays, intense cold accompanied by snow, with the regular harmonious alternations of the yearly seasons turned into disharmony" (*On the Special Laws* II, 190–191).

The "elements of the world" in Colossians 2:8 and 20 are, consequently, not spiritual beings in heaven. But that does not imply that they are outside the reconciliation of all things through Christ's making peace (1:20).

The subservience to the "elements of the world" among Christians in Colossae displays signs of a Jewish filter through which the Hellenistic theory of the four elements has passed. The Sabbath is a part of the regulations imposed by the Colossian philosophy (2:16), the sequence "festivals, new moons, sabbaths" echoes Old Testament language (2:16; cf. Hosea 2:11; Ezek. 45:17), and the veneration of "angels" adopts Jewish wording (2:18). This Jewish filter may well have produced a concept of the "elements of the world," which gave them a position and an effect comparable to that of the "principalities and powers."

A saying of Empedocles has been preserved which states that the elements were gods (Diels-Kranz I, 311.15–312.2; see Select Bibliography), and Herodotus reports of the Persians that they "sacrifice to the sun and moon and earth and fire and water and winds" (*Histories* I, 131). The option of understanding the four elements of the universe as divine powers was known to Philo, who mentions those "who revere the elements, earth, water, air, fire" under the names of Hephaestus, Hera, Poseidon, and Demeter (*On the Contemplative Life* 3). The Jewish tendency to transform pagan divinities into spiritual beings subservient to the one God may explain the fact that Philo can call the four elements the "four rules (*archai*) and powers (*dynameis*) from which the world has been framed, earth, water, air, and fire" (*Who Is the Heir* 281). Philo is also capable of substituting the word "heaven" for the purest and finest of the four elements: "We find the constituents that make up the whole to be four: earth, water, air, heaven" (*On Dreams* I, 16).

We assume, therefore, that a Jewish recasting of the Hellenistic teaching about the four elements of the world tended to blur the difference between the "elements" and the "powers and principalities." The "thrones, dominions, rules, and authorities" (1:16), "every rule and authority" (2:10), and "the rules and authorities" (2:15) in Colossians belong to the transworldly force of the single God of Judaism who exercises his government with the help of a court of aides and servants to which the functions of pagan divinities have been reduced. God is in command of "all the fiery armies of the great archangels, and the incorporeal forces and the dominions and the origins and the authorities, the cherubim and the sera-phim and the many-eyed thrones" (*2 Enoch* 20:1; Rec. J) who are "the angels who are over seasons and years, and angels who are over rivers and the ocean, and angels who are over the fruit of the earth and over every kind of grass, and who give every kind of food to every kind of living thing" (*2 Enoch* 19:4; Rec. J).

The assumption of a Jewish molding of the Hellenistic doctrine of the four elements of the world can explain why "elements" and "powers" are so closely proximate in Colossians. "Every rule and authority" has its head in Christ (2:10), but he is also the head to whom the human tradition (2:8) and regulations (2:20) enjoined by the elements have to yield (2:19, concluding the summary of the regulations in 2:16–18). The Christian has died to the elements (2:20) as the Christian has put off the body of flesh and has been buried in baptism with Christ in finding life in the head of all rule and authority (2:10–12).

It is now possible to summarize our understanding of the Colossian philosophy. (1) It is developed on the basis of the widespread theory that everything in existence is composed of four basic elements, all of which we would today consider natural substances. But this philosophy was influenced in Colossae by some Jewish modifications of the theory which allowed heavenly forces to be associated with it. (2) The harmony of the world, cosmic peace, depends on the estab-lishment and maintenance of a balance between the elements, which have different properties tending to upset the equilibri-um between them. The disturbance of the balance causes cosmic and terrestrial catastrophes that can be understood as war between the elements. Whether or not the practices recommended by the Colossian philosophy aimed at safe-guarding the natural order, e.g., through the worship of angels, cannot be determined by the letter. (3) The Colossian philosophy embraced an anthropology which sought to assure that the human soul, consisting of the lightest and purest of the elements, would be enabled to ascend to its home in the highest spheres after death. A certain affinity to later Gnostic ideas is likely at this point, but a full-fledged metaphysical dualism denying the goodness of the earth cannot be substantiated through the letter. (4) The philosophy in Colossae insisted on a set of instructions and rules in harmony with their convictions concerning the power of the elements of the world. They seem to have emphasized calendric, dietary, and purifying regulations designed to conform to the proper balance of the elements as steps to lead their participants to share in, or perhaps produce, the cosmic peace.

We can now return to the poem in Colossians 1:15–20. It is structured in two parts whose beginnings conform closely to each other: "[Christ] is the image of the invisible God, the firstborn of all creation," and "he is the beginning, the firstborn from the dead" (1:15 and 18). Creation into being and a new creation out of death are set side by side, and Christ is central and active in both.

Colossians 1:15–20 concentrates entirely on the praise of Christ in the work of creation and of re-creation. The "firstborn from the dead" presupposes the rule of death in creation, but the introduction of death into the world, the character and extension of its reign, and the history which it initiated, remain unmentioned in the poem. The hymn moves from the origin of all that exists, to its destiny in an act of God that conforms and surpasses creation itself in the resurrection of Christ from the dead. Anything between these acts of God is left unmentioned because it cannot compare in dignity and importance to the primal acts of creation and re-creation.

God's act of re-creation in Christ's resurrection is said to be a peacemaking through which all things in heaven and on earth were reconciled to the creator (1:20). But this re-creation through the firstborn from the dead is described in close analogy to creation itself, so that it can only be understood if the two parts of the poem are allowed to interpret each other.

The declaration that "[Christ] is the image of the invisible God, the firstborn of all creation" (1:15) is rooted in Jewish thought about the Wisdom of God which was with God at the beginning, and even before the beginning of creation. Already in Proverbs 8, God's Wisdom, speaking like a person, says of herself, "The Lord created me at the beginning of his work, the first of his acts of long ago. Ages ago I was set up, at the first, before the beginning of the earth. . . . Then I was beside him, like a master worker [or perhaps, "like a darling daughter"; the reading is uncertain]; and I was daily his delight, rejoicing before him always, rejoicing in his inhabited world and delighting in the human race" (Prov. 8:22–23; 30–31). The apocryphal book of Sirach goes even farther: Wisdom speaks again about herself: "I came forth from the mouth of the Most High, and as a mist I covered the earth [cf. Gen. 1:2] . . . [The creator of all things] created me in the beginning, before the world" (Sirach 24:3, 9). The Wisdom of Solomon, written probably about the middle of the first century B.C., in praise of God's Wisdom, has this to say: "She is a breath of the power of God, and a clear reflection of the glory of the Almighty. . . . She is a radiance from everlasting light, and a spotless mirror of the working of God, and an image of his goodness" (7:25f.).

Especially the last passage suggests that "image" is not understood in the sense of an accurate copy of someone, but as a highly dynamic force which represents the source from which it springs. It is a living power which participates in the life of its source and communicates it to others far distant from the source itself. It is the "image" of the invisible God who cannot be represented by any copy, not only because the invisible is logically nonrepresentable by anything visible, but because the majesty and holiness of God are protected in Old Testament and Jewish tradition from all human craving to worship elements of creation through the second commandment of the Decalogue, which prohibits images of Yahweh by any likeness in the universe, be it celestial, terrestrial, or chthonic. God's Wisdom as God's image, in Jewish tradition, is an act of God through which he grants his own presence, opens his own riches, and so communicates himself to everything that lives as a part of his creation.

The emergence of the figure of Wisdom in Old Testament and later Jewish wisdom literature is a profound reflection on the nature of Yahweh and his relation to the created world. God who cannot be imaged by anything in nature is, by the prohibition of images, so distanced from everything in the natural world that he would appear to be forever removed in unapproachable solitude. If God is without analogy in the universe, if there is no natural bridge between him and the product of his word and will, how can there be any communication between him and created beings, any understandable and expressible dialogue between him who dwells in mystery utterly beyond our reach, and ourselves who are not God? The personalized figure of God's Wisdom provided an answer to that question because it differentiated between God in essential distinction from everything in creation, on the one hand, and God in his gracious self-direction toward a world completely different from him, on the other. First in the form of a created companion of God before creation, and later in the idea of an ongoing radiance from God, God's Wisdom was God in his active, powerful and gracious relation to all of creation. In Sirach 24, Wisdom, although still created by God, is coming forth from God's mouth, i.e., she is the word of God with which God communicates to a cosmos which, in and of itself, can furnish no image of God. Wisdom is God himself in the act, in the incomprehensible miracle, of making himself present through his word, which is to say through the meaningful and personal self-communication that occurs in the act of one person speaking to another. The figure of Wisdom is the metaphor for the act of an imageless God who communicates himself as person to person through his word. This was God's intention from the beginning of time, therefore Wisdom is preexistent with him before creation; and there is purpose, order, meaning, and joy in creation, because Wisdom was with God when creation began.

The first stanza of the poem in Colossians 1:15–20 identifies Christ with God's Wisdom before all creation. He embraces all of creation from its inception ("In him all things . . . were created," v. 16); he is the creative power of God himself ("All things were created through him," v. 16); and he is the destiny of creation ("for him," or "toward him," v. 16). He is creation's home, origin, and goal. Regarding the Colossian philosophy, one may conclude that the poem is introduced into the letter to state that the four basic "elements of the world," together with all "thrones or dominions or rules or authorities" (1:16), have no independent existence or power. They are created in, through, and for Christ, and they are therefore entirely subject to Christ's dominance over all.

Somehow—the poem does not explain why—creation did not remain under the dominion of Christ. The "elements of the world" and the "rules and authorities" were no longer held together in him (1:17), and the body of the universe ceased to have Christ as its head (1:18). Consequently, hostility arose in heaven and on earth so great that only an act of God, comparable in magnitude and consequence to the first creation, could restore peace. This act of making peace is the reconciliation of all things to God through Christ's resurrection from the dead (1:18, 20).

Looking back now on the discussion of the Colossian philosophy and the background of the poem, Colossians 1:15–20, in the Jewish wisdom tradition, we can ask the question: What is the peace won by Christ's resurrection which is, in 1:20, said to be identical with the reconciliation of all things?

1. The peace in heaven and on earth is won by the firstborn from the dead. This implies that death is seen as the enemy, as in 1 Corinthians 15:26, who is defeated in the resurrection of Jesus Christ. In 1 Corinthians 15:24–26 death is in company with "every rule, and every authority and power," as the firstborn from the dead in Colossians 1:18 is associated with these heavenly forces (Col. 1:16). But while in 1 Corinthians 15 death is the "last enemy" whose ultimate defeat lies still in the future, in Colossians 1:18–20 the victory of Christ is already accomplished. The attention of the poem is drawn completely to the triumph of the firstborn alone, and in him—in him alone—the victory is won.

Within the context of the whole letter, the victory of the first-born over death is imaged in pictures of a military exploit. The "rules and authorities" are marched through the streets as captives taken in war (2:15). They are vanquished by a superior force, subdued in chains, and displayed in public as impotent. Their reduction to powerlessness is analogous to the pacification with which the Roman legions secure the Roman peace. It is, once more, manifest how much the Old Testament tradition of Yahweh's wars against his human and metahuman opponents remain in full force. But this pacification campaign is also the reconciliation to God of all that is in heaven and on earth. God's conquest of the powers in heaven and on earth is not aimed at their eventual destruction but at their restoration to a place and function in which resurrection unleashes its power to re-create. No terrestrial or celestial reality is left outside the resurrection power of the firstborn from the dead.

The poem in Colossians 1:15–20 is placed in the letter as part of an answer to the Colossian philosophy with its preoccupation with the elements of the world. This philosophy offered, in modern terms, a complete philosophy of nature. The basic substances of all being were thought to be known, their admixture and effect upon one another was classified, and the goal of the system was the overcoming of the war throughout the universe which caused the permanent disposition to natural catastrophes and to the subjection of humans to the vicissitudes of an unpredictable fate. Peace, to the Colossian Christian philosophers, was bound up with a number of regulations designed to bring human life into conformity with its nature-given order, offering escape to the soul destined to its aerial home. The claim of Christ as the peacemaker and reconciler of all things (Col. 1:20) denies the viability of this philosophy. The will is declared invalid to derive, from observations of the natural world, an insight into that which makes for the salvation of human life and the whole universe. The elements of the world are pacified and reconciled through Christ's resurrection alone, in which the "elemental" force of the creator of the universe acts in triumph. But the denial of the Colossian philosophy also has a positive side. In the firstborn from the dead the elements of the world are reconstituted and therefore also affirmed. Their reconstitution and affirmation has not happened through their own power; they are forced into a new order of all things through the event, comparable only to creation itself, in which God re-creates nature in resurrection. But in this re-creation, nature throughout heaven and earth has come into its own. The universe with its myriads of known and unknown realities is, in the event of Christ's resurrection, reinstalled as God's good creation. In and through this event it deserves honor, love, and gratitude.

2. The affirmation of nature in the reconciliation of all things through Christ's resurrection does not produce, in Colossians, some kind of Christian philosophy of nature. The Colossian philosophers, who aim at the introduction of some ecclesiastical version into the system of the four elements of the world, are attacked as troublers of the community and as false guides to wisdom.

Colossians makes no attempt to explain in what way the substances of nature might have collaborated in the resurrection. Christ's resurrection is understood as a primal event whose facticity and consequence can only be acknowledged without the endeavor to undergird or verify it by means of previous insight into the nature of the universe. Christ's resurrection is a primal datum for nature outside of which no perception of the universe is possible, any more than thought on any aspect of being is thinkable without the datum of creation.

The knowledge of the peace gained by the firstborn from the dead is, in Colossians, the incorporation into the life-giving power of the risen Christ. The Christian is planted into a relationship in which God's power of creation and re-creation is at work through partnership in Christ's death and resurrection (2:11-12). This partnership is built on "the forgiveness of all our trespasses" (2:13) and it calls for putting to death attitudes and acts that deny the newness of life, and for putting on a form of life created by the power of the risen Lord (3:5-17). The secret of the attainment of peace lies in the participation in the death-dealing and life-bestowing energy of the firstborn of creation and the firstborn from the dead. No system of a philosophy of nature can validate, supplant, or augment this primal reality.

3. The peace of the universe, and the reconciliation of all things, are praised, in Colossians 1:20, as being established. No glance is cast at a creation that is still groaning in travail, being still in subjection to futility and in the bondage to decay (Rom. 8:20-22). As the poem concentrates entirely on creation and re-creation, leaving out the drama of a corruption of God's good work and any consequence it may yet have for nature and human life within it, so Christ is viewed entirely as origin, sphere, and goal of creation and re-creation alike. He is the will, act, and purpose of God as God directs himself to that which is, as creation, not God. Christ is throughout the poem, in both stanzas, glorified as one who stands on the side of God.

Therefore, the insistent exclusiveness in the entire poem is on him alone, and the accompanying summation of all that exists is in complete dependence on him. He is the image of God and firstborn of creation, he is the beginning and first-born from the dead; for him, in him, and through him is everything that has life; he is before all things and preeminent over all; in him is God's fullness, the head of all creation who holds together in divine greatness all of creation. Corre-spondingly, everything is subject to his reign, all creation whether in heaven or on earth is his domain, all things— repeated five times—are included in his government. It is clear that the identification of Christ with God's creative will and act is rooted in the adoption of Jewish thought on God's wisdom. But this explanation of its origin points only to a dependency in the stream of tradition that shaped Jewish language and reflection. Behind this dependency on a tradition, however, stands the conviction of Christian faith, long before the writing of Colossians, that Jesus Christ is in person the act, presence, and purpose of God in the world which is called into being by the one single God who spoke to Israel.

The praise of Yahweh in Israel had, centuries before New Testament times, found expressions in which nature appeared in pristine purity as a reality freed from signs of imperfection. In this praise, a new song is chanted to the King of kings in whose presence, and in whose reign, the worshiping people are encouraged to "let the sea roar, and all that fills it; the world and those who live in it. Let the floods clap their hands; let the hills sing together for joy at the presence of the Lord" (Ps. 98:7–9). Their song will "let the heavens be glad, and let the earth rejoice" (Ps. 96:11). In this praise, the rule of the only God and creator of all of nature is already honored without the shackles of corruption: "Sing, O heavens, for the Lord has done it; shout, O depths of the earth; break forth into singing, O mountains, O forest, and every tree in it! For the Lord has redeemed Jacob, and will be glorified in Israel" (Isa. 44:23).

The praise of Christ in Colossians 1:15–20 partakes in the characteristics of the praise of Yahweh in the Old Testament. Although it is put in a confessional form, the third person being used throughout, it shares in the forms of prayer and praise whose genuine expression is the address of God as "thou," in the second person. The poem makes statements about Christ representing God to all of creation. When it speaks of him, therefore, it expresses claims that can be uttered only in the voice of a community of faith which has in God the only, but also the fully sufficient, pledge of an all-inclusive comprehensiveness of power and grace.

Therefore the peacemaker Christ, the reconciler of all things, can be glorified only in the prayerful adoration that worships the beginning and the end of all things, leaping from the foundation of the universe in God directly to its consummation. This language of praise cannot be reduced to statements of fact based on the ordinary condition and apparent regularity of the world of nature. But the form of language rooted in prayer does not at all invalidate the statement itself;

rather it may provide occasion for the reminder that every sentence about God is as fleeting mist unless it is conceived and born of prayer, in which all language of God has its origin. The peace of nature, won in Christ's resurrection, is confessed truthfully and adequately only in the voice of one praying; in whose prayer God, who governs beginning and end, is at work.

2. Ephesians: Global Peace

Ephesians 2:11–22 concentrates on peace more directly than any other passage in the New Testament. In four verses (vs. 14–17) the word *eirēnē* is used four times, and into the whole section is woven a dialogue with three Old Testament oracles that are held together by the theme of peace.

> [11]So then, remember that at one time you Gentiles by birth, called "the uncircumcision" by those who are called "the circumcision"—a physical circumcision made in the flesh by human hands—[12]remember that you were at that time without Christ, being aliens from the commonwealth of Israel, and strangers to the covenants of promise, having no hope and without God in the world. [13]But now in Christ Jesus you who once were far off have been brought near by the blood of Christ. [14]For he is our peace; in his flesh he has made both groups into one and has broken down the dividing wall, that is, the hostility between us. [15]He has abolished the law with its commandments and ordinances, that he might create in himself one new humanity in place of the two, thus making peace, [16]and might reconcile both groups to God in one body through the cross, thus putting to death that hostility through it. [17]So he came and proclaimed peace to you who were far off and peace to those who were near, [18]for through him both of us have access in one Spirit to the Father. [19]So then you are no longer strangers and aliens, but you are citizens with the saints and also members of the household of God, [20]built upon the foundation of the apostles and prophets, with Christ Jesus himself as the cornerstone. [21]In him the whole structure is joined together and grows into a holy temple in the Lord; [22]in whom you also are built together spiritually into a dwelling place for God. (Eph. 2:11–22)

Ephesians begins and ends with greetings of peace (1:2 and 6:23), as is customary in Pauline letters. In 4:3, the statement about the essential unity of the church is introduced with the admonition to be eager "to maintain the unity of the Spirit in the bond of peace," and the description of the armor of God speaks, among other things, about being ready to proclaim the gospel of peace" (6:15). Neither Ephesians 4:3 nor 6:15 needs to be discussed separately because the linkage of peace and unity, and peace and gospel, is the essence of chapter 2:11–22 and will have to be considered there. All in all, however, peace is one of the dominating themes in Ephesians that contributes to the unique flavor of this letter in the New Testament.

The emphasis on peace in Ephesians 2:14–18 is connected to a strikingly large number of words that are also found in Colossians 1:15–20 and its immediate context. "Reconciliation," "hostility," "body," "through the cross," and "ordinances" (*dogmasin*) in Ephesians 2:15 and 16 are clearly reminiscent of Colossians 1:18, 20 and 2:14 (*dogma* meaning "regulation" appears in the New Testament only in Eph. 2:15 and Col. 2:14). But a dependency does not imply an identity of thought. In spite of the use of a common vocabulary, Ephesians 2:11–22 is quite different from the praise of the reconciliation of all things resulting in peace in heaven and on earth that triumphantly concludes the poem in Colossians 1:15–20. Peace in the Colossian hymn is associated with cosmic concerns, with the end points of history in creation and re-creation. Not so in Ephesians, where in 2:11–22, as well as in 4:3 and 6:15, the emphasis lies entirely on the establishment of peace at a time in history, for the human population of the earth, and on the announcement of this peace to all people near and far. Ephesians has a pronounced cosmological interest (1:10; 20f.; 3:10; 4:9f.). But it is not connected with the topic of peace, in contrast to Colossians 1:20, where this combination of themes predominates.

Three Isaiah oracles are woven into the texture of Ephesians 2:11–22. In all of them peace is at the core of the saying; they are Isaiah 9:6f.; 52:7; and 57:19. The birth of a prince from the house of David is announced in Isaiah 9:6–7. He will be given throne-names that designate him as a messianic ruler with unique powers. One of the names signifiying his unparalleled authority is the title "prince of peace." He will initiate a period of lasting peace: "His authority shall grow continually, and there shall be endless peace." Isaiah 52:7 speaks of a messenger who is dispatched to the Jewish exiles in Babylon to spread the good news (LXX *euangelizomenos*) that Yahweh has again affirmed his actual kingship on the holy mountain of Zion, and that therefore peace and salvation can be proclaimed for an Israel in captivity. In Isaiah 57:19, the announcement of peace is directed to all Jews, whether they are still living dispersed among a pagan population or whether they have already returned to their homeland: "Peace, peace, to the far and the near, says the Lord."

The author of Ephesians has, in accustomed Jewish manner, combined widely scattered sayings of scripture connected by a common topic. The use of Isaiah 52:7 and 57:19 in Ephesians 2:11–22 is clear. But Isaiah 5:6f., the prince of peace, is not directly introduced into the wording of Ephesians 2:14–18; yet there are very early rabbinical traditions suggesting that the sentence "He is our peace" (Eph. 2:14) echoes a virtual identification of the messiah with peace, based both on Isaiah 9:6 and on Isaiah 52:7. One of these traditions reports of Rabbi Yose Hagelili, who said around A.D. 110, "The name of the messiah is called peace, as it is said: Everlasting Father, Prince of Peace [Isa. 9:6]," and the same Rabbi made the statement, "Great is peace, because when the king messiah will reveal himself to Israel, he will begin with peace alone, as it is said: How beautiful upon the mountains are the feet of him who publishes good news, who announces peace [Isa. 52:7]." It appears probable that Jewish identifications of the prince of peace in Isaiah 9:6 with the messiah, as well as the messianic interpretation of the messenger of the good news of peace in Isaiah 52:7, have helped to produce the sentence in Ephesians 2:14, "[Christ] is our peace."

Ephesians 2:11–22 is addressed to Christians of Gentile origin (2:11). Their incorporation into the Christian community implies that Israel's history with God is made accessible to them; more than that, they have become implanted into this history so that they can become rightful heirs of its benefits. Ephesians 2:12 puts it this way: Before they had become members of the Christian community, the former Gentiles were separated from Christ, alienated from the citizens' right of Israel, estranged from the promise enshrined in God's commitment to Israel's history, caught in a life without hope, and, in the last analysis, stumbling through the world as though there was no God. In this sentence it is remarkable that separation from Christ is conceived to be, at the same time, alienation from Israel's privileges. Conversely, the end of the separation from Christ is simultaneously initiation into the special status of Israel before God. The presupposition for this argument is the view that Christ is already present in Israel's past history with God (cf. 1 Cor. 10:1–4). The benefits of Israel's life with God are concentrated in the person and name of Jesus Christ; and conversely, the riches of Israel's history with God are manifestations of a hidden presence of Christ within it. Israel's history, seen from this point of view, displays the rights of a citizenship in God's dominion whose powers are ultimately realized in Israel's messiah; it moves forward through several forms of covenant to a final promise that is kept in the messiah's work; it never comes to rest at any point till it reaches its culmination, from which it can be seen that Israel's life was one great history of hope in comparison to which all other hopes fade; and it drove toward a form of divine presence in the world, in the person of the messiah, that demotes other appearances of divine realities to a condition of godlessness. The announcements of peace in the oracles of Isaiah, in Ephesians 2:14–18, are the content of Israel's citizenship, of all the promises ever made to it, of all the hope it ever engendered, and of the truth of God's presence in the world. Citizenship, promises, hope, and the presence of God are collected into that peace of God which is one and the same as the person of Israel's messiah who, in person, is our peace (Eph. 2:14).

But that tells only part of the story, because the endorsement of Israel's history is peace also in a new sense. It removes a division which has so far rent the people of the world into two separate camps; it unites two hitherto hostile segments of humanity into a new body at peace with itself; and it does away with a distance established between some who were, as citizens, at home with God and some who were, as aliens, far away from God's rule. This messianic peace, which is Christ in person, is the elimination of a hostility which had so far split the world into two parts between which real peace was impossible.

Although written for a Christian community of pagan origin, Ephesians 2:11–22 is written from a standpoint set by the acceptance of God's election of Israel as the one single factor dominating the history of the world. Yahweh's election separates humanity, before the arrival of Christ, into two parts, and in view of this separation all other distinctions between nations and races are secondary. This way of dividing humanity is, of course, not the only one possible, and it helps the appreciation of the claim made by Ephesians 2:11–22 if we cast a glance at different divisions of the human population in the world which were commonly known some time before and during the emergence of the Christian communities in the Greco-Roman civilization.

After the conquest of the Persian empire by Alexander the Great, and the development of the Hellenistic successor states at the end of the fourth century B.C., Hellenistic society was divided by the consciousness of belonging either to the Greeks or to the barbarians. The ruling class of Greeks and Macedonians maintained a sense of superiority over the members of all subjected nations, who were uniformly classified as barbarians. These barbarians were not in full command of the Greek language, the language of the educated who ruled their foreign subjects, and they had only limited access to citizenship in a Hellenistic *polis,* which was restricted to those who had received their education in the Greek *gymnasion.* The prejudice against the barbarians was severe. They were considered uneducated and brutish, born slaves with a bent toward despotic attitudes, and between Greeks and barbarians there was an inequality so deep that, in spite of the necessary accommodations in practice, their relation was perceived to be an eternal war between them (Livy, *History* XXXI, 29, 15). The gradual sweep of Rome's conquests of Alexander's successor states changed this twofold division into a tripartite classification. The distinction between Greeks and barbarians was maintained, but the Romans are now added as a new element among the ruling class, dividing the world population into Romans, Greeks, and barbarians.

Among Jews of this period, the accustomed separation of all human life into Jews and Gentiles was maintained. The pull of Hellenistic civilization produced, during the reign of Antiochus Epiphanes in Syria, a Jewish movement that attempted cultural integration into Hellenistic society. Had it succeeded, it would have greatly modified the ancestral ways of separating Jews from Gentiles. Also, it carried attitudes liable to consider purely Jewish life as a form of barbarism. But this attempt at cultural integration was soon squelched by the victory of the Maccabean revolutionaries, who fully reestablished the traditional distinction between Jew and

Gentile. In spite of this, during New Testament times some Jewish writers were able to combine the Jewish view of the division Jew-Gentile with the Hellenistic habit of differentiating between Greeks and barbarians. Josephus can describe three groups that make up the population of Seleucia (Greeks, Syrians, and Jews; *Ant.* XVIII, 372), or a different composition of three basic population segments in Alexandria (Jews, Greeks, and Egyptians; *Against Apion* II, 68–70). This possibility of recognizing three essential components of humanity can also be traced in the New Testament. Paul can state that he is obliged to spread the gospel "both to Greeks and to barbarians," while he can also say, almost in the same breath, that he owes the gospel "to the Jew first and also to the Greek" (Rom. 1:16; cf. 1:14), and in Colossians 3:11 the world of humanity is divided into "Greek and Jew, . . . barbarian, Scythian," the Scythian being a particularly convincing example of what it means to be a barbarian.

These ways of dividing humanity into its basic parts were, however, counteracted in some measure by the rise of cosmopolitan convictions advanced by the dominant philosophy of the time, Stoicism. Stoic philosophers propagated the idea that, by nature, all human beings were the same. Refusing to yield to any of the popular divisions of the human race, they suggested that the true distinctions among humans were due neither to birth nor to education, but to the character an individual was able to produce, so that the evidence of a virtuous life, or the lack of it, provided the measure that alone truly separates one human life from the other. Thus, the whole world was the Stoics' home. They sponsored a feeling for the possibility of a cosmopolitan order encouraging the ideal of a citizenship in the world which could prevail over the prejudicial separations dividing humanity into falsely construed classes. A certain similarity to Stoic ideas in Ephesians 2:11–22 is undeniable, and it is possible that indirect influences from Stoicism contributed to the image of the one church in the whole letter.

In contrast to Stoic ideals, however, Ephesians 2:11–22 considers the separation between Jews and non-Jews, and the resulting mutual hostility, serious enough to require the destruction of a wall of separation (2:14). This involves far more than the elimination of superficial prejudices and the introduction of an enlightened view of the essential unity of all humanity. Christ is our peace because he has created a new reality and order of human community, imaged by the phrase "one new humanity." It stands in the place of two old communities alienated from each other by enmity (2:15). This new creation could be called into life only by the destruction of a dividing wall which is identified with "the law of commandments and ordinances."

The barrier of partition, consisting of a fence or wall, which is mentioned in Ephesians 2:14, has given rise to a variety of cosmological, mythological, and parabolic interpretations, often connected to a possible Gnostic or pre-Gnostic background of the passage. We adopt a straightforward understanding of the phrase, in keeping with the explanation in 2:15 that the wall of partition means the law with its commandments expressed in ordinances. The law of Moses was often likened, in Jewish thought, to the erection of a fence around Israel which was to safeguard its purity of life and guarantee the necessary separation from pagan life-styles and customs whenever a Jewish community lived together with non-Jewish populations. Passages from the *Letter of Aristeas,* written probably within the first century B.C., are so close to Ephesians 2:14 that they deserve to be quoted. The letter says that Moses, the wise legislator, "surrounded us [i.e., the Jews] with unbroken [or unbreakable] palisades and iron walls to prevent our mixing with any of the other peoples in any matter, being thus kept pure in body and soul, preserved from false beliefs, and worshiping the only God omnipotent over all creation" (v. 139). A little later it is stated that "to prevent our being perverted by contact with others or by mixing with bad influences, he hedged us in on all sides with strict observances connected with meat and drink and touch and hearing and sight, after the manner of the law" (v. 142). Obedience to the law of Moses is interpreted, in the *Letter of Aristeas,* not as capricious subservience to a set of external regulations, but as the form of human life that is lived in purity and justice and that conforms to the laws of nature and so produces a life in harmony with the cosmic order. The fence of the law preserves the necessary distinctiveness of this life and enables a pattern of conduct through which human life is elevated to a quality in keeping with the will of the one creator of all things. Jewish separateness, enforced and guarded by the Mosaic law, became constantly a source of irritation, and often the cause of downright hatred, among the pagan population, who ridiculed, resented, and oppressed the Jewish inhabitants of their cities. When Ephesians 2:14 speaks of the Mosaic law as "the dividing wall of hostility," the word "hostility" must be taken in the full and literal sense. There is plenty of evidence that the law brought about both an attitude of hostility on the part of Jews against their pagan neighbors and intense enmity on the part of pagans against Jews.

The attitude of moral superiority over their pagan neighbors is frequently very pronounced in the writings of the Jews. Although there are some teachers who were ready to admit high moral achievements by some individual pagans, including the expectation that those pagans were worthy of being granted life eternal in the world to come, the emphasis lies on a pronouncedly negative judgment on the Gentiles as individuals and as nations. Since the time of Abraham and Moses, God has bound himself in a covenantal relation to Israel that implies the rejection of the Gentile world. Pagans are before God like the chaff that the wind drives away, even like rubbish that is burnt by fire. They are rightly despised by Jews, and even hated. Although characteristic of only a segment of Judaism in New Testament times, a few sentences from the Qumran community can typify an orientation that was everywhere at least a latent possibility for Jews. It was incumbent on true Jews "to love all the children of light" but also "to hate all the children of darkness," because God had commanded them through Moses and the prophets "to love all that He has chosen and hate all that He has despised" (1QS 1:3–4 and 9–10). (For this paragraph, see the evidence in the collection of rabbinical material by H. L. Strack and P. Billerbeck, vol. III, 139–155, and the long essay in vol. IV/1, 353–414, listed in the Select Bibliography to this chapter.)

But resentment, hatred, and hostility were by no means reserved for the Jewish side. Pagan society was, for its part, vigorously engaged in the effort to malign the Jews. Privileges granted to Jews by the Roman administration were resented. Particularly the Jews' freedom from military service and the right to maintain their own legal system were eyed with envy by the Gentile population. Judgment by individual Roman writers reflect a deep-seated distrust of Jews that is caused by the seemingly impious refusal to honor the gods, excepting One who could not even be venerated in images; by their tendency to isolation; and by their insistence on opposing all attempts at integration into the larger cultural body. At the beginning of the first century B.C., Appolonius Molon declares Jews to be atheists, misanthropic creatures who have to be held as the most stupid of all the barbarians who have not contributed a single useful invention to better human life. Cicero is unable to see in Judaism anything but a barbarous superstition, and practically at the same time as the writing of Ephesians, a man of the fairness and character of Tacitus produces in his *Histories* a fairly lengthy description of the history and nature of Judaism that is highly unfavorable. Tacitus' account is a curious mixture of grossly erroneous information, some glimpses of sympathetic understanding, and an inability to do justice to so strange a phenomenon. Tacitus knows of the exodus from Egypt, which was however, according to his information, enforced by the Pharaoh because he wanted "to purge his kingdom and to transport this race into other lands, since it was hateful to the gods." Being exhausted by a lack of water in the wilderness, the expelled Jews were conducted to an oasis by a herd of asses, and proceeded later to worship the ass in memory of this event. "The Jews regard as profane all that we hold sacred; on the other hand, they permit all that we abhor." They first celebrated the seventh day in memory of the day of their liberation, "but after a time they were led by the charms of indolence to give over the seventh year as well to inactivity." Their rites are preserved by their antiquity, but "the other customs of the Jews are base and abominable, and owe their persistence to their depravity." As a nation, they are "extremely loyal toward one another, and always ready to show compassion; but toward every other people they feel only hate and enmity" (Tacitus, *Histories* V, 3–5). If such was the judgment of a man of the nobility of a Tacitus, it is little wonder that relations between Jews and non-Jews in Hellenistic cities were frequently marred by ugly incidents often resulting in the murder and expulsion of Jews. In Josephus's report, Jews and pagans in Alexandria live in perpetual strife (*JW* II, 487); in Antioch bloody conflict occurs during the time of Vespasian (*JW* VII, 46–53); in Caesarea repeated clashes take place which claim lives (*JW* II, 266–270, 284–292, 457–460); and the hatred of Gentile mobs is vented against Jews in murderous persecutions in Ashkelon, Ptolemais, Tyre, Hippos, Gadara, and Damascus (*JW* II, 477–480, 559–561).

The "dividing wall of hostility" (Eph. 2:14, RSV) erected

by the law (2:15) between Jews and non-Jews is a stark and concrete reality at the time of the writing of Ephesians. Jewish awareness of a special place on the scene of world history, often resulting in suspicion, fear, and even hatred of the vastly more numerous pagan population, is as real as the pagan resentment of Jews, which expresses itself on a scale of feelings and acts ranging from bafflement, credulity of fantastic rumors, to contempt and organized massacres. The declaration of peace in Ephesians 2:14–18 is to be understood against this background as offering a new reality of peace in which the old enmity is effectively removed.

By the use of a variety of images, Ephesians 2:11–22 lays the greatest stress on the formation and growth of a new community strong enough to overcome the old division. The pagan world, once far away from the place for which it was in God's mystery destined to belong, has now, in the new community, been brought home (2:13, 17). Both Jews and pagans are now, in a new society, made one (2:14) because they share the same spirit (2:18). Both are now reconciled to God through one event, valid for both, and made into a single body so that they can be likened to a new individual into which the two formerly hostile persons are merged (2:16–17). The concern of Ephesians 2:11–22 is the emergence of an alternative society, grounded on peace, spreading peace, and preserving peace.

Ephesians 2:11–22 states its case for peace on the assumption that the world of human history is divided into two groups. Other divisions may and do exist, but they are reduced to insignificance once the split between Jew and pagan has entered consciousness. We have seen that the Hellenistic world knew of other basic divisions that dominated the realities of daily life. Ephesians disregards these possibilities of drawing lines to determine essential differences among populations. The letter affirms the abiding validity and truth of the history of the one God with one unique human community down to the event of a reconciliation—an event through which the special community of Israel and a large body of people who until now were "without God in the world" (2:12) became recreated into a new "nation." To Ephesians, the division of Israel from non-Israel is deeper and more consequential than any other division affecting the human race through its cultural, societal, and religious realities. Set against this basic division, all other distinctions become relegated to the twilight of a fundamental sameness. The removal of the only division that matters leads to the creation of a oneness of humanity as a whole. This takes the form of a token which is put into the world of a thousand divisions and proceeds to incorporate a new humanity of global dimensions. The peace Ephesians has in mind is nothing less than the peace of the human family as a whole.

Ephesians 2:16 emphasizes that the new people of peace were brought to their new condition by an act of reconciliation through which Jews and non-Jews were equally liberated from their enmity against God. Christ, who came to make peace, lived so that he "might reconcile both groups to God in one body, through the cross, thus putting to death that hostility through it." In the execution of Christ on a cross, the ground for hostility between Jew and pagan has been removed. After all, both Jews and pagans share the responsibility for this execution. While our Gospels in the New Testament distribute the burden of guilt differently, some stressing more the Jewish responsibility for Jesus' death and some giving a larger share of the blame to the Roman administration, they are unanimous in providing a picture of the events in which both the Roman governor and the Jewish leadership unite in pronouncing a verdict and in carrying out a sentence that imposes the penalty of death on the Son of God. In this verdict and its execution, Jew and non-Jew are acting as one. The dividing wall erected through the law was, in this joint judicial act, in fact removed because it did not prevent the Jewish supreme court from consorting with the pagan power to effect a killing on whose necessity, for different reasons, they did in fact agree.

The dividing wall of hostility is rendered ineffectual by the actual joining of Jews and pagans on one all-important decision amounting to the forced exclusion of God's living presence and grace. But it is also removed in another, positive, sense. The death of Christ is, in continuation of the Pauline tradition, understood as the sacrifice of a life given by a righteous person on behalf of others who need atonement with God. If the phrase "in one body" in Ephesians 2:16 should refer to Christ's death, meaning "in the one body of the crucified," the atoning power of Christ's sacrifice would be underscored. This is, however, not likely to be the intent of the verse. In agreement with the consistent use of the phrase in other sections of Ephesians, "in the one body" is more probably to be understood to mean "in the church." The verse, then, immediately places the weight on the ecclesiolog-ical aspect, drawing the consequences of Christ's atoning death for the existence and mission of the one new communi-ty which is founded on peace and exists for peace.

The notion of oneness is already dominant in Ephesians 2:11–22, and the peace that the passage announces is indis-solubly connected to this unity. Two estranged societies have been made one in this peace (2:14), and one new person has been created out of two former enemies, establishing peace (2:15). This joining of peace and unity is reinforced in Ephesians 4:3 and its immediate sequel. There the encour-agement "to maintain the unity of the Spirit in the bond of peace" is followed by a statement that underlines the theme of unity with a listing of the special gifts of the one God to the one church. "There is one body and one Spirit, just as you were called to the one hope of your calling,

> one Lord, one faith, one baptism,
> one God and Father of all,
> who is above all and through all and in all." (4:4–6)

In this sequence of verses the gifts of God, which make the Christian community what it is, are thematically connected with the oneness of God, of Christ, and of the Spirit. This way of combining the special characteristics of a community with the oneness of God has precedents in Hellenistic Judaism, and it helps our understanding of Ephesians if this evidence is given some consideration. By way of an example, some passages from Josephus may be mentioned here. Josephus can refer to unique institutions and people, and to particular historical facts, to claim their function as witnesses to the one God. Moses, that unique historical personality, introduced Israel to the conviction that there was one God alone, and he consequently initiated a theocracy in Israel that would corre-spond in terms of historical reality to the faith in one single God (*Against Apion* II, 164–167). Although Josephus does not do so, one could well reduce his sentences to the formula "one God, one Moses, one law." The singularity of God is also reflected in the world through the existence of the one people of Israel, who, alone among all other nations, subject themselves to the government of the one God. Therefore, theirs is only one holy city, only one temple, and only one altar; these, excluding all other holy cities, temples, and altars, function as the representation of the one God by his one people: "for God is one and the Hebrew race is one" (*Ant.* IV, 200–201). Exactly that which is most particular in Israel's existence—its exclusive place of worship and its unique institutions—is representative of the one God in a world that pays homage to scores of deities. In the same manner, Ephesians 4:4–6 enumerates the gifts of God to the church, those which are most unmistakably Christian, as the signs of a oneness representing the oneness of God in a world split by discord and strife. The peace on which the church is founded, in which and for which the church lives, is a visible, concrete, and societal reality. It is charged to give evidence of the one God by maintaining in its unity the peace that has overcome even the most severe of all divisions.

We do not know how numerous the Christians were in the area addressed by Ephesians in the last quarter of the first century A.D., but it is safe to assume that they were still a small minority. Their task was to image a new vision and reality: that of a global human community no longer torn apart by hostility. This, however, could be achieved only in the form of a sign for a society at large that continued to be organized along very different lines. Ephesians, however, looks forward to the growth of the one body of Christ toward a completion in which this body replaces everything else in the world. Thus the victory of Christ will bring about a total unity in which a total peace has been accomplished. Christ is installed as God's co-regent over the entire world, subduing all hostile powers in the heavens, and is made "the head over all things for the church, which is his body, the fullness of him who fills all in all" (Eph. 1:22–23). The growth of the church into a holy temple of the one God (Eph. 2:21) is therefore also the growth of a new unity in the human race and an expansion of the peace realized in this unity. The growth of the church is intended to advance the unity and peace of this new community, the signpost and pioneer of an ultimate unity and peace in which all who are members of the global human family are united.

The growth of the church, and with it the advance of the peace and unity of the human family, cannot be won without a struggle. Precisely as instruments of God's peace, Christians require an armor of God; and to this belongs being ready to proclaim "the gospel of peace" (6:15). The conflict to be endured is, however, not with "blood and flesh" (6:12), but precisely with those forces and powers above and beyond human enmities, parties, and divisions. Such forces represent might ungoverned and opposed to the one God (6:12), the God whose innermost mystery was disclosed in the making of peace (3:9–10). Christian guardianship for peace is the sustained resistance to those forces which divide the world into opposing camps, worship power for its own sake, and capitulate to a concept of reality in which disunity and hostility is considered inevitable. Christian peacemaking is, at its root, not the advocacy of any given system, form of government, or cause, but rather the resistance to any claim of any powers whatsoever that would establish a dependency on anything or anyone except the rule of God in Christ through the presence of the Spirit. Christian peacemaking goes to the roots of evil. It cannot be content with seeking remedies for the symptoms of the world's malady in its fever for conflict. Rather, it penetrates to the cause of divisions and overcomes the proclivity to conflict by abdicating every loyalty except that which resides in the one God. For it is the one God who has brought peace to all of humanity—in the death of the one Lord on whose presence in the Spirit the building of a truly united humanity depends.

Select Bibliography

Diels, H., and W. Kranz. *Die Fragmente der Vorsokratiker.* 6th ed. Zurich: Weidmann, 1985.

Hengel, Martin. *Jews, Greeks and Barbarians: Aspects of the Hellenization of Judaism in the Pre-Christian Period.* Philadelphia: Fortress Press, 1980.

Martin, Ralph P. *Reconciliation: A Study of Paul's Theology.* Atlanta: John Knox Press, 1981.

Schweizer, Eduard. *Der Brief an die Kolosser.* Evangelisch-Katholischer Kommentar zum Neuen Testament 12. Zurich: Benziger Verlag; Neukirchen/Vluyn: Neukirchener Verlag, 1980. (This commentary lists, on p. 17, five essays of the author on Col. 1:20 and the question of the "elements of the world," to which may be added the author's interesting account in more autobiographical style in his recent book *Jesus Christ, The Man from Nazareth and the Exalted Lord,* Macon, Ga.: Mercer University Press, 1987, pp. 72–81.) Very convenient for the reader of

English is the author's translation of the pertinent texts in the article "Slaves of the Elements and Worshipers of Angels: Gal 4:3, 9 and Col 2:8, 18, 20," *Journal of Biblical Literature* 107/3 (1988): 455–468.

Strack, Hermann L., and Paul Billerbeck. *Kommentar zum Neuen Testament aus Talmud und Midrasch,* vols. III and IV, 1. 6th ed. Munich: C. H. Beck, 1975.

Stuhlmacher, Peter. "'He Is Our Peace' (Eph. 2:14): On the Exegesis and Significance of Eph. 2:14–18." In idem, *Reconciliation, Law & Righteousness: Essays in Biblical Theology.* Philadelphia: Fortress Press, 1986, 180–200. Eng. Trans. of "'Er ist unser Friede' (Eph 2, 14): Zur Exegese und Bedeutung von Eph 2, 14–18." In *Versöhnung, Gesetz und Gerechtigkeit: Aufsätze zur biblischen Theologie,* 224–245. Göttingen: Vandenhoeck & Ruprecht, 1981. (The essay emphasizes the importance of the Old Testament references in Eph. 2:14–18.)

8

Peace
in the New Testament
and Peace Today

This book is written with the conviction that now, more urgently than ever before, is the time for peace (chapter 1). The study of the aspects of peace in the Bible, and particularly in the New Testament, is presented in the interests of the search for peace today (chapters 2–7). In this concluding chapter we will return to our own time and ask how the Christian concern for peace, and Christian work for peace, may be guided and shaped by attention to the subject of peace in the Old Testament, and above all in the New Testament. Both the questions we explore, and the answers we seek, in respect to peace at the close of the twentieth century will have to be informed by this dialogue with the Bible. But the goal before us in this last chapter is set by the necessities of our own time.

In the preceding chapters, images and concepts of peace in the Bible have emerged whose variety is remarkable. The meaning of *shalom* and *eirene* is unusually wide. Even if one concentrates exclusively on the New Testament, "peace" cannot be reduced to a uniform idea. Different Christian communities contribute distinctive shades of meaning to the word. New Testament passages utilize previously developed Jewish traditions about "peace" that have quite distinct connotations. Some books in the New Testament emphasize a particular meaning of "peace" that is not repeated anywhere else in the canonical collection (Colossians and Ephesians). Sometimes *eirene* is subject to the social conditions of the Christian communities in a specific time and place, lending a meaning to the word that is somewhat in conflict with the understanding arrived at by other communities. For example, "peace" for the Matthean communities under the threat of governmental oppression is quite clearly different from the relatively positive evaluation of the Pax Romana in Acts.

It is not possible, therefore, to extract from the New Testament a set of direct instructions about peacemaking. On this point, as on any other, the New Testament, as much as the Old Testament, cannot be treated like a code of law whose content requires only contemporary interpretation and application. What is required of us is the effort to let the many, distant, and sometimes disturbing voices of the Bible speak to us in their manifold variety.

A summary of New Testament teaching is not of itself a ready and sufficient instruction for the Christian community's responsibility concerning peace today. The conditions of life at the close of the twentieth century need to be addressed by what we can hear the New Testament say, and in that dialogue perceptions and directives will be found by contemporary Christian theology and ethics that are not merely copies of biblical concepts and commands. Precisely because the New Testament, and indeed the Bible in its entirety, is to the Christian community a living word of God, it must inspire responses and responsibilities today that are new answers in a new day. We shall attempt, in this concluding section, to state the case for Christian peacemaking in our time in answer to the New Testament's guidance.

1. The Gift of Peace

In the New Testament, God makes peace. The Christian community receives the gift of peace. Long before it can get involved in its own efforts to establish peace, the Christian community is founded in the act of God which makes peace. The community lives in the enjoyment of this treasure which makes its very existence possible. It has not produced God's peace, nor will it ever improve on it. The peace of God is already established for the Christian community once and for all, and the community can add nothing to it. In the Son of God, the gracious and effective rule of God over human history has come with its peace, and the Christian community is constituted by this peacemaking act of God. For all Christian efforts at making peace, it remains forever basic that the peace of God is received as an unearned divine gift, given as freely as the grace of God itself.

The Christian community *remembers* God's gift of peace. God's act of peacemaking is identical with the life, death, and resurrection of Jesus Christ. The good news of this one act of making peace is, first and foremost, remembered in the Christian community. As the gospels in the New Testament preserve this memory, so the Christian community today can do no more than keep the same memory alive. The church, in teaching and doctrine, in preaching and mission, in service and not least in making peace, is permanently and essentially indebted to that memory. Therefore, the church's first responsibility in its peacemaking is the resolve to keep the remembrance of God's peacemaking in Christ as vigorous and as true as possible. The church's task to spread the peace of God is, seen from this primary point, the task of a constantly renewed vigilance to express in new language, and in new thinking, the declaration of God's peace in ways that do not abridge or dilute the gospel. The primary vehicle that transmits memory is the spoken or written word in which the subject of the memory presents itself. The church acknowledges and honors God as the first and sufficient peacemaker by the energy and devotion with which it goes about the business of caring for words that transmit God's act as memory.

This is not to say, of course, that Christian peacemaking does not marshal will and activity. Christian peacemaking calls for acts. But that must not obscure the fact that it is God who is the primary peacemaker, and that the divine act of making peace through Christ charges the church with the primary responsibility to ascertain the gospel of peace as the vehicle of the memory of God's peacemaking.

It must be said quite bluntly: Christian peacemaking is at root a farewell to self-reliance. Christians are people who hear and heed the word of God. They are, first and foremost and permanently, listeners and students of this word, which makes them what they are. In the matter of peacemaking this primary condition is not changed in the least. If a church rushes into all kinds of peace activities without first being ready to hear what the good news of peace says about God as peacemaker, it will fall prey to an arbitrary set of convictions about what peace is and how it can be achieved. The degree of faithfulness to its status as listener is, for the church, also the degree of its effectiveness as witness to God's peacemaking.

The gift of God's peace is, however, not only remembered. The Christian community also *puts this gift to use,* and the way in which it is used honors the primacy of God as peacemaker. We recall at this point how frequently, in the Gospels of the New Testament, peacemaking is cast in the form of narratives that tell of totally inexplicable and novel acts of healing and restoration—acts that cancel out the bondage to conditions in which human life, together with its corresponding experience of nature, is at odds with God. And we recall also the stress in the epistles of the New Testament on the formation of a new quality of human life through the power of the Spirit of God, in which peace is made.

The Christian community, in its life in peace and its concern and work for peace, is encouraged to take seriously God's peacemaking by putting it to use in a way that expects miracles to happen. By this we mean the successful break-through of new and amazing events in which the gracious will of God restores the health of individuals and corporate units, and even the life of nature, and does so in a way that denies and actually eliminates the habits of thought, conventions, attitudes, and acts that, even in much Christian theology, are called "real life" and that are "in reality" the consequences of a wholesale rebellion against God. If Christian peacemaking is occupied with this kind of reversal, it will have no option but to implore the power of God, the peacemaker, to accomplish the miraculous. The Christian peacemakers' feet are, then, set on a ground that is beyond our control, defies our calculations, and runs counter to the vast majority of our experiences, together with the "wisdom" about "real life" that we have accumulated on the basis of those experiences. Events in the area of international politics should not be excluded from this consideration; rather, the Christian community has plenty of reasons to feel deeply ashamed in view of the fact that a Gandhi of India, a Sadat of Egypt, and in recent years a Gorbachev of the Soviet Union have, each in different ways, demonstrated the courage to abandon dusty prejudices and have ventured to conduct "real politics" in risking fashion to advance peace in ways contrary to deeply ingrained habits. It should be a cause for serious soul searching, not to say repentance, that those three men were and are not members of the Christian community, and that the Christian communities with which they were acquainted have not been the stimulus that drove them, or at least assisted them, in their actions.

Finally, the gift of God's peace to the Christian community is not only remembered, and not only put to use, it is also *expected in hope*. The Christian peacemaker preserves the primacy of God's act in establishing peace by having been put on a road on which the miraculous is the norm. This implies that no step on this road can be taken unless it is taken in the hope that the power of God, which we can in no way ever domesticate, will accompany our steps in re-creating what has sadly come to grief. And even if miracles of restoration happen here and there on this road—they do!—there will also be a lot of territory that remains arid and intractable because no dew of God has yet fallen on it. There simply is no shortage of Christian experience in which peacemaking has not yet happened, as plenty of the stuff of life holds on stubbornly to a condition that cries out for future liberation from its fetters. The "once and for all" of God's making peace remains unverifiable by our senses and perceptions in a great many real situations, yet it summons us to the expectation that this "once and for all" will in the end become "sensible" and perceptible to all in all. Therefore, Christian peacemaking can, precisely when it is serious about its own business, be only the beginning of a journey whose end we cannot see, but on which we embark confidently because hope in the God of peace envisions the completion of God's own act of making peace for all the world.

2. The Process of Peace

The New Testament participates with the Old Testament in offering an astonishing wealth of meanings for the words *shalom* and *eirēnē*. This richness of scope challenges modern peace efforts through the realization of the highly dynamic nature of the biblical understanding of peace.

Health and money, food and clothing, justice and security are factors in the establishment and preservation of peace, as much as are a good conscience before God and a life that draws its strength from the ever-renewed forgiveness of God. To put it into more technically modern terms: Medical science and practice, economic theories and systems, the production and distribution of food, shelter, and clothing, the development of laws and the administration of legal practice, protection from threats against the freedom and good order of public life—all these areas affect peace in the understanding of the Christian community as long as it is guided by the wide range of the biblical concept. Conversely, peace is not maintained by harmonious relations between governments of nations and states alone. Economic exploitation of people and their relegation to mass poverty, caused by whatever economic theory and system, amounts to a declaration of war against them even if no bullet is ever fired. Carelessness and neglect in the provision of health services is a serious disturbance of the peace. The toleration of injustice—be it through the formation of different standards for different people, or weakness in the prosecution of criminality, or the elimination of equality before the law through the domination of an ideology of elitism—is in all cases the irruption of a chaos that banishes peace from the land.

Peace, guided by a biblical understanding, can therefore not be understood as a static condition. It is reached in a process in which a multiplicity of forces interact. Everything in peace is life and movement, and any standing still on a point once achieved constitutes a danger to peace. It was said above that the primacy of God as peacemaker implies an abiding limitation to all human self-reliance. Nothing can be taken back from this statement. The Christian community receives God's peace as a free gift, and it remains forever with regard to this gift a learner and listener whose actions on behalf of peace can neither produce nor modify nor supplement the peace of God. But that does not mean that the Christian community is, in matters of making peace, condemned to passivity. On the contrary, it is precisely the peace from God which initiates, prods, and impels the community to ceaseless activity for the sake of peace. It is, as a community of the God of peace, empowered to constant vigilance and to heightened sensitivity for peace in the world. And this vigilance and sensitivity reaches into all areas of life in the effort to open every aspect of human history to the blessing of peace.

By virtue of its calling through the God of peace, the Christian community knows that peace is God's design in every reality in which it lives. It is involved in the process of letting peace come to power, of letting peace subdue any and all forces hostile to it. But every Christian community lives in a particular place and time within which it accepts its commission to make peace. Since peace is a process in the flux of human history, it is not always and everywhere impeded by the same forces. For the Christian community this has the consequence that it will need to discern, at the place and time allocated to it, the particular shape of those factors which endanger peace. Christian peacemaking is, for that reason, not the same thing at every time and in every place. The first task for the Christian community is the discernment of what, in the configuration of power at this community's special location, is the particular set of potencies that make for the loss of peace. In one place, the archenemy of peace may well be an oppressive political system that subjects its victims to indignity and impotence. In another place, it may be an unrestrained ideology that grants license to every form of greed at the expense of all whose conscience does not permit the unbridled lust for accumulating riches and possessions. Somewhere else, it may be a condition of cultural, educational, and technological backwardness that results in permanent dependence on more advanced populations who can and will use this dependence to enforce their own will and further their own advantage, to the virtual enslavement of the less advanced. And it can be, in yet another area, the emergence of a martial spirit in a nation that worships brute force for the attainment of its presumed position of preeminence in the world. The shapes and faces of those forces which destroy peace in the world are changeable. Like God's antagonist in the Bible, they have many names, and they refuse to be pinned down to a hierarchy of evil that could provide the Christian community with a permanent measuring stick with which to gauge the dimensions of the threat to peace.

It is therefore to be expected that Christian communities the world over will, even at the same moment of history, not find the same answer to the question of what is the basic counterforce to peace. Their differences may well be situated in their different circumstances, and the differences are then a sign that their response is alive. The virus that infects the peace of the world is not everywhere the same, and consequently proper diagnoses of the infection must differ. Of course, the differences in the diagnosis by the Christian communities may also be caused by a lack of discernment, by a shallow insight into the realities impeding peace, and by a lack of commitment to the spirit that makes Christian discernment possible. But even the deepest and most insightful recognition of what needs to be done to enhance peace will be different in separate Christian communities. On the worldwide scale, and in ecumenical cooperation, what is expected of Christian communities in the pursuit of peace, then, is the sharing of analyses and projects, the exploration of possible joint strategies, and the patience and openness required to endure, and even encourage, each other's frank criticism.

3. The Discipline of Peace

Christian prayer for kings and leaders in government is said (1 Tim. 2:2) to aim at the community's "quiet and peaceable life" in society. The ideal of tranquillity is perhaps more pronounced in the pastoral epistles than anywhere else in the New Testament, but it cannot be said to be unparalleled elsewhere. The favorable estimate of the Pax Romana in Acts and the positive view of the power of the Roman empire to assure a measure of justice and safety (Rom. 13:1–7 and 1 Peter 2:13–17) are sufficient evidence, among other indicators, that the New Testament holds in high regard the existence of a civil order in which strife and turmoil are reduced to a minimum.

But this aspect of peace in the New Testament must not be misconstrued in arriving at the conclusion that the Christian community's attitude toward state and society, and its orientation to peace among its own members, consists in a quietism which avoids at all cost any involvement in struggle and controversy. The infamous German slogan "Ruhe ist die erste Bürgerpflicht" ("Quietness is the citizen's first duty") is in no way a true conclusion from the New Testament. On the contrary, peace in the New Testament is the result of a battle in which a whole army of forces hostile to God is defeated. The arrival of God's kingdom is conditioned by the subjection of "every rule and every authority and power" other than God's own, which entails a conquest in which all enemies are put under God's feet (1 Cor. 15:24–25). To be sure, the enemy is not human. "Our struggle is not against enemies of blood and flesh, but against the rulers, against the authorities, against the cosmic powers of this present darkness, against the spiritual forces of evil in the heavenly places" (Eph. 6:12). The whole struggle is not against but, without abridgment and reservation, for the benefit and on behalf of all human life, including the human adversary. The battle against Satan does include the command, "Love your enemies and pray for those who persecute you" (Matt. 5:44); in fact, love to the human enemy is the very battle line at which the victory over God's adversary is decided. But the Christian fight remains real. It is a struggle against the idolatry of human power and, beyond that, a fight against the idolization of presumed "laws of nature" that contravene the grace and truth of God.

In what sense, then, is Christian peacemaking today drawn into the fight against powers denying the fullness and sufficiency of God's rule in the world? In order to avoid misleading associations caused by the use of military terminology, we choose to think about this aspect of peace as a consequence of Christian discipline for peace. The Christian pursuit of peace today may be described as a struggle involving two forms of Christian discipline: (a) the discipline of discernment, and (b) the discipline of being radical.

a. The Discipline of Discernment

Ancient polytheistic religions had apprehended the universe in pictures of personalized, superior divinities whose lives expressed the dignity and order, the relationship and limitation, of a total reality that modern linguistic custom has chosen to abstract into the single word "nature." Under the impact of a philosophical enlightenment in the Greek world, the personification of nature's forces, in particular the anthropomorphism of the gods and goddesses, was successfully criticized, and the divinities became abstract cosmic forces comprehensible by rational thought. At the fringe of this development, Israel had been entrusted with a faith unparalleled in all of Western antiquity, one that denied not so much the existence of the gods as their ultimacy and universality, affirming a God who was unimageable and therefore in principle without analogy to any force of nature, accessible primarily through his self-communication as personal will in his Word. The reality of the gods, or in abstract form the existence of a natural universe, was not negated in Israel, but it was robbed of its claim to be the fountain of human worship and obeisance. Early Judaism maintained this protest against the veneration of the powers of the universe by transmuting pagan divinities into a host of subordinate entities with names like powers, principalities, hosts, rules, and thrones. They remained strictly subordinate to Yahweh, the One without image, sometimes as willing aides and lieutenants, sometimes as rebellious antagonists whose host could be headed by Satan as the personified protagonist of resistance to Yahweh's rule over the whole cosmos.

From this observation we derive the right to claim that the biblical language of Satan and angels, of principalities and powers, is the language of protest against the pagan disposition to venerate the universe of nature as the source of ultimate human allegiance and of the appropriate form of human conduct. Israel is Israel in its act of unmasking the powers of nature as idols. And the church is the church in the obedience of faith, by which it refuses to listen to the lure that elevates the laws of nature to subjects demanding ultimate honor, holding rather in single devotion to the life, death, and resurrection of Jesus Christ as the only binding disclosure of the true Lord of the cosmos.

Peace in both Old and New Testaments is that life of well-being in which the powers of nature, the harmony of human society, and the health of the individual are nurtured in the exclusive veneration of the unimageable God whose act and will rules nature. If this exclusive bond to the one God is lost; or in New Testament terms, if the totality of faith in Jesus Christ is lost, nature, society, and individual assume the form of wild and dangerous animals who trample on every good order and devour all benefits of peace.

The struggle against the bestial encroachments of a nature without its Lord is, therefore, a requirement of the Christian obligation to make peace. This struggle is a matter of the discernment of faith in which the Spirit of God guides the Christian community into insights in which nature's powers and laws are liberated from their power to create illusions of ultimate dependencies in the human mind.

It may help to illustrate from one example of modern history what is at stake in the Christian struggle for peace in the form of that discernment which is empowered by God to call the bluff of the idols. On June 6, 1932, more than six months before the ascendency to power by Adolf Hitler in Germany, the "Faith Movement of German Christians" published a set of guiding principles meant to reform the Protestant German churches into a force auxiliary to the aims of Hitler's party. The church was to be invigorated by some natural endowment of the German nation which only now, in a newly revelatory moment of its history, had become intelligible to Germany as an unchangeable law of nature. "We see in race, folk, and nation," the seventh principle declares, "orders of existence granted and entrusted to us by God." The preservation of these orders is no less than "God's law for us." Since those orders of nature are lodged in a specifically German conduct and attitude, the future German church is to be "rooted in our nationhood" (principle 10). No longer is Christian faith expected to mold a specific nation in its history into its own unmistakable character; rather, the starting point is now a fact of nature, that of being German, which has the power to make legitimate what is to be tolerated as Christian. Now, "an affirmative and typical faith in Christ" is by no means determined by what the Christ of the New Testament affirmed and typified, but through "the German spirit of Luther" and a "heroic piety" (principle 4). This heroic piety will wage its fight according to its own spirit (especially against "atheistic Marxism" and the Catholic Center Party, principle 5) and thus will force its way into the kingdom of God: "The way into the Kingdom of God is through struggle, cross, and sacrifice, not through a false peace" (principle 6), it being understood, of course, that "struggle," "cross," and "sacrifice" are words whose content is determined by the deep and urgent voice of the German blood which has discovered that the foremost orders of existence reside in the purity of race, in the folk-inheritance, and in the preeminence of the German nation. The German church of the future, therefore, is not to be shackled any longer by the limitations of denominational or confessional history. In answer to the beckoning of its blood it will supersede those relativities and become "a vital national church that will express all the spiritual forces of our people" (principle 3). (Quotations of the guiding principles are taken from Arthur C. Cochrane, *The Church's Confession Under Hitler,* pp. 222–223; Philadelphia: Westminster Press, 1962.)

What had happened to make it possible that these guiding principles could be promulgated by representatives of a Christian movement who were convinced that their proposals would lead to a renewed sense of mission to the nation and to a revitalized understanding of the relevancy of the church? It was assumed that a historic movement in history had occurred which burst into the open carrying its own revelatory power. In the strength of this revelation it was now incumbent on every believer to recognize that "orders of existence" needed to be acknowledged which demanded integration into the Christian faith. The purity of the race, the manifest destiny of the nation, the excellence of the national tradition were considered ideas of such power that Christian faith had to be reinterpreted in accordance with the dictates of these ideas.

It is interesting, indeed it remains profoundly disturbing, to realize what could be made of the guiding principles of the Faith Movement of German Christians in the mind of a person whose allegiance to the presumed new revelation in history was uninhibited by some remaining loyalty to Christian faith and life. Alfred Rosenberg, the official ideologue of Hitler's movement, produced some "guiding principles" of his own for a future national German church. Rosenberg's articles, formulated during World War II, sound like radical conclusions from the principles of the German Christians drawn up some ten years earlier. The idea of a "vital national church" of the German Christians has become for Rosenberg a national church with total dictatorial power: "The National Reich Church of Germany categorically claims the exclusive right and the exclusive power to control all churches within the borders of the Reich" (article 1). The new "insight" of the German Christians into the law of God expressed in the orders of existence which are manifest in race, folk, and nation is stripped, by Rosenberg, of all attempts to coordinate it with the Christian confession: "The National Church is determined to exterminate irrevocably . . . the strange and foreign Christian faith imported into Germany in the ill-omened year 800" (article 5). What to the German Christians encouraged a partial and truncated retention of the Bible became to Rosenberg a radical principle of disavowal: "The National Church demands immediate cessation of the publishing and dissemination of the Bible in Germany" (article 14). (Quotations from Rosenberg's articles are from William L. Shirer, *The Rise and Fall of the Third Reich,* p. 240; New York: Simon & Schuster, 1960.)

It would be unfair to blame the German Christians of 1932 for the manifesto of Alfred Rosenberg in World War II. If they had heard of Rosenberg's conclusions, they would have disassociated themselves from them. But that does not alter the fact that they operated, together with Hitler's ideologue, on the basis of shared premises: the celebration of a historic time in which God has provided a new revelation aside from that confessed by the church; a law of God at work in the national capacities of a special race and nation; and the elevation of that new revelation and that new divine law to a position which effectively predetermines the understanding of the Bible and the confessions of the church. By doing this, they opened the floodgates of an ideology into the faith of the church. Not only did they advocate a correlation of their new revelation on equal terms with the scriptures and the confessions of the church, but they insisted in practice that everything which their ideology considered to be desirable was in fact the measure to be applied to scripture and confessions. Whatever did not meet that standard was to be corrected or abandoned. In advocating this approach, the German Christians weakened the vigilance of the church. With the discipline of discernment sapped, large portions of the church in Germany had no defense in their faith that could topple the idols of the time. The disaster ran its course largely unopposed by those charged with the responsibility to discern between the spirits of truth and the spirits of idolatry.

b. The Discipline of Being Radical

So far in this section it has been argued that the Christian struggle for peace depends, in the first place, on an act of discernment. It is a conflict that rages on the level of judgment and thought, and it is decided, prior to any actions or overt policies, in the area of a discipline in which idolatry is recognized and rejected. Peace, in the Christian sense of the word, cannot be established unless the struggle for peace is initially won on this ground.

That is not to say, however, that there is not also a public and political side to this struggle. Idolatries have an external aspect in the form of political programs, legal enactments, trade practices, and the like. And whenever the idols totter and fall, freedom from the compunction to serve false gods shows itself equally in public measures and actions. The struggle for peace, therefore, involves the Christian community also inevitably in participation in a strenuous effort to achieve good, healthy, and just orders in public life. Peace needs its Christian advocates who do not fear controversy. It will not be pursued without the Christian community producing its protesters and its critics of public life who apply the acid test of their criticism to all public systems and structures. No form of human civilization is exempt from this attack on behalf of peace. Political systems and practices, economic theories and management, social conventions and orders, presuppositions and realities of ethical conduct, all are constantly subject to attack from a Christian community that is serious about its quest for peace. A Christian community that is not capable of initiating the continued struggle for the realization of peace in the wide connotations the word has in the biblical sense is not worth its existence: it has lost its salt. Precisely as a community of peace, the Christian community must constantly be expected to infuse an element of disquietude into public life.

In raising the voice of criticism and protest on behalf of peace, the church cannot avoid becoming embroiled in political battles with all the attendant compromises and intrigues. In being an advocate for peace in public issues on a very broad scale, the Christian community will have to aim at concrete and measurable improvements in the area of secular administration and legislation. Small steps forward, limited advances toward betterment, are all that can be expected on the front of public policy. Relative changes in public life must not be discredited by the Christian community because of their limited effect. But the involvement for the sake of peace in secular politics brings with it also a danger to the church that must not be forgotten. The achievement of improved forms of public policies, in Western democracies, is realized through the formation of parties, or political action groups, that function as advocates of certain causes. Causes spawn caucuses and caucuses beget adversarial attitudes. Viewpoints are not only researched, they are also promoted to the public through extremely high expenditures. Slogans capturing half-truths are floated to the public, the more injurious to the antagonist the better. Political advocacy unavoidably breeds a division of the public into friend and foe, it tends dangerously toward the dissemination of propaganda, and it habitually instills in the followers of a cause the illusion of a moral superiority over political opponents. A vicious circle, repeating itself over and over again, is running its course: A grievance produces its protesters, the critics fashion a cause for liberation, the political action needed to advance the cause gives birth to mass propaganda, vilification of the enemy, and a fanatical zeal to absolutize the cause. If successful, the "liberation" will install itself as the final solution in its victory over its antagonists; in due time it cannot fail to show its own clay feet by producing new forms of oppression and misery.

If the Christian community, in its advocacy of peace, gets drawn into this vortex, it will loose its own identity, betray the uniqueness of its own mission, and become no more than an additional pawn in the political game. Having allowed itself to become absorbed into this political process, it may win a few skirmishes, but it has already lost the war. And it has lost the war not because its criticism and protest was too radical but because it was not radical enough. The Latin word *radix* means root, and a process is radical when it issues from the root. A Christian community that is radically critical of society in its pursuit of peace will take the greatest care to let its protest well up from its own roots and to remain constantly self-critical, so that its every criticism will remain connected to the root.

If it is radical in this sense, Christian criticism of society does not spring from observations of symptoms of sickness in public life, but from its knowledge of the root of human ills, be they societal or communal. Considered from its root, the sickness of human life is, for the Christian community, the refusal or the lack of knowledge of the gospel of Jesus Christ, which claims that the peace of God is fully established in the gospel. All human beings, without regard to their point in history and without regard to any and all forms of societal differences, whether between races or nations, rich or poor, old or young, male or female, are—whether they know it or not—included in the peace of God which Jesus Christ has declared and initiated once and for all. This peace provides healing for body and soul; it extends to the most basic needs of corporeal existence as well as to the most sublime reaches of the human soul. The discipline of the Christian community keeps its struggle for peace open to this root and expects all healing of the symptoms to occur only as consequences of the flow of healing that arises from the root and removes the sickness itself.

The Christian struggle for peace, as a radical criticism of human society, will then exhibit some characteristics that will prevent it from ever being simply absorbed into the secular political fight for power. It will make clear and compelling that even its most severe criticisms are not reflections of the desires and needs of one group against another, but criticisms that follow from the insight of what is needful and necessary for the peace of all. It will insist that political analyses, including the church's own, be continually subjected to the most vigorous objective standards of evidence available. It will therefore resist all efforts, including those coming from its own ranks, to plunge political processes into adversarial confrontations, reduce reality to propagandistic simplifications, and blow up differences of opinion into political dogma separating the just from the unjust. In standing fast for this radical criticism on behalf of one undivided peace, it will continue to be guided by its effort to lay bare the idols of the time as the only real enemy of the peace of all.

4. The Way of Peace

In considering the struggle of peace as a form of discipline, in the previous section, a far-reaching transformation of language about the warrior Yahweh and of military metaphors was necessary. To capture the New Testament's intention, we suggested that the Christian fight for peace be understood as a form of Christian discipline in which forces in the history and nature of humanity and the world that impose themselves as religious claims are exposed and combatted as idols, and in which Christian opposition to conditions injurious to peace are attacked from the root up by addressing the sickness itself and not only its symptoms. This obviously implies a marked deviation from any idea of the use of war, violence, and compulsion in the service of God as temporary means to establish and secure peace.

But we need to go farther than that. The vision of peace in the New Testament displays at crucial points an inner consistency in which the aim of peace, the power of its presence, and the means of achieving it are so correlated that no allowance is left for any experience or calculation that would offer a serious challenge to the omnipotence of peace. We see in this consistency of vision the specifically Christian way of peace that is meant to be gained and lived in a world filled with violence and war, with military and police forces, with prisons, legalized coercion, and incarceration. What is the way of peace for the Christian community surrounded by an ocean of constitutionally protected and institutionally established forms of aggression?

Since the time of Constantine and the transformation of the Christian movement into the state religion of the Roman empire, the question at hand has been approached from the vantage point of some distinctive theories about the relation between church and state. The history of Western Christianity has produced some basic types of systems, a Medieval Catholic, a Lutheran and Calvinist, and a Nonconformist model, all of them in several variations, whose study is of great interest. But we shall here not even attempt a sketch of these theories; rather, we choose to work toward the question from a different angle. One reason for doing so is a reading of the New Testament which suggests that in none of its documents is there any attempt made to stipulate a systematic key for the relation of church and state. Not only is the relation of government and Christian community depicted very differently in different books and at different times; but also, and what is more important, the few passages that address the relation of the Christian community to the authority of the Roman government are not intended to express a systematic theory.

We will have to come closer to the heart of the matter and search for a point of departure sufficiently central to the New Testament itself. It has often been suggested that this point of departure is the attitude of nonviolence espoused by the New Testament. But it would seem to us that even this suggestion does not reach the core of what some important passages in the New Testament indicate. In Matthew 5:39b–41, for example, three sayings are coordinated that discuss the disciples' answer to injury: a blow on the cheek, the loss of a piece of property through procedures established by law, and forced service imposed by some governmental authority. In each case, a response is described that issues in a definite action utterly baffling to accustomed standards. The other cheek is offered for another blow, an additional piece of property is given in addition to the one taken, and the forced service is rendered for twice the distance demanded. Since all three cases involve some kind of violence done to a person, one is justified in concluding that the recommended responses counsel nonviolence. But it is hard to miss the point that all three examples are given to encourage a positive action through which the chain of injury leading to further injury is broken. The sayings breathe the fiery spirit of a confidence that now is the time to reply to hostile acts with totally surprising answers of active love in which hostility is no longer perpetuated. The reaction to this act of love by the perpetrators of injury is not contemplated in the sayings. It may be hoped that they would be won over by this act; however, the force of the sayings rests in the call to risk the most compromising personal decision to act in accordance with the faith that the rule of God here and now allows wagering everything on it, and in so doing breaking the rule of retaliation and revenge altogether.

We conclude that the attitude and action of nonviolence is not in itself the motivating force envisaged in the New Testament as response to violence. Rather, we are confronted with texts that dare to announce the reality of the one God, merciful to all, whose rule may be trusted in courageous actions that break the allegiance to all other rules of behavior. In such daring acts of obedience to the kingship of God, hatred, hostility, injury, and violence are defeated by the love that includes the enemy. Strictly speaking, there is no enemy left. The rule of the one gracious God is such that it suffers no reservations and exceptions. The mercy and kindness of this God extend to all without limit, to good and bad, to Jews and pagans. The disciple who is called to spread the announcement that the time of this omnipresence and omnipotence of God's totally inclusive grace has come is transported to a position in which enmity as such is left behind. This has nothing in common with a rose-colored optimism which expects that the inherent goodness in every enemy will yield to the superiority of an ethical ideal constructed on nonviolence. There are enemies right and left and the community of the disciples knows them well. But the announcement that now is the time for God's kingship carries with it the conviction that customs and habits, rules and regulations, laws and structures not in tune with the time of God's kingship do not deserve enough respect to be accepted as serious contributors to the making of decisions that draw on God's total rule. The disciples' action in the midst of violence and enmity is therefore liberated from calculations of outcomes, from the accounting of likely effects and consequences, and from compromises that mix the time of God's rule with the time of the rule of competitors to God's exclusive right to govern. What is at stake in the disciples' response to enmity is the truth and power of the coming of God's kingship itself, not its possible results, effects, and consequences. As the disciples engage in this novel encounter with hostility, they do so with open eyes. They know that persevering in it cost their Lord his life, and they have no illusions that they might themselves be exempt from the hatred of those who insist on remaining enemies. But in spite of that, they insist for their part that even continued enmity against them, and consequently the possible loss of their own *shalom,* will not defeat the truth of their announcement that now is the time to reckon with God's gracious rule first and last.

This, it seems to us, is the starting point of the New Testament's attitude to hatred, oppression, war, and all forms of violence. Therefore it does not start with the consideration of social problems, nor does it expect their cure from methods derived from social realities as such. It is also logical, for the same reason, that the New Testament does not pronounce a blanket condemnation of persons in military service, or on the institution of slavery, or on the practice of economic exploitation. Had it done so, it would have reintroduced the notion of enemies whose form of life renders them immune to the power of faith. Nor has the New Testament staked its claim on the dignity of the individual conscience which alone can decide what is right in the solitude of the encounter between the individual and God.

This leads us to the conclusion that in respect to war and oppression the New Testament begins with the Christian community, which has expressed in the baptism of all its members that all claims of human laws and human orders are dead for the community so that it may live entirely from the gift of God's unrestricted and universal grace for the entire world. From this starting point, we must attempt to draw some concrete conclusions for our time and day.

We concentrate on the problem of war and would only indicate that the problems of coercion by police would be subject to similar considerations. Nobody has ever even postulated, to my knowledge, that members of the different Christian communities reflected in the New Testament could possibly have met on a field of battle armed to kill each other.

This is unthinkable not only because no Christian communities at that time had sufficient power and identity to wage war, but also because the sense of being the exponent of a new order was so keen as to dominate the relation of one community to the other, and in this new order war was a contradiction in terms. The apostle Paul took the emergence of party ideologies in Corinth so seriously that in his view a final division of the community into dissenting groups amounted to a division of Christ (1 Cor. 1:11–13). There is no doubt that the absurd notion of Christians taking up the sword against Christians would have provoked from him the question: Is Christ slaughtered? This question allows no other response but a firm "No."

We have come a long way since New Testament times. But we also need to remind ourselves that, continuing after the Constantinian changes, the greatest pioneers of Christian doctrine and ethics have preserved the claim that the Christian as a person cannot participate in war and violence. Not only have the classical peace churches retained the awareness that mortal conflict between communities and nations is irreconcilable with the nature of faith. They were joined, with respect to the Christian as private individual, by the greatest figures in church history, who justified Christian participation in war only on the assumption that the individual Christian was also a member of the civil community whose decisions were dictated by the necessities of the common good. There was a presumed natural law, or there were presumed orders of creation that supplemented—or at least went alongside—the commitment of faith, and in accordance with those laws and orders the Christian could be expected, even commanded, to participate in war.

In our attempt to hear the gospel of peace in our time, we move a long way toward the position of the classical peace churches and modify greatly the assumptions of the mainline denominations, Catholic or Protestant. We do so not on the basis of a different judgment as to whether or not there can be a just war, but on grounds of the inner consistency of life and faith in the Christian community. It appears to us undeniable that the vitality of the Christian community in all Western mainline churches is so eroded that it has ceased seriously to consider what forms of communal behavior it can use to demonstrate an alternative to civil societies, one that concretely manifests the claims of its own faith. In terms of political reality we have become largely conditioned to accept as final the judgments and decisions of the civil government, so that a declaration of war by a national government entails the duty to its Christian citizens to serve in the military forces. The theory of the just war—designed by Christians and still defended by its good Christian proponents—has actually functioned for centuries as an opiate lulling Christian conscience into submission to the state, whose leaders it was thought necessary to obey out of reverence for their office, their supposedly superior knowledge, and their responsibility for the welfare of their people. But we know far too much today about the circumstances, motivations, and appetites—not to speak of downright stupidity—of those who governed, for example prior to the outbreak of World War I, to accept this kind of assumption. A great deal more critical vigilance on the part of Christian citizens is demanded in our time.

But a disenchantment with the wisdom of rulers, and a critical distance toward policies that contain the germs of armed conflict, can only reinforce that reorientation of Christian thinking in respect to war which grows out of its own being. The Christian community is faced today with two mass demonstrations—before the eyes of the whole world—of the complete political ineffectiveness of Christians' claim to honor, support, and protect each other as a new community called to demonstrate the God of peace, and the peace of God, to the world. The horrifying atrocity of two world wars, conducted preeminently by Christian nations pitted against each other, disproves the pretense that Christians are effectively witnessing to God in any socially or politically verifiable manner.

If this starting point is granted, it would seem to us that a massive task of re-education in the Christian community is necessary, a task which with regard to war amounts to a reformation of the Christian social consciousness. Some specific points would have to appear on the agenda of this re-education.

- The Christian "no" to all nuclear weapons must be absolute. The danger to the continued existence of our world in a condition in any way comparable to the *shalom* of God's creation is so great that the destruction

of all nuclear stockpiles is mandatory even if they tempo-
rarily contribute to the prevention of war by the superpowers with each other. An ecumenical consensus must
be sought that commits the Christian churches to a
common and uncompromising "no" against further continuance of the arms race in nuclear weaponry and
against reliance on the presumed nuclear deterrence to
war.

- The Christian community can preserve its social and
political witness for peace only if refusal to take part in
the preparation and conduct of armed conflict is considered the norm for all members of the community. What is
today, among most Christian denominations, considered
a legitimate exception should become tomorrow's general rule.

- The Christian community within the world of nations
should understand itself in analogy to an internationally
recognized organization such as the Red Cross. As the
International Red Cross does not arm its members but
participates in war only as a force upholding the power
and hope of rescuing, healing, and reconciliation, so the
Christian community should seek global recognition by
international agreements as an organization dedicated to
peace beyond national rivalries.

- The great number of Christians in churches other than
the classical peace denominations who are, through centuries of tradition and often by deeply felt personal
conviction, committed to the notion that peace is best
served through military preparedness, are not to be
ostracized within the community. The transformation of
Christian consciousness, advocated here, cannot undo in
one instant what centuries of tradition in confessions,
catechisms, and preaching and teaching have produced.
But their position must be challenged by an understanding of Christian community that preserves its uniqueness
and social viability over against all dictates of secular
reasoning.

- The Christian community, if it is true to its own nature,
must deny that compulsion and deadly force are the only
available means to combat threat and aggression. It will
therefore, in the political arena of public life, support and
encourage any practical steps that lead to the eventual
elimination, by international agreements, of the accept-

ance of war as a legitimate continuation of international politics.

• Prior to its taking a position of advocacy for or against public policies in support of peace, the Christian community will, in its preaching and teaching, work against the admiration, and indeed the worship, of revenge as the motivation for political and civil actions. The heroic ideal of the Christian community is not the fighter for justice who, smoking gun in hand, stands as survivor on a pile of slaughtered villains, but the advocate of the peace of God for all without exception who defends the freedom of God's grace through the offering of his own life for the benefit of every villain in the world.

5. The Peace of the Gospel

It is possible to describe the entire ministry of Jesus as a single act of peacemaking. If one takes into account that the healing of the sick, the feeding of the hungry, the care of the neglected and despised, and the forgiveness of sins are all aspects of the restoration of God's peace through the powers unleashed by the dawn of God's kingship on earth, one may fairly say that the core both of Jesus' preaching and of his acts is captured in the phrase: Jesus the peacemaker.

The doctrinal tradition of the Western church used language drawn from the areas of law and cult almost exclusively to clarify the meaning of Jesus' Messianic life. Western soteriology is couched in terms of justification, sanctification, and redemption—that is to say, in sets of concepts that derive from law courts and from the realm of priestly service. It is not at all the intention here to criticize, let alone invalidate, the appropriateness of this terminology in Christian theology. After all, forensic and cultic language plays a very large role in biblical modes of speech and imagination. But we would suggest that the aspect of peacemaking provides a different and wider possibility in the service of critical thought devoted to both Christology and soteriology. The concept of peace introduces the aspect of well-being into the data of the theological search for adequate and responsible expressions for the nature and the benefits of Jesus Christ. If peace is taken into account, christological and soteriological thought will then be opened up to the material side of human existence, which has to face human reality lived in sickness and poverty as well as in depravity and estrangement. Such opening of christological and soteriological reflection toward the question posed by the dust and dirt of human existence cannot replace the older doctrinal formulations which moved within the ambience of legal and cultic language. But this opening can enrich and widen the comprehensiveness of Christian theology seeking to understand who Jesus Christ was and is and what he has accomplished.

An understanding of the entire work of Jesus Christ as peacemaker can also help to secure the positive character of Christian faith and life. The Christian knowledge of human history and the human condition will never be grasped if the realities of corruption and disease are denied. But human sin and its consequences are not given their due in the Christian form of understanding if they are left to dominate the picture, producing a morbid and defeatist view of human life. The gospel does not put aside the dark aspects of humanity. But it brings them into focus as a darkness that is recognized in its starkness only because it has already been overcome and displaced by the brightest light. The appearing of the light itself is the heart of the gospel. It proclaims peace, it grants peace, and it spreads peace into the darkest corner. As the gospel of peace it is the most affirmative, encouraging, and joyous thing, which rings in the era of the cessation of all hostilities and the glad enjoyment of its fruits.

Index of Scripture
and Ancient Writings

Index of Subjects